AMONG *the* SUNFLOWERS

*A Memoir of a Mother's Love for her Son
and his Poems of Addiction, Relapse, and Recovery*

GAIL MEHLAN | M. M. MEHLAN

Published by Gail Mehlan/GM Sunflower Creative Arts
1155 Coral Springs Dr. Cicero, IN 46034
For more information: g.meh1974@gmail.com

Scripture quotations marked NIV are taken from the Holy Bible, New International Version® NIV® Copyright © 1973, 1978, 1984, 2011 by Biblica, Inc.™
Used by permission. All rights reserved worldwide.

Scripture quotations marked NRSV are taken from the New Revised Standard Version Bible, copyright © 1989 National Council of the Churches of Christ in the United States of America.
Used by permission. All rights reserved worldwide.

Scripture quotations marked MSG are taken from THE MESSAGE, copyright © 1993, 2002, 2018 by Eugene H Peterson. Used by permission of NavPress, represented by Tyndale House Publishers. All rights reserved.

First Edition

Cover and Interior Design by David Provolo
Cover Art by M. M. Mehlan with E. Mehlan

Library of Congress Cataloging-in-Publication: 9798986625508

ISBN (paperback) 979-8-9866255-0-8
ISBN (ebook) 9798986625522

Among the Sunflowers: A Memoir of a Mother's Love for her Son and his Poems of Addiction, Relapse and Recovery is a memoir. The author changed or altered names to protect the privacy of individuals.

Dedicated to *all* who struggle with addiction
and the families who love them.

"Sometimes I have to fight the old urge to keep quiet at all costs, but I have found that sharing is the key to healing."

TABLE OF CONTENTS

Prologue 9
Introduction 10

Part One: First You Have to Name It

Chapter 1—Darkness. 16
Chapter 2—Bad Mother 19
Chapter 3—Sometime in the Year 2001 27
Chapter 4—Why Did You Even Have Me? *by Jolly Jackson* . . 32
Chapter 5—Here I Am Lord 36
Chapter 6—Help. 42
Chapter 7—September 11, 2001 48
Chapter 8—Clear Lake. 55
Chapter 9—Phone Call. 60
Chapter 10—Oh! Oh! Oh! Another Day 68
Chapter 11—Kaleidoscope 76
Chapter 12—Escaping to Europe. 82
Chapter 13—You've Got to Have Friends 87
Chapter 14—God Needs More Time. 93
Chapter 15—Arrested 100
Chapter 16—Being Judged. 107
Chapter 17—Stolen Love. 114
Chapter 18—Rearview Mirror 119
Chapter 19—Tough Decisions 124
Chapter 20—Time Out 134
Chapter 21—A Presence to Walk With 137

Part Two: A Long Reach of Hopes

Chapter 22—Among the Sunflowers 145

Written by Michael M. Mehlan—Hey W' Happens?!!

Chapter 23—The Beds Were Empty 150

Chapter 24—New Every Morning 154

Chapter 25—Always Second Chances 160

Chapter 26— First Letters 166

Chapter 27— The Good Servant *by Jolly Jackson* 171

Chapter 28— Among the Sunflowers 2. 175

by Michael M. Mehlan—This is My Dreams Come True

Chapter 29—Seeing the Prodigal. 179

Chapter 30—Thoughts. 186

Chapter 31—Reflections *by Jolly Jackson* 191

Chapter 32—Among the Sunflowers 3 194

by Michael M. Mehlan—Jet Airliner

Chapter 33—Possibilities. 196

Chapter 34—It's Not Your Life. 201

Chapter 35—No Sleep and a Wedding. 206

Chapter 36—Honorable Intentions 212

Chapter 37—I Don't Like Failure. 218

Part Three: Regards from the Land of the Living

Chapter 38—Astronaut 227

Chapter 39—Heroin 230

Chapter 40—Darkness Continues 234

Chapter 41—Miracles of Life and Love 237

Chapter 42—Holy Ghost 242

Chapter 43—Meeting Douggie 250

Chapter 44—Present Still 257

Chapter 45—Powerless 260

Chapter 46—I Don't Want This to be Our Story Anymore . . 267

Chapter 47—Sometimes Prayers Aren't Enough 274

Chapter 48—Who *is* Jolly Jackson? *by Jolly Jackson* 284

Chapter 49—Why Did We Have Children? 291

Chapter 50—Is That a Monster Under the Bed? *by Jolly Jackson* 296

Chapter 51—The Edge 303

Chapter 52—Recovery is Lonely *by Jolly Jackson* 307

Chapter 53—The Walk Home *by Jolly Jackson* 310

Chapter 54—The Good Day 314

Chapter 55—Epilogue 319

Postscript—Rainbow Connection *by Jolly Jackson* 336

Update—Breath and Life 341

About the Authors 346

Comments, Notes, Permissions, and Resources 347

Acknowledgments 369

Recommended Reading 372

Bibliography 374

"Though I sit in darkness,
the Lord will be my light."
Micah 7:8 (NIV)

A PROLOGUE

To My Dearest Mother,
I cannot remember how we met. I could not see your face when you saw my face for the first time, but I knew then, as I know now, that I loved you, and you loved me. You were going to be my protector. You then made me a promise that day that no harm would ever come to me as the years played on. Oh, how I tested your resolve! I left you wondering for my future and pushed your temperance beyond fortitude, but your promise never waned too far from me or from the faith I had in your promise.

I never knew how hard it was.

Until one day, fear and weakness crept into my fearful heart with the birth of my beautiful son. I only hope I can keep the same promise you made to me. Oh! How all the years feel like a dream! I spend every night lying awake telling myself I will do everything to keep that promise, but I know it's only partially in my hands. I will have to let go. I will have to let him fall and fail. My only wish is that when the time comes, he will make the same promise I made him and the same one that you made me.

I love you forever.
I'm sorry for all the heartache.
Always love, your son,
Michael

INTRODUCTION

Even as a child, I envisioned being a mom and having a family. My young heart knew the exact number of children I would have, the color of the house we would live in, and other now forgotten details. I wanted to grow up, get married, and live happily ever after.

I grew up in a northwestern suburb of Chicago. My parents were well educated, and my dad was a Navy veteran who came home from serving in the Korean War right before I was born. They were transplants from the East Coast to the Midwest, purchasing a brand-new home in a developing suburb called Hoffman Estates. The developers promised new schools, roads, churches, and shopping; as I grew up, so did Hoffman Estates. My parents held all four of us to high standards of conduct. Education was always vital. Being involved with a faith community was a big part of growing up. I remember attending services and Sunday School in the newly-built school gym, sitting on metal folding chairs and stomping our feet as we sang *Onward Christian Soldiers*.

I loved being a part of a large family, and I married a wonderful man from the South Side of Chicago. We settled in the same suburb as my parents. When we had children, the grandparents, aunts, uncles, cousins, and good friends were nearby. For me, it was all that I ever hoped for. I believed that my fairy tale would have a happy ending. I had things figured out.

Life's *ups* were joyous, but the *downs* shook me to the core of my being. When I lost my father unexpectedly and my daughter, Michelle, broke her neck the following year in a gymnastics accident, I thought the worst that could happen to a family was behind us. Michelle's miraculous recovery as she regained her strength and went on to college led me to believe that life could only get better. I remained faithful.

I was not prepared for the next low. Our youngest child would become addicted to heroin.

This story of my son's addiction has been sitting in my heart for many years. It is the true-life story of our family. Even now, I dread sharing all of these thoughts and memories because they are intensely personal and painful for our whole family. Most days, I simply want to move on to the next *positive* thing, the scrapbook page image that shows happy times. I was naïve about mental health and addiction. These issues rocked my world and shattered my unrealistic dreams.

It has been a tough season for me as a mother. Somehow, I found a way to climb up and out of this challenging time. As I reflect on these years, I can still see moments of love, life, laughter, and hope. I also see that God never left me alone in the struggle, even when I didn't recognize that presence.

Our son is still working hard to battle his demons and seek recovery and a better future for himself. His poems richly express the experience and struggle of his journey. The collaboration of writing our story together has been healing and transformative for both of us.

A friend once told me that when a woman shares her experiences, there is always someone who has experienced something similar and will benefit from the sharing. If this writing is a way for me to document my healing process, my walk with the Lord through this time, and my deep love for my family, it will serve its purpose.

May the reading of our story be a blessing to you.

Gail Mehlan
June 2022

PART ONE:

First You Have to Name It

THE WILDERNESS IS A PLACE WHERE WE ARE BRAVE

First, we have to name it—
The heartbreak,
The addiction,
The shame,
The grief.

Whatever your wilderness is,
First, we have to name it.

And once we've said the words out loud,
We let the truth hang in the air.
And we let ourselves feel what we feel,
For in this moment,
We are close to the surface.

And after a few deep breaths,
We begin the removing.
Piece by piece, we take our amour off,
For truth-telling days are
Soft skin kind of days.
And once we are armor-free,
Hearts on our sleeves
And tears in our throats,
We stand toe-to-toe
With every hurt that wrecked us.
And we don't try to swallow that pain away.

And there,
In all our beautiful God-given honesty,
We say to that monster,
"I have love on my side.
And her name is God,
And no wilderness can separate me
From that north star."

And I believe
It will be the bravest thing you ever do.
And your knees might shake,
And you might lose your way,
But our God is a God of second chances,
So, take my hand.
You are close to the surface.
Let's be brave together.

Sarah Are

"Shades of a sober temperament
How long have I suffered in pain, in darkness?
Through angry "spirits" and drunken teardrops?
It came in calm winds through red-headed beauties
Laughing through the broken hearts
Fair-skinned brilliance through
hard work and earned duties."

Jolly Jackson *
Excerpt from *The Cracks*

Gail

CHAPTER 1—DARKNESS

2009

As I opened the heavy church door and walked into the darkness that led to the pastor's office, I was full to the breaking point with emotion. I knew why, but I didn't understand the power of these feelings. It had been years, yet they still attacked and choked me. A rock was stuck in the back of my throat. Breathing felt difficult.

I knocked on the door.

"Hello, Gail. Come on in." My pastor greeted me softly as he opened the door. He knew by the look on my face that something had happened. We had been getting together every week for spiritual direction sessions and counseling. My son's ongoing behavioral problems and addiction issues left me heartbroken. Where was God in all of this?

That very day, my son had walked out of our home after I caught him up in my bedroom, rifling through my jewelry box.

"What the hell are you doing in my room?" I shouted, knowing that there was nothing of value in that box.

"NOTHING, NOTHING, NOTHING!"

My heart was pounding as if it would beat its way out of my chest. The fine hairs on my arm stood at attention. I held onto the doorframe to keep myself steady. "Get out! And DO NOT COME BACK! I am about to call the police." In a few moments, he was gone.

He didn't take anything, but something precious *was* stolen. My heart was broken. I was broken. Trust was broken. Love violated.

I lamented to my pastor that I was about to explode and couldn't stop the tears leaking from my eyes. He looked at me and said, "Your tears are beautiful, Gail. They are the tears of a mother who loves deeply. Don't ever be afraid of them. They are the Holy Spirit moving in and through you. They *are* prayers for your son."

I waited for answers to this darkness. I prayed for wisdom and help for my son. The answers came in strange and unusual ways over the years, never the way I expected.

We waited late into the night to hear from Mike. When he called to let us know he was safe, Doug reminded me that we had welcomed our children into our lives. We enjoyed many loving moments together. We were committed to having and caring for our children. We were a family. We would work through this darkness together.

After a mix of starts and stops, beginnings and endings, the choice was always *life*.

"This day, I call the heavens and
the earth as witnesses against
you that I have set before you, life and death,
blessings, and curses.
Now choose life so that you
and your children may live."

Deuteronomy 30:19 (NIV)

* Throughout this book, Michael, the author's son, is referred to as *Jolly Jackson* (pen name), *Mike, Michael* or *M. M. Mehlan.*

"Her vehement desire stands like that of searing wrath
With penetrating eyes, swimming with fearful loss
Sadness bought and sold for too high a cost
A raging war of attrition seething inside her
The casualties too high to number
This lioness now protecting her den"

Jolly Jackson
Excerpt from *Motherhood—A War*

Gail

CHAPTER 2—BAD MOTHER

2001

It was early in the morning as I tiptoed into my son's room to wake him up for school. As I opened the door, the whiff of a boy, slightly stale and sweaty, permeated the space. I was surprised that the room was so neat. The shades were drawn tight, and it was dark. The alarm was beeping next to his bed, ignored. I turned it off as I gently rubbed his forehead and moved the hair away from his eyes. He rolled over on his back and let out a soft moan.

"I don't feel good, Mom."

"What's wrong, honey? Do you have a headache?"

"No, I just don't feel good. I don't think I can go to school today."

"But you *have* to go to school today. You've missed too many days so far this year."

"I know, but I really don't feel good."

"I know. I understand. Get up and take a shower, and we'll

see if you feel any better after that."

I walked out of the room but left the door open so that I could check on him in a few minutes. As I turned the corner into the kitchen, I heard the door slam. *Sigh.*

It was a pattern. He didn't want to go to school. I'd try to be patient. He wouldn't go to school. I'd lose my patience. He might go to school but wouldn't stay for the day. I walked over to the counter to get myself a cup of coffee and sat down at the table to think. How could I get him to school on *this* day?

This child was in eighth grade, not a kid, but not quite a teenager, and we were fast approaching the end of the school year. I was a wreck. All I could think of was *what* I was supposed to do to parent this child who could care less about anything. He was not completing the work required to graduate and go to high school. Yet, imagine this, *I* was *trying* to hold him accountable. Am I a fool or what? We had gone to counseling. He was on medication for depression. We talked on and on and on and on about what was expected here at home. He agreed to some specific bottom-line standards that were still not yet met. He *was* allowed:

- No friends
- No computer
- No TV
- No snacks
- Nothing
- Period.

I questioned myself all the time. The dam holding back *my* tears was about to burst, and I was afraid *I* would fall apart. I held it together but was a long way from acceptance. I was holding on to a great deal of desire to *control* this situation. But what? Control what? Accept what? Less than I had hoped? For my child, for my family? I wanted to throw all my expectations out the window, cave in, and let him sleep. I felt drained from the constant struggle.

No. I refused to take the blame for expecting my child to fulfill his obligations. As I thought about all of this, my anxiety and frustration grew. I took a deep breath and a sip of coffee and pushed the chair away from the table, ready to face the battle again. But suddenly, I heard the shower start in the upstairs bathroom. Phew!

Sometimes all of this seemed so petty. Other parents talked about curfews and getting their kids to do the dishes and straighten their rooms. We dealt with school failure, complete avoidance of school-related work, depression, self-esteem issues, lack of cooperation, anger management, and what *else*? My mind imagined the worst. Sex? Drugs?

While this constant and unbearable struggle was going on at home, I worked full-time as the director of early childhood ministries for our church preschool program. My days were busy planning with staff and public outreach to ensure enrollment for the following year. I had many responsibilities, and as I prepared to close up the program for the summer, my heart wasn't in the job. I often felt like I was sitting on pins and needles, waiting for the next phone call about Mike. I wasn't working up to my high standards, but I was blessed that my coworkers understood and were patient with me each day. My closest coworker covered for me whenever needed. Every time the school called, I spent what seemed like hours on the phone with a teacher or the school counselor when I should have been working. Sometimes I needed to leave school to pick Mike up if he wasn't feeling well. Often he wasn't actually ill, just out of sorts. He would end up unsupervised at home while I returned to work.

I blew things out of proportion, worrying about him all the time. The situation *was* affecting my work.

My two older children were living away from home. My daughter was a senior in college, getting ready to graduate and start her student teaching in the fall. She had called me the day before, and I related some of what was happening with her brother. Although she was tired of hearing that he frustrated me, she reassured me: "It's not your fault, Mom."

I neglected to thank her for her encouragement, but I felt it in my heart.

My other son, also away at college, had called and listened to my complaints too. He had often gotten angry with his brother for his bad attitude and lack of initiative in the past. I didn't say much about the situation with his brother when he called. When I asked how life was going for him, he replied, "Things are going well, very well, actually!"

I breathed a sigh of relief. Maybe I hadn't been such a bad mother after all.

"Love you!" I said to each of them as I hung up, a little less depressed.

How could this one child make me feel so incompetent as a mother? I had so many other *blessings* in my life that it struck me as a little over the top crazy that this one child, and this one situation, could dig into my heart and make me feel out of balance. Did he know the power that he had over me?

After about a half-hour or so, the shower turned off, and Mike made his way downstairs in time for us to fly out the door, so I could drop him off at school and not be late for work.

On Tuesdays, my husband, a physical therapist, saw patients from early morning until late in the evenings, so it was my turn to get Mike where he needed to be.

After school, my troubled son left the house in direct disobedience to my orders. We were supposed to go to a counseling session together, but he was nowhere to be found. Frustrated, I gave up looking for him and went on to see the counselor alone. Worried and sick to my stomach the whole time, I sat in the counselor's office discussing the scenario.

My husband got home at about 9:30 PM. My heart was aching, and I felt close to tears. Fear was stirring in me.

"He's not home yet. He left at about 4:30 PM. I don't know what to do! Why didn't you come home sooner?" I asked my husband. The anger in my voice reflected my resentment. *My husband* was somehow responsible for this. Before we had time to discuss it further, we heard the garage door open. It was after 10:00 PM.

"We were so worried!" my husband said with a voice that sounded more angry than worried.

"Where were you? You weren't supposed to leave the house!"

"I didn't want to go see that f**king counselor."

He stormed through the kitchen and off to his room. I was relieved that he was home, but still, I was unsettled. I refused to take the blame for these problems we faced. In many ways, going to the counselor alone had been good for me. He gave me some helpful suggestions.

Think of it as a disability.
Don't take it personally.
Refuse to join the fight.
Keep your composure.
Ease up controls.
Establish simple, enforceable consequences.
Count to 20.
Reframe requests.
Give genuine choices.
Praise whenever possible.
Connect with what you like about your child.
TAKE CARE OF YOURSELF!

I *tried* hard to work on many of these ideas and apply them to our situation. I was disillusioned because I couldn't get them to work most of the time. Sometimes the "oughts" and "shoulds" added to my frustration. They seemed like an unmovable and formidable mountain that I could not climb. The suggestion made by the counselor that popped out at me the most was *TAKE CARE OF YOURSELF*. Do I do that? Can I do that? Are my emotions *hooked* on *his* problems? And how am I to separate myself and my feelings from Mike's behavior? I've asked for guidance from God. What should I do? Can I change? I struggled with the notion that I cared too much. It didn't seem logical to me. I was too emotional about it. Could a mother's love *be* the problem? Was that even possible? What was the counselor's word? *Enmeshed.*

Later I learned that an enmeshed relationship is one in which you are obsessed with thoughts about another person's life. Your own happiness or contentment relies on what is happening with the other. The relationship affects your feelings of self-worth. You feel extreme anxiety or fear and have a compulsion to *fix* the problem when there are conflicts in the relationship.

I didn't realize at the time that I *was* playing God.

Lord, I am looking to your word right now to guide me.
"Do not judge others, and you will not be judged.
Do not condemn, and you will not be condemned.
Forgive, and you will be forgiven.
Give, and it will be given to you.
A good measure pressed down, shaken together,
and running over will be put into your lap;
for with the measure you give, will be the measure you get back."

Luke 6:37 (NRSV)

Please help me, Lord. I am not faltering in my faith. It's my actions that are not pouring out a measure of kindness, gentleness, patience, or love. My well feels dry today.

Come and be with me. Help me to say the things that will be helpful, not hurtful. I need some kind words directed towards me today as well.

Today-

—I forgive my son for his faltering steps and his weaknesses. Help me do and say the things that will build him up and support him.

—I forgive my husband for requiring me to be strong instead of allowing me to wallow in self-pity and place the blame on his shoulders. I'm secretly glad he holds me to a high standard. It's so hard!

—I forgive myself for my weaknesses and struggles.

—I forgive myself for not being able to let go.

Somehow, even though I was constantly in prayer, there were no answers. God remained silent.

? (QUESTIONS)

Where is the grave in which I have buried myself?
Where is the vat in which I can drown my sorrows?
Where is the key to chains in which I have locked my heart?
Are they in the cave of sadness I have carved into my mind?
Am I bruised and broken, beyond repair?
Are my harsh words cold like swords and daggers?
Are they to be pulled from my body?
ONE? BY ONE? BY ONE?
What is the name I shall go by?
Misery, perhaps?
Is that the "ME" that I defend?
I'll try to see the journey through, the questions lost forever
Sinking deep into the impacted snow.
Is it in a rainbow in spring rains, perhaps that I will shine?
Shining bright with an everlasting glow?
I DOUBT IT.........BUT?
Who knows?

Jolly Jackson

"Tell them how you really feel and they say
you have no right
Ha! To take my own life? I have nothing to say,
'But who gave you this right?'"

Michael M. Mehlan
Excerpt from *None*

Gail

CHAPTER 3—SOMETIME IN THE YEAR

2001

After school, we went for a haircut together. Mike was his typical self, sitting in the chair next to me, spinning around and around as he waited for my hairdresser to finish. I had to speak to him several times, and he finally went to the front of the shop, where he sat and poked holes in a Styrofoam cup with a straw.

Mike kept whining about having to go to orchestra practice that evening. He was having a hard time. I thought to myself. *He's about ready to quit.* The music was complex, and the behavior expected of the students was impeccable. The director often spoke to Mike because he had a hard time *not playing* when she was working with the other sections. The bass was loud and annoying, and these reprimands were just more negative feedback for Mike. He had missed two rehearsals, the maximum for this session. I convinced him to go, and we put off the decision to quit for at least a week.

Mike was so proud of himself when he tried out for and made the community youth orchestra. It was a big deal that this elite organization accepted him. I was proud of him too. He took private bass lessons from a gentleman we knew from our church who was an absolute saint. He was so patient with Mike, and he never lost his temper. Don, a loving and dedicated teacher, shared his faith with Mike and taught him jazz and classical music. Mike's talent for music is one of his strengths.

After our haircuts and before orchestra, we went to eat dinner at Steak and Shake, Mike's favorite place to eat, and a bribe to get him to go to practice.

Over dinner, he commented in a soft-spoken, serious voice, "I think I'm about to have a nervous breakdown."

"Are you nervous about orchestra practice or something else?"

"Not really. I'm just so stressed out."

"I know, honey—you can get easily frustrated, and sometimes you get *stuck*." Mike nodded his head in agreement.

"Mom, why did you even have me?" he asked, looking at me with eyes that could pierce a soul.

A million and one thoughts raced through my mind. My son didn't want to be here? What was he thinking? My soul recognized this question as alluding to suicide, but I shut my conscious mind at that door. He couldn't be making such a comment. That would indicate that this was much more serious, and I jumped right back into the conversation like nothing was amiss. I wanted to get back to talking to him about getting through school this year. I ignored the foreboding feeling.

"Of course, I wanted to have you! You are a very special child of mine. I went through a lot to have you. I love you so much! You are such an important part of our family."

And then the conversation went right back to school and the mundaneness of life. I promised to help him get his work done whenever I could. We also talked about getting things done in class and right after school before getting tired when his meds wore off.

"I really need a break, though. I can't deal with it."

Maybe he wasn't talking about schoolwork, but I was. I didn't want him to give up.

"Are you talking about orchestra? I would hate for you to give up on orchestra, Mike. You're so talented! Or are you worried about the graduation ceremony? It would be great if you were in the graduation ceremony, but if you are too stressed out over it, it's not worth it."

"No, it's not that—it's just that—I miss painting because I know that I can do it and then put it on hold until I get back to it." He sounded like he was going to cry.

Somehow, we went on to have a conversation about when he had tried out for the variety show not too long ago, singing the song *Wish You Were Here* by Pink Floyd.

"I had a revelation about the words to the song, *Wish You Were Here*. Remember? The song I sang for the v-show?"

"Yes, of course, I remember."

"I feel like I miss the me who was involved with stuff—like—"

"Like what?"

"Like painting, scouts, maybe soccer, and even orchestra. I miss the *old* me."

Perhaps he felt in that moment that he could handle things better *before* all that was going on in his mixed-up, sad brain. He wished his old *little boy* self could be here now.

"Well, um—it's time. We need to get going, or we'll be late for orchestra practice. Do you want a shake or something to take with you in the car?" I asked. I didn't know what to say. I dismissed the problem, and we went on our way.

Later, I wrote:

I must confess that I enjoyed the little boy I remember too, an enthusiastic player, looking forward to activities, wanting to try out for orchestra, and taking a painting class. He was confident and energetic. I miss that child, too. BUT FOR NOW, I AM CONTENT WITH WHO HE IS, *not afraid of his great potential and not afraid to make mistakes—to learn from them—continuing to plug away at some things that are challenging for him.*

It seemed like I had missed an opportunity that evening to talk about forgiveness, the essence of what my faith is all about. I didn't explain that God's promises are new every morning or that he could start fresh anytime. I didn't say that he was loved and forgiven for all the *things* that were troubling him. I didn't tell him we would somehow get through these *things* together. I was speculating about what the problems were because he kept them to himself. Even still, I didn't tell him I was content with who he was at that moment, even though I had written it in my journal. I kept emphasizing that I wanted him to plug away at things that seemed so important to *me*.

I didn't understand at the time that depression and substance abuse were stealing from him, a mere boy, the enthusiasm, the confidence, the spunkiness of his *LIFE*. I thought he had to push through it, plug away at it. I felt that medication and counseling would *fix* him. As the Pink Floyd song says, I kept "going over the same old ground." I didn't get that he was unhappy with who he was. I didn't realize that he thought maybe *my* life would have been simpler if I hadn't had *him*. He wanted to be written out of my life because he was disappointing *me*. I didn't realize that this was a cry for help, a sign of desperation, a signal. I had no idea that things were getting so hard for him. I was in denial.

This conversation would haunt me over the next several years because I *had* missed a *moment*. It's so scary to think that my son didn't see the value of his own life. I was naïve and didn't pick up on the signs of his deep depression. I didn't create the problems faced by our family. It wasn't my fault. I wasn't to blame for the trouble. But because I couldn't fix it, I would brush it under the rug. I carried on like it was all about school, graduation, and orchestra when it was so much more. I have learned since that day that most of those problems were the effects of adolescent depression. School problems, drug and alcohol use, low self-esteem, reckless behavior, running away, and self-hatred are all associated with depression. Suicide warning signs were right there. When Mike asked me, "Why did you even have me?" I didn't realize how close the possibility of losing him to suicide was.

We were lucky that nothing happened on that day. I was holding on to the thread of hope that if I were a good parent, the things just below the surface wouldn't happen. I thought life was a balance of love, good things, discipline, and hard work. My expectations of Mike were based on how *I* felt as a parent. I wasn't considering what he wanted or needed. I had to grow up *myself* and learn that *I* was no longer a kid trying to be good enough. I was an adult, and I *was* good enough, even when I *did* have shortcomings as a parent. I was doing the best that I could.

UNDER THE SEAS OF THIS REVOLUTION

I sing a sad song every time I wake up.
I sing a love song, not for me, but for your sake.
I don't know if I can stand on my two feet all alone.
I'm locked inside this tomb without a telephone.
So, I can't call my friends to help me roll away my stone.
Sit back and relax. We can still get out of this place.
You look at my lips, you hoped for a kiss,
and to my surprise, we miss.
Some would say that's not up to us but up to fate.
We came into this world too late.
But we are the ones who feel the reactions,
the guilt, and pain, pleasure, and satisfaction.
The world is a stage, and we are the actors.
We choose our own player, and we play from a reaction.
Which one are you, and who am I?
Which am I to be, and how am I willing to try?

Jolly Jackson

Michael

CHAPTER 4—WHY DID YOU EVEN HAVE ME?

2001

That's not a question you ask your mother. Frankly, you know about love and biology because it's what your parents decided to do. It's not that you were some accident at birth. They chose to love you. They chose it, and I always knew it.

I never felt like I fit. I wasn't part of the world. I didn't see the real reality. I was an invader to this universe.

There was something more to be learned in my life, more to experience, that I was somehow missing. There had to be more to life than the mundane routine of going to school going to orchestra practice. Why was I doing any of these things? I was smart, smarter than most, and as a result, I was bored, bored but unchallenged, but definitely not disciplined enough. I was Peter Pan. I wanted all the adults to go away. I wanted to be free from being told that I was broken or different when in truth, I was, and I am. Honestly, the only thing that made me different was that I was too sensitive, like someone turned up the gain too loud on this Mike- rophone, and when it's turned up too loud, it hurts.

Girls didn't like me. My friends found me to be a clown. I was too childish and fantastical. They wanted to smoke cigarettes, do drugs, smoke pot, and get with girls. Frankly, I did too, but I wanted it to be an adventure. What I found was more pain, always more pain. The more pain I found, the less I wanted to feel, so I numbed it out of existence until this Mike-rophone was utterly broken.

I loathed school. I was small and insignificant to everyone that I wanted to notice me. That pain became too much. I had a girlfriend at the time, and we were best friends, but she didn't like me like that. She wanted cooler high school guys, not the short, stocky nerd who played the orchestra's stupidly large bass. I hung out with the misfits who had troubles at home, who felt like outcasts, but I wasn't one of them. To be honest, I had love at home. I had a good family. My parents cared for each other, but for some reason, I preferred when they ignored me. And to be honest, other than having empathy for others and seeing just how damn bleak the world could be, I was sad and couldn't understand how to grow up. I still feel that pain even as I write this as an adult.

I saw my friend Jay's parents getting divorced and doing cocaine openly in the house. I saw my friend's father and brothers abuse her sexually. All those friends wanted to escape too, but they had reasons. I just wanted not *to be a disappointment anymore. I thought growing up meant more freedom, more love. I thought my high school years were gonna be like* Grease. *I thought college was gonna be like* Animal House. *I had false hopes, and those became cracks that began to dissolve into canyons by the time I was fourteen. It seemed better to quickly and easily steal drugs than endure another day with the gain on this Mike-rophone turned up to torture, and my mother didn't get it. I couldn't explain it to her, so what came out was: "Why did you even have me?"*

Those words make me cringe. But I was in pain and saw never existing as a better resolution, a way to justify why I should die. And if I had accidentally died, I could've justified it. If my mother didn't give me a good enough answer, I could justify my non-existence in this world to my friends, my family, and the universe. Maybe I could justify my invisibility. But this should not have been the question. Perhaps a better one would've been:

"Why do I feel so much?"

"Why does all of this life hurt so much?"

"Why does everyone think I'm broken?"

"Why do I feel like I'm not enough?"

"Why do I feel like a terrible son?"

"Why do I exist?"

"Why doesn't God love me?"

Any of these would've sufficed. Instead, I stabbed a knife into my mother's heart.

If I had asked any of those other questions, maybe then we would have understood each other, but I was hiding all the pain and suffering, all the secrets of puberty, friendships, and caring for others. I hid it all because I was afraid that I'd be thrown into treatment and put under a microscope. They would be giving me medication that turned me off, and I didn't want that. I didn't know how to ask for help. I didn't know how not to suffer this pain, and I couldn't tell the woman who loved and created me: "I don't feel like living anymore."

So, I made it her problem. It's what a teenager does, I suppose, but I couldn't see clearly. I didn't want to stay sober long enough to learn the answers. The world was too loud, and I couldn't find the volume control.

PILLS

I do not wish to take these pills
I thought I was sad, moving by others' wills
I fear the medicine is making me ill
I had amassed the confidence, but now giving me chills
I really don't trust 'em, Doc, these colorful pills.
I do not wish to do what the colorful pills will.

Jolly Jackson

Gail

CHAPTER 5—HERE I AM, LORD

2001

May 24, 2001

Here I am, Lord. It's 4:30 AM. I can't sleep. I awoke at 3:00 AM from a phone call from Matt's girlfriend's mom, looking for her. She wasn't home yet, but Matt was here. Unexpected phone calls in the middle of the night always bother me. I had such a nasty headache afterward. I took two ibuprofen tablets and still couldn't get back to sleep. So here I sit at the kitchen table, trying to find some inspiration to keep me going forward. You, Lord, and you alone understand the depth of my anxious feelings.

My Bible opens to this verse:

"Search me, O God, and know my heart;
test me and know my anxious thoughts.
See if there is any offensive way in me,
and lead me in the way everlasting."

Psalm 139:23 (NIV)

I witnessed the full extent of Michael's trouble yesterday as I entered the room to pick him up after his first day at the behavioral health hospital. He became *stuck* and was immobilized, irrational, and easily provoked by a brief comment I made to one of the counselors,

"Wait a minute. I have a quick question."

"You are such a bitch. I hate you, Mom!" he shouted at me with an oppositional and defiant tone.

He tried to storm out of the hospital, but a therapist stopped and restrained him as he continued to scream and curse, causing a scene in the lobby. A team of four therapists and some other students escorted him to the backroom. Finally, he calmed down enough to say he was sorry, and the staff permitted us to leave. I was mortified and angry. I didn't know how to react.

Mike attended a partial-day outpatient program at the local behavioral health hospital, brought on by his outbursts and continued school failures. His school counselor had advised us to have an evaluation done several weeks earlier, and we finally did. At that evaluation, the therapist recommended that he participate in an outpatient program to help him with his depression and oppositional behavior. He had just started there, and I had to drop him off in the morning and pick him up in the afternoon.

That day I left the church early before locking the door to the preschool entrance. After picking him up, when I stopped at the church to lock up, I told him, "Let's go, Mike. This'll only take a second." I wasn't supposed to leave him unattended.

"Geez, Mom, I don't want to go in. I'll be fine."

"Well, I want to keep an eye on you, but okay—If you try anything, I'll call the police," I said, half-jokingly, as I smiled at him.

"Mom—I said, I'll be *fine*." I felt unsure about this but hurried inside to lock up as quickly as possible.

When I returned to the car, he was gone. In the few minutes I was inside, he had gotten out of the car! I looked in all directions, thinking maybe he was having a smoke nearby, but I couldn't see him anywhere. *Maybe he had walked.* Frustrated, I decided to head home, only a few blocks away. When I got there, he was nowhere to be found. So, I immediately called the police.

Mike walked through the door just as I was giving the officer who had shown up the report. I looked up at him with a face that spoke for itself.

"He's here," I told the officer. "No report is necessary." My tone was full of anger and contempt.

But because I *had* called the police, things escalated between us for another twenty minutes after the officer left. Mike began screaming at me, calling me names.

"You're such a bitch. I hate you! This is my *HOME* and not a prison! Why did you call the POLICE? God, I HATE you!"

I was at my wit's end and didn't know what else to do or say to de-escalate the situation. I didn't say anything to Mike, but I picked up the phone to call the hospital. I wanted to talk to one of the therapists. While waiting to speak to one of his counselors, he grabbed the phone, unplugged it, and threw it at me. It just missed my shoulder but hit the wall behind me, making a hole in the drywall. He stood there in desperation, grabbed plastic spoons from the counter, and began throwing them at me. Part of me was trying not to laugh.

"Calm down, Mike. We won't go back to the hospital today

if you can stay in my sight and follow my directions for the rest of the evening," I said.

"Can I go for a bike ride?"

"No. What part of 'stay in my sight' did you not hear?"

"Can I just watch TV for a few minutes?

"I guess so. In fifteen minutes, we leave to go food shopping."

He sat and watched TV for a few minutes before turning it off.

"Take me back to the hospital," he said, coming over to me. "I want to get better and have all this stuff out of me."

"But honey, you are calm now. There's no reason to go. If you feel the need later, in the evening, we will go," I said, misunderstanding the urgency of the moment.

So, we went shopping together. Mike was a different person at that point. It was almost as if somebody had reconnected a circuit breaker. He was pleasant. He was smiling. He helped me with the heavy items. We picked out good food for meals. I allowed him to go look at the books and movies while I finished up. When I went to find him, he looked a little sheepish.

"What's going on?" I asked.

"Nothing."

His hands were in his pocket, and I intuitively felt something wasn't right.

"What do you have in your pocket, Mike?"

"Nothing!"

"Well, let's go then."

We proceeded to the checkout line, and as we were standing there, a small orange object fell out of a hole in his jacket pocket. Mike stood there holding his pocket together as I bent over to grab it to see what it was, but someone we knew called to me, and I looked up, distracted.

"Hi, Gail! How are you? I haven't seen you for a while!" An old friend stopped us to say hello.

"I'm fine. How are you? It's good to see you! Hey, have you ever met my son, Michael?"

"No! Hi, Michael. Nice to meet you!"

I slipped the item into my pocket, assuming it was a piece of candy.

On the way home, we had a fascinating discussion about good and evil, sin, and repentance. He was challenging my beliefs, which was normal for us. He wasn't arguing with me—what a miracle. I let the incident slide.

When we got home, he asked if he could go for a bike ride again, and this time I conceded, "Yes, but only for twenty minutes."

Something was suspicious about Mike wanting to go off riding his bike all the time, but I was trying to reward him for cooperating. I started getting dinner together. He returned in less than twenty minutes and helped me unload the car. All in all, he was quite pleasant and agreeable.

When his father came home, Mike didn't want to talk about what had happened earlier, the police, or the incident at the store, and we didn't push the issue. We ate dinner together as a family and had a decent conversation. After dinner, Mike said he would do the dishes, but I said, I'd do them so he could get started on his schoolwork. It was unusual for him to sit down and work on his assignments for an hour without complaining. He went to bed at 10:15 PM.

"Good night. I'll have a good day tomorrow," he said before heading to his room.

Later that evening, I looked again at the little orange candy. Of course, it was not candy. It was a round orange pill with three small "Cs" in a triangular pattern. I researched online and found that this pill was *Coricidin HPB*, a brand of cough medicine containing a drug called dextromethorphan.

HUNGER

Hunger like a dog
Hungry and potent feed for the hogs

Digging sweet things into the muck and mud
Praying for pity in empty troughs
Burning down these paper walls
Wailing mares in the sight of studs

Hunger down into the pits
Hungry deep, a wrenching stomach stitch

Eating feasts with starving paupers
Cooking peas in laundry soup
Turning glazed eyes into sticky goop
Leaning into oiled kettle stirs

Hunger to stave off the burning souls
Hungry to score the winning goal

Craving gold for these swollen bellies
Rising dough for lusts licking lips

Hunger be gone on shrinking hips
Hunger be gone while drinking sweet shining drips-
Drip- Drip- Drip-

Jolly Jackson

HEADACHE #1

Pounding blisters into the back of my spine,
a sugared pulse of pain
Strain in my ignorance
Temperance has led to spastic interceptions
Of necessary brain-trained responses
Sweet liquor of the attention deficit dispensers
Brewed mind aches of lost mood enhancers

HEADACHE #2

Bang! Smack! Slap!
BOOM! BOOM! BOOM!
Doomed at the end of a rope
Choking down the sweet strokes of harsh, blinding obliteration
Doomed to sleepless hardship, pulsating joints
Divining rough considerations
Last resorts of my thoughts tender less suffocation

Jolly Jackson

Gail

CHAPTER 6—HELP

2001

May 25, 2001
I felt like I had a good night's sleep last night, and, after yesterday, I
was drained of all emotion, numb.

But we were not done yet.

Early the next morning, as I went into Mike's room to check that he was up and moving so he wouldn't be late for the out-patient program, I got the same old run around. A hoarse voice moaned from underneath the comforter, "I don't feel good."

I thought we were getting some help for the issues that plagued us. I needed the help as much as my son did. I was at the end of my rope.

"There is no option to stay home today, Mike. You *must* get up and go to your program. Period."

"No! I don't want to go to that stupid, f**king program! I'm NOT going!"

"Yes. You ARE going."

"I AM NOT GOING! LEAVE ME ALONE!"

"I'm NOT going to leave you alone about this! Do you want me to call your dad?"

"NO! Mom—PLEASE! NO!"

"I'm going to count to three, and if you're not out of bed, I WILL call your dad. If that doesn't work, I WILL call the police!"

"The POLICE? What the f**k is wrong with you? I didn't do ANYTHING WRONG! DON'T you DARE call the police, MOM! You are a f**king idiot! YOU BITCH! I can't believe this right now! This is so f**king ridiculous. There is NOTHING wrong with me!"

"Mike, I mean it! We can't continue pretending there's nothing wrong! I'm going to start counting NOW!

One—

Two—

Three!"

No movement. No response. Mike's eyes were closed tight as he pretended to be asleep. I walked out of the room to get the phone. I said what I meant, and I meant what I said. He knew this about me.

Suddenly he jumped out of bed, rushed into the hallway, and pushed me aside. He forced himself right past me and grabbed the phone before I could get it. I panicked, wondering what I would do now that I'd made an ultimatum. I felt determined, though. I intended to follow through.

I tried to appear calm. Below the surface, my thoughts were racing out of control. I walked downstairs to retrieve my cell phone charging in the kitchen. I heard Mike slam his bedroom door and lock it. I called his dad. My husband, Doug, who was in the middle of treating patients, sensed my frustration. He apologized but said he couldn't do anything at that moment. He couldn't leave work while there were patients there. I understood.

"Then I'm calling 911," I said.

"Do what you have to do, honey."

I'm not sure why I felt like this was such an emergency, but I was big on following through with the threats.

The 911 dispatcher told me to talk Mike down and convince him to ride with me to the outpatient program. They told me to call back if he refused. I think the dispatcher sensed my desperation, but there was no calming my anxious heart. I thanked her and hung up the phone. Back up the stairs, I went to try again.

I pleaded through the locked door, "Mike, calm down, and *please* open the door so we can talk about this!"

No answer.

"Mike, PLEASE talk to me! *I* will take you, and we can get some help with whatever is going on! I want to *HELP* you!"

No answer.

Then I tried to unlock the door with a bobby pin, but he had it barricaded with a chair. He was not responding to my pleas, and I began to worry about what he was doing in his room alone. An eerie sense that he might harm himself filtered through my mind. He was pushing me to the limit, so I called 911 again.

They said they would send someone.

Two police officers soon arrived at the house and went up to Mike's room to talk with him. Mike opened the door but refused to calm down. He continued to escalate his verbal tirade and emotional outburst with them. One of the police officers shrugged his shoulders and called the paramedics.

Michael was carried off, restrained, in an ambulance. I stood in the doorway, stunned and emotional, watching as the ambulance drove off in an eerie silence, the lights flashing.

It was a harrowing day for me, but somehow, we needed to get to this point. Stunned and shocked to see this outburst from my son, I cried as I watched the ambulance drive down the street. But even then, I breathed a deep sigh and felt a sense of relief, knowing we would get some help now. I followed the ambulance to the hospital. When he arrived, they admitted him to the behavioral health hospital inpatient program. I was, for the moment, hopeful.

After four days as an inpatient, Mike seemed to be doing a little better. He still didn't want to talk about it. My husband and I tried to step back and didn't push the conversation. It felt like I was walking on eggshells whenever I was with Mike. I *wanted* to give him the chance to show us that he could make changes. I *wanted* to provide him with positive feedback when he did well. It was good to talk to the therapists at the hospital and work with them on a plan. I admit I was skeptical, and I knew it was because I'd been down this road before.

Mike was intelligent enough to portray himself as being able to cope. He was always a gifted thinker. He knew all the right things to say and do so the therapists would *think* he was making progress. Mike could talk about everything and was excellent at writing things down. He made an official contract with us about what would happen when he came home and made all sorts of promises. Mike showed improvement in front of the counselors. The teens have a word for this. They call it *fronting*. Mike was great at it, he could put up a great front, but he resisted the deep work of actually *doing* any of it when he got home.

I needed help too. I needed to learn to use words that calmed instead of escalated. I still waited for Mike to say, "I am responsible for my decisions and how I responded." I admit that I acted as immature and stubborn as my son. He resolved things by making a zillion excuses and blaming me, the mom, for everything. I took the blame, along with his teachers, the meds, and the therapists. We *all* were in this together.

I blamed Mike for everything too. As his parent, I was still holding out. *I was reluctant* to see *my* part in any of this. I wanted *him* to say *he* was sorry to *me*.

June 6, 2001
Yesterday was an emotional day for me, going to the junior high to get my son's things, thinking about how the year ended with no graduation ceremony, no positives. Yet, I realize he cannot stay my baby all his life. It just feels lousy.

A few days later, I wrote:
June 12, 2001
I am thinking about my husband today. He's the father in our family, and his words are sometimes so very wise. I am thinking in particular about what he said to Michael while in the hospital.

He told Mike: "I can't wait to be a part of your high school experiences. I imagine you being involved and active in art and music. I see myself attending a musical production at the high school to see you perform. I can't wait to do that and share those experiences with you."

His words touched my soul. It was a gift to visualize the positives and put them forth in words for Michael. I wish I could be more uplifting. Doug gave ME the gift, too. I've struggled to see the next few years positively. I appreciate Doug's ability to see a promising future for Mike. I need to work on that. I have been very negative lately. Thank you, honey, for giving me that gift.

DRY

Tepid air for empty rooms
The smoky smell clears out the gloom
The sticky turns to dry when the world of words
closes in on the one
Soon.
At once, the morning forest of reflections
had meditated on dreaded regret
The impending calamity the only mantra
known as ticking clocks hands click
A solemn tune
Soon.
Soon.

Jolly Jackson

Gail

CHAPTER 7—
SEPTEMBER 11, 2001

It was September 11, 2001. The clear blue skies and bright sun filled my car with light as I heard the radio announcer's booming voice, "*Domingo, domingo, domingo!*" echo throughout the car. I turned the volume down because it was deafening. I was listening to the news in Spanish as I drove to school because I was nervous about a scheduled Spanish proficiency exam I was to take to qualify for my bilingual education teacher's certificate. I needed the practice.

A small plane had crashed into a skyscraper in New York City? That's what I thought I heard. A building called the *Centro de Comercio Mundial*, also known as *Las Torres Gemelas*, had been struck. I paid closer attention to what the announcers were saying and thought I heard something about a *choque*, a crash. I assumed that it was an accident with a small plane, that the pilot had gotten confused—perhaps *I* did *not* understand what they were saying.

Then my mind began to wander back to the day ahead. This year Mike seemed to be doing reasonably well, but the school year had only started a few weeks ago. Had Doug been able to get Mike out the door to school that morning? We had a meeting scheduled that afternoon at the high school, and I made a mental note to remind Doug to meet me there. Mike was on a different combination of medications that seemed to help him focus, and I wondered if Doug remembered to give him his meds. My husband had stepped up and was the go-to parent for getting Mike up and out the door in the morning. He also fielded any problems that cropped up during the day. His help was a relief for me, but my *thoughts* always snapped back to the situations I had relinquished to Doug at home. I was having a hard time focusing on the news in Spanish.

As I continued to drive, I heard that a second plane had crashed into the towers. I felt that I *must* be mistaken. I leaned forward, turned up the volume, and tried to focus. The second plane was a *commercial* jet full of American citizens. They were talking about how this appeared to be *intentional*. What did they mean, intentional? Why would someone purposefully crash into a building? It was too unbelievable to be true.

When I arrived at school, I stopped and stood in silence with other teachers watching the television in the staff lounge. Most of us were in shock, hands over our mouths in disbelief. The scent of freshly brewed coffee was the only interruption to our focus. We watched, horrified at the events occurring before our eyes. Two prominent skyscrapers were burning to the ground, thousands of Americans were missing, and shocked newscasters were trying to mask their terror as the story unfolded. It was an unsettling way to start the school day. The principal came into the lounge and asked us not to discuss the day's events with the children. She didn't want to frighten them. She asked us to carry on as usual, and we did. We managed to teach that day, trying to contain our fear and uncertainty.

I had understood *perfectly* what was being said on the radio earlier that morning.

In June, after Mike's hospitalization, I interviewed with the public school system for a full-time position as a bilingual resource teacher. Since graduating from college with a dual degree in Spanish and elementary education, I had wanted to work with Spanish-speaking children and families. After nine years at the church as the director of early childhood ministries, I felt called to do something different. I prepared a resume and submitted it. By the grace of God, or perhaps in answer to my prayers for direction, the district offered me a position.

The new job was very challenging. The district required that I learn new skills, and I enrolled in graduate classes to earn my bilingual certification. I began working with various grade levels, including older children instead of preschoolers, preparing multiple lesson plans, and speaking Spanish daily. The job was demanding but was also a blessing for me in many ways. One significant benefit was better insurance for medical *and* mental health. We had been slammed with outrageous medical bills after Mike's hospitalization due to limits our previous insurance had on mental health services. Another blessing was that I was so busy teaching, preparing, and working at school that my job reduced my laser-focused efforts to control and intervene on Mike's behalf. I began to put my focus on other areas.

That afternoon, we had a meeting scheduled at the high school about starting the paperwork necessary for Michael's special education diagnosis of emotional disturbance (ED). We wanted to get him on an Individualized Educational Plan (IEP) for high school. The IEP would make it easier for Mike to receive accommodations and support for his school work. After listening to the news about the attacks all day, I called the high school, fearing they might cancel the meeting as they had already canceled most other after-school activities. The school psychologist said we should go ahead with it anyway. I'm glad we did and that, for the time being, we had a plan in place for Michael and some extra help for him at school. After all that happened that day, these decisions seemed like small things.

After the meeting, I decided to go for a walk. I needed to walk off the emotion of this horrific day. It was so calm that I could hear birds singing and the gentle breeze blowing. I perceived no airplanes overhead or traffic sounds from the highway. It was breathtakingly quiet, and it was beautiful.

September 4, 2001
Yesterday I realized that I had missed two birthdays, spent hours at school, and still feel no further ahead than I have ever been. Some days I feel so very overwhelmed. Tomorrow, I take my Spanish proficiency test—Lord, calm my anxiousness!

Lord. I am asking you NOT to desert me! I long for your hand to guide me in my work, relationships, and ALL that I do. I may be unprepared, yet I must continue to grow as a teacher. In many ways, you blessed me with this challenge. Teach ME. Help me to be the best teacher I am capable of being. In the comment section of my first formal teaching evaluation for this new job, the words "The students have found a warm, sensitive, caring teacher." jump out at me and warm my heart. I hope that what her comment said is true.

It has been a crazy and complicated week. So much has happened to our great country. Sometimes it feels like nothing because my little immediate world does not appear to have been affected, yet we HAVE been. The news reporters say that there are over 3,000 people still missing. I cannot even begin to imagine the pain that so many families face. I take a deep breath and move forward. Lord, your Spirit is within me.

Keep my family and me from evil. There seems to be so much out there! I fight against that force! I pray, and I continue to work hard. I trust that YOU will protect me and those I love

Guide me.

Bless us.

Stay with us.

SHOEBOX

Mike gave up his shoes this week
Old, beat-up, dirty "hole"—y worn-out
Shedding his old skin
Letting the new shoes be worn
Be comfortable
Become familiar
What else did Mike give up this week?
Did he give up his old feelings
Anger, resentment, frustration
Did he give up dirty, "hole"—y
thoughts?
Wrong-way, out the door, off the wall
Did he give up his worn-out attitude?
Don't, wait, can't, NO
Shedding his old skin
To make way for the new
Trying the new
Feelings—
Happiness, comfort, safety
Wearing the thoughts
Follow along
Success
On the ball
Go with the flow
Way to go!
Finding them comfortable?
Breaking them in
Finding them familiar?
Allowing his soul, as opposed to sole
To absorb the positive

To accept
Happiness, laughter, success!
YES!

Put on the shoes, make them the way
Out of the low of this past year.

Walk in the new shoes toward
The light
Of tomorrow
Of a future
Of hope—

Put the old shoes in a box to remember
But wear the new
Making them
your own

When will he break in a new hat?
Coat?

Gail Mehlan
October 2001

"And if these walls could talk
They'd tell a story
of my family
so candidly

And if these old trees
could see
They wouldn't understand
what they mean to me

They share all these things you see
They're loving things
Like a canopy

But the water will rise
and consume the fire."

Michael M. Mehlan
Excerpt from a song called, "Clear Lake" about
the family home of his grandparents.

Gail

CHAPTER 8—CLEAR LAKE

2002

When I was ten years old, my parents purchased a piece of property on Clear Lake, a small lake in Wisconsin. The water in the lake was so crystal clear that you could see all the way to the bottom in all but the deepest water. It was beautiful.

Through the years, my family visited the lake often—almost every weekend. We started by cutting through the brush and trees to make paths and set up a tent in a small clearing. There was always so much work to do, clearing brush, putting in a well, and a little outhouse in the woods. We cooked over an open fire and a hibachi grill and swam in the lake at a beach down the way. My dad purchased an aluminum boat and some oars, and my sisters and I would go out in the boat for hours, singing camp songs and enjoying the lake. I caught my first fish at Clear Lake, and, once, a giant snapping turtle was on the line. One summer, I collected 21 frogs in my Girl Scout sweatshirt pocket and brought them back to show my parents. Finally, after my dad suggested *frog legs* for a snack, we let them all go.

Over the years, our little campsite grew into a garage for storing the camping gear, a garage with a porch and windows where we stayed instead of the tent. Later they added a garage with bedrooms, a kitchen, and a basement that evolved into my parents' summer home and, in 1986, their retirement home.

Clear Lake is what we call the place now. "Let's go up to Clear Lake" means "Let's go up to Wisconsin and stay at Grandma's house." My children experienced many firsts there: first fish caught, first boat rides, first barbecues cooked, and first card games. It is more than just a beautiful, clear little lake. It is a place where we make memories.

We came to Wisconsin to stay at my mom's lake house for a few days around Thanksgiving. It was a relief to sit at her kitchen table, look out the window at the lake, listen to the birds, and watch the neighbor fishing on the dock. The bright blue November sky was a stark contrast to the dark branches of the beautiful trees. I loved coming here and breathing in the restful healing of this place, restoration for the soul.

When I am at the lake, my mind floats to images of the past—the wonderful yesterdays of my childhood, with Mom and Dad working so hard to make this a home, the kids playing in the water, learning how to fish, boat, and water ski. Dad's spirit seems to be here some-times, and I felt it. I could almost picture him leaning against his rake, looking out on the water, watching.

Mike was only seven when his grandfather passed away. My dad was so special to him, and when he died, Mike cried, "How will I learn about the stars and the trees and the rocks? Grandpa knew ev-erything!" He missed my father so much, even though it had been a few years. Being at the lake brought Mike joy and peace, and we thought being there would help him get out of his depressed funk.

After a good start to the year, he hadn't been keeping up with his classwork. He continued to have many absences. The school counsel-or suggested that he attend a program that had him sitting in front of a computer all day doing online work. He wasn't happy there but liked being on his own schedule for learning. I needed a break from the day-to-day struggles of making sure he went, and so did Doug. We were delighted to be away.

It was hard to watch Mike waste the weekend sleeping on the couch. His grandmother tried to engage him in conversation, bless her heart. He would roll over and barely open his eyes to look at her, grunting, "I'm okay, Grandma."

On Saturday morning, my mom spoke to Mike as if he were a little child, "Mike, would you please go over to the neighbors' house and check on their dogs, let them out, and make sure they have food and water? They're going to be gone for the day. Can you do that for me? Here's the key to their cottage."

" Sure." He agreed and headed down the road to take care of it. I thought it was a good idea.

"You could give them some love too. They're older dogs, so be gentle." My mom added, smiling. Mike liked dogs and needed to have something to do. So, he went, let the dogs out, checked on things, and returned.

Later that day, Mike left to go for a walk alone. He was gone for what seemed to be quite a long time. Doug asked me, "How long has Mike been gone?"

"I'm not sure, but it's been a while," I said as I looked up at the clock.

"I'm going to take a walk and see if I can find him." My husband seemed worried.

He found Mike back inside the neighbors' house.

"What are you doing in here, Mike?" Doug asked angrily. Mike was completely soaked in sweat and acting agitated and very defensive.

"I just came back to check on the dogs again. I didn't do anything wrong, Dad! Why are you always on my case?"

"You didn't need to come back here, Mike. Give me the key, and let's get out of here."

Doug was anxious that Mike had taken something, so he looked around. He double-checked everything; nothing was amiss except the mirror to the medicine cabinet was opened slightly. Doug suspected that Mike had been rummaging through their medications but couldn't be positive. He brushed it off. The dogs were okay and had their food and water. When he returned, he whispered, "I have so little trust in Mike right now, and who knows? Maybe it was nothing."

However, it *was* suspicious that Mike went back into their house using the key my mother had given him earlier. It was hard to remain calm when my mother had such trust in Mike. I felt *no* confidence in my son.

November 2002
I am powerless, Lord. Take this anxiousness from me and give me the strength to function. I am counting on you! I must keep my eyes on you, Lord, while the storm rages around me!

When we were home again, I walked into Mike's room one evening. His room was surprisingly neat, with only a few things lying on the top of his dresser. I saw a piece of paper folded into tiny squares that looked like it came from his pocket, coins, and some gum. I couldn't help myself and took the paper. Curious and nosey, I unfolded it. It was a print-out from the internet of how to get high using DXM, dextromethorphan, the medication in cough medicine. I recalled that orange pill I had scooped up off the floor at the grocery store over a year ago. Could Mike have been getting high on those pills all this time? I was conflicted about whether to leave the paper there or not, fearful that Mike would accuse me of going through his belongings. I carefully folded it and slipped it into my pocket anyway. I planned to do some more research on it later. I was suspicious of *everything* Mike was doing.

I finally sat down at the computer late one evening. When I typed in the web address on that folded-up paper, I was taken to a site that spoke of "Robotripping on DXM." As I read through the page, I felt a sick feeling creep over me. The article described different phases of tripping on cough medicine depending on how much was taken. It described the experience as something similar to tripping on other hallucinogens, but DXM was legal and available over the counter at most pharmacies. Most users favored the liquid Robitussin hence the name "Robotripping." Another common way to get high was to take large doses of *Triple C*, the street name for Coricidin HPB cough and cold tablets. I knew those were the same tablets that had fallen out of Mike's pocket at the grocery store.

Reading further in the article, I found that common side effects of using DXM were lethargy, increased body temperature, sweating, slow breathing, dangerous behavior, and hallucinations. There was no information about whether or not this drug was addictive, but it did say that taking too much of it could cause *death*.

"If I knew what they said
I wouldn't have so many questions
If I knew what they said
I wouldn't need a thing."

Matthew D. Mehlan
Excerpt from *What They Said*

Gail

CHAPTER 9—PHONE CALL

2002

It was about 10:00 PM when the phone rang. Surprise, surprise! It was my older son, Matt, calling from college in Ohio. My husband and I had just walked in the door after driving back from a weekend visiting him at school. It had been a wonderful weekend listening to his music and watching his video production for his junior year recital.

"Hello?"

"Hey, Mom, it's Matt. You guys make it back, okay?"

"Yes, we just got home. It's a long drive, but we made good time." I was surprised to hear from him so soon after getting home.

"Cool. Hey, Mom, I wanted to talk to you about something."

"Okay?" My mind began to race. What's wrong? What happened? Tiny wisps of fear filtered into my body and around my heart, squeezing it.

"What's up?"

"Well—um—like—you know how Mike spent the night

in the apartment with my friends and me over the weekend? Well—I thought you should know—I don't want you to think badly of my friends or me, but after I went to sleep—I mean after I went to bed—um—I found out that Mike smoked weed with some of my friends here. I just wanted to let you know. I'm kind of worried about him. He told my friend that he uses every day, sometimes three times a day. I think that's a lot. I wanted you and Dad to know. I'm worried."

"Oh."

"I mean, some of the guys were drinking and stuff, and I wasn't with them at the time. One of my buddies told me about it this afternoon after you guys left."

"Oh. Okay, honey, thanks for letting me know. I—um—um am frankly not surprised. I didn't know it was that much, though. Huh—um." I was stuttering, almost speechless.

A sense of foreboding settled over me. Of course, all the signs were there. I knew Mike had tried getting high on cough medicine, but we had done drug testing several times, and it showed nothing, not even marijuana. I didn't believe that cough medicine could be addictive. Marijuana use seemed like typical teenage experimentation, but Matt seemed concerned that it was more than just experimentation.

DENIAL. I convinced myself that it was other things—mental health issues, depression, and anxiety. This was a huge wake-up call for me. Drug use wasn't going to *continue* to happen on *MY* watch. As Mike's parents, we needed to do *something*!

Mike was already going to therapy weekly with a counselor, and so was I. Sometimes my husband would come with us. We would all go simultaneously and split up, each seeing our own counselor or therapist. Mike's counselor was a compassionate young man, and we were able to speak with him about Mike's drug use when we were at the counseling sessions together. I wanted to protect Matt from Mike's wrath for ratting him out about marijuana use, so I waited until we were in the calm environment of the counseling sessions to address the issue. It felt like a safe place. Mike's counselor was very understanding and addressed the drug use with Mike. He helped Mike quite a bit with behavioral and social issues, but he was *not* an addictions specialist. He recommended that we all see a friend of his who was trained in addictions and shared office space at the same location. We set up sessions for Mike with her, and she also met with Doug and me when he was with his other counselor. She kept encouraging us to let go and let the consequences of his actions lead our interventions. I tried hard, but letting go didn't feel right. Letting go felt like abandoning my child. I couldn't *NOT* do something.

"My son started using when he was 15. Now he's 40 and just entered a methadone clinic for treatment." I listened as I sat at my first Twelve-Step meeting for families of children and adults who use drugs and alcohol. I heard different stories from each person. There was laughter. There were tears, too, sprinkled with hope.

"My son is 34 and still drinks. His liver isn't functioning, and he's in the hospital now, clinging to life. I don't know what to do!"

"My daughter has been clean for seven years and wants to start a sober living house for women."

"My son is 17, and I just found out he's using marijuana daily," I'd said.

I felt very naïve, but when I opened up to others after the meeting, I felt welcomed and cared for. These folks had been there, understood the situation, and listened with a sympathetic ear. They saw me in my struggle and gave me honest feedback when they saw me trying to manipulate and control our situation. I no longer felt alone. I learned so much in these rooms. I began to recover even though I hadn't entirely accepted that addiction was a disease. It is not an easy *fix*. Recovery is a lifestyle.

Working the steps was a way to move beyond the struggle and create a better life for *me*, whether my loved one found recovery or not. I held on tight to the experience, strength, and hope of the other people in the program, especially those whose children *had* found recovery.

After the phone call, I began to look for ways to get Mike into treatment. I was sure that going to a drug treatment program would benefit him and take care of the problem. I didn't want to let this go and wait until my child was 40 to influence the outcome. I checked into all of the treatment facilities in the area. I asked about what our insurance covered and where we could send him. All of the treatment programs required an intake interview. Mike wouldn't cooperate with us, so I looked for other options. I investigated boot camps, where parents sent their troubled teens to detox and learn hard lessons out in the wilderness. I researched boarding schools, military, and special education programs. Despite all my efforts, we never came up with a plan that seemed workable. I had a stockpile of brochures and many emails from facilities hoping to convince us to send our son to them. It isn't easy to *force* your child into recovery. I tried to communicate the information to Doug, but he always responded, "Let's keep a wait-and-see attitude."

After one semester of doing the online course work, Mike went back to the regular high school. Once there, he didn't go to class or do any work. He participated in the Jazz Band for a while and even worked on the school yearbook. I used these activities to justify that there were *some* positives. But these involvements ended up going by the wayside as he continued to spiral downwards into what seemed to be a pit of depression.

My husband would drop Mike off at the high school's front door and leave for work. As soon as he arrived at work, there would be a message from the school secretary.

"Mr. Mehlan? This is the attendance office from Hoffman Estates High School calling to inform you that Michael was not in his homeroom class this morning. We have not received a call today that he will be out. Please call to verify his absence." Doug would be frustrated, knowing he couldn't leave immediately to check on Mike with patients waiting for treatment. He would have to call the high school *and* find a break in his busy schedule to head home.

Nine times out of ten, Mike would be sleeping in his bed by the time my husband could get away. Some days, he got Mike to go back to school, but some days not. Doug never admitted that Mike was high when he saw him. He would often tell me with a sigh that Mike was fine. Mostly, he was worried that he would harm himself. Doug was just glad Mike was *alive*.

My new job kept me very busy. I was difficult to reach during school hours, so the brunt of responsibility surrounding the school's phone calls went to Doug. It was a relief, but I was always frustrated when I got home and found out what had happened. Doug continued to be more matter-of-fact about the cough medicine and marijuana use, chalking it up to teen experimentation.

Anxious to return to Spain to visit the family I had stayed with as a young college student, I spent time planning a memorable family trip to Europe for three weeks during the summer. I could use the trip as part of my continuing education plan because I needed to use the Spanish language for my teaching role and wanted to gain additional practice. It was also the diversion I needed during this rough patch. I needed to escape to a foreign country and forget the issues that continued to present themselves.

I purchased tickets and set up hotel reservations. We invited our daughter to go on the trip with us. We were also going to meet up with our middle son, Matt, who would be traveling

GAIL MEHLAN | M. M. MEHLAN

in Spain simultaneously. We were all excited about this planned vacation, but it seemed that traveling with Mike would not be a good idea as time got closer and closer. The addictions therapist kept telling me, "You simply can't reward Mike for this behavior with a trip to Europe!"

Of course, I *knew* that. But I was still in denial.

CHESS WITH MYSELF

I played a game of chess with Myself and lost
I had a friend who
lost his mind
Maybe there's some
rope on sale in heaven

This is the part of the story
when my brother
moves away

When I try, I fall
When I move, I cry
When I talk, I lie
When I see, I'm blind

The air is cold
It takes a breath
to see the stars

Sister, can you be there?
Mother, why are you?
Father, listen to me
I can't do it alone
I can't be alone

Shaking
I lift my head
F**k you
I'm tired and
I can't sleep

I can *Not* try
I can *Not* lie
I can *Not* do it

Michael M. Mehlan
Poetry found in a notebook, March 2003

Gail

CHAPTER 10—OH! OH! OH! ANOTHER DAY

2003

"Gail, what do you need from Doug when Mike gets emotional?" The counselor's question had me thinking. We had been talking for over an hour already, long past the time allotted for the session.

"I'm not sure—but I think I want him to take over, be more in charge. I feel alone in all of this—I don't know."

"I have to work, Gail, and I can't be there all the time. You can always call me, but sometimes you just have to deal with it. You called the other day, and I had three patients lined up in the waiting room, and I couldn't talk."

"I know, I do, but—I have to work too... " I tried to respond.

"You're not alone in this, Gail. I'm doing the best I can."

"I just don't feel respected sometimes—Mike doesn't listen to me." Mike gets up and swings around to face me.

"You are nuts, Mom. You always call the damn police on me! I'm not a criminal!"

"I know, Mike," my husband replied, sympathizing with Mike.

I thought: *So, you agree with Mike. I'm **nuts**?*

Doug continued talking, telling a story about something irrelevant that happened in the past. The counselor shifted his body from side to side, crossed and uncrossed his legs, impatient for Doug to wrap up his thoughts. Were we making any progress at all?

When the counselor suggested that we have another evaluation at the behavioral health hospital, Mike became agitated and walked out of the session.

A few days later, I was going about my business getting ready for school when I heard Mike yelling at Doug downstairs. Mike was upset because Doug was *watching* him leave.

"He must have something in the garage he wants," Doug said.

Or needs, I thought to myself.

"I won't leave with you standing there! Quit watching me, Dad!"

"I'm watching you until you leave. Now, go! You'll miss the bus."

Mike was frozen and wouldn't move.

"No! Dad, you're an asshole. I want you to leave me alone. You're pissing me off right now!" Mike turned around and stormed into the house, crying.

"Why won't you two just leave me alone? You're treating me like a baby! I'm not a baby!" He put his head down on the kitchen table, sobbing inconsolably.

I could not help but say, "When you act like a two-year-old, you get treated like a two-year-old!" It was time for me to leave, so I asked him, "Do you want me to drive you to school today?"

"No way! Just leave me alone! You're making me so anxious watching me! F**k you, Dad. Leave me alone!"

"I have to get ready for work, Mike. I don't have time for this nonsense." My husband turned and went upstairs.

Doug was trying to hold Mike accountable but having a hard time with it. I felt a camaraderie with Doug, knowing that we were both struggling. I went outside to my car to leave but decided to wait for a few extra minutes to see how this played out.

The garage door went down for about one or two minutes, then up again. Mike came out and saw me in the car. I rolled down my window to speak to him, and he went ballistic. "Why are you *still* here? Just leave. I'm not leaving until you go!" I sat there patiently, totally baffled.

"You'll have a drug test," I informed him, and I left. I worried about how I handled the situation on the drive to school. How do we keep doing this day after day? I began to worry about his mental health, especially if the drug test was negative.

That evening, I was lying in bed reading and trying to relax after a busy day. Mike opened the door and said, "Can I talk to you for a minute, Mom?"

"Of course," I said as I patted the side of the bed next to me. Mike was always the child who would creep into bed with us and seek comfort by lying next to me for a little while before he surrendered to sleep.

He snuggled in next to me, and we started talking about the possibility of going to Spain again. "Are we really going to go this summer, Mom?" He asked me. I hated to put conditions on this trip but had to reply with a question for him.

"How are things going with the counselor, and are you trying to work your program? He says you shouldn't come with us if you're using *anything*. That's the reality, honey."

"Geez, Mom, why is it always about that? I just want to go back to Spain, see your family, and spend time with you guys. I've been doing so good lately—I've been clean for 23 days now."

"That's great!" I tried to sound supportive. His behavior that morning had been so questionable. I loved this kid so much, but I had *strong* feelings about what was happening.

"I don't understand why you were so angry with Dad today. He wasn't doing anything to you before you left for school. Why the meltdown?"

"I know, Mom, I just get so frustrated with you guys. You don't trust me. You never leave me alone, and I still get stuck sometimes. I'm sorry, I don't know why I do that."

"We'll see about Spain, Mike. I did purchase the plane tickets the other day. Keep on keeping on. I *want* you to come with us too." Mike rolled over and got up.

"I want to go so bad, Mom. Please?"

"We'll see," I sighed, feeling so much doubt. We had come together briefly after being so far apart. It was a moment of quiet congruity between us, yet the shadows around us stayed dark. Mike was up and down the stairs many times that night and was still up at 2:00 AM. I couldn't sleep either, and I wondered if there was a reasonable consequence for his late-night wanderings.

In the morning, I called the behavioral health hospital and set up the evaluation for Mike that afternoon after school. I called Doug and told him that I would need his help to get Mike there, so we agreed to pick him up from school early together and take him for the promised drug test first. I needed to follow through with my threat.

After school, Mike was surprised to see his father with me when I picked him up.

"Why are you here?" Mike asked with a sarcastic edge in his voice.

"I care about you, Mike. I am going to be involved," Doug said.

"Yeah, right." Mike retorted as he got into the back seat.

We drove in silence to the hospital for the drug test. Doug waited outside in the car while I went in with Mike.

I signed him in, and a few minutes later, the nurse called us to get the supplies for the test. I told Mike that I would go into the bathroom with him to make sure he peed in the cup.

"No way, Mom. I can do this alone." He walked into the bathroom ahead of me, and I followed closely behind. My instincts told me he was up to something.

I put my foot against the door to hold it open and tried to get myself in there with him. Then I saw him reach into his pocket and pull out a small bottle. It looked like a Visine container without the label. "What the heck are you doing, Mike? What's that in your hand?"

"Get out of here, Mom! I told you I could do this myself!" He stumbled forward a bit, so I came in and closed the door.

"It's just some eyedrops, that's all."

I felt my heart speed up with anxiety, but I was victorious that I had gotten *into* the bathroom. I handed Mike the cup to pee in, and he dropped his drawers and started peeing. I saw him stop, and then, like a magician, he whipped out the little bottle and started to spray it into the sample.

"Stop that, Mike!" I reached out to stop him, and he dropped the bottle.

"Give me the sample," I said sternly. I didn't yell. I just took a deep breath to steady myself. Surprisingly, Mike handed it over, zipped up his pants, and said, "Let's get out of here."

I didn't get a chance to tell Doug what happened until later, but I knew that Mike had tried to *alter* the drug test. We would know in a few days what the results were.

When we arrived at the behavioral health hospital for the evaluation, Mike was outraged. He had no idea that we had set this up. Doug was prepared and had locked the child locks on the car. When Doug opened the door for Mike, he tried to run, but Doug grabbed him, wrapped his arms around his body, and wrestled him to the ground. Doug had a few words with Mike that I couldn't hear, and after a few minutes, they got up and walked calmly arm in arm into the building for the assessment. I followed, amazed.

The counselor recommended a six-week outpatient program for Mike. I was worried that he would refuse because of what had happened the last time he was an outpatient. We warned Mike that he would *NOT* go to Spain with us unless he cooperated. Mike wanted to go with us to Spain so much that, miraculously, he reluctantly attended the outpatient drug rehab program each day.

When I received the results from the drug test, it was positive for PCP, *Phencyclidine*, also known as *angel dust,* a hallucinogenic drug, *and* marijuana. I know now that DXM, dextromethorphan, often shows up on a drug test as PCP.

LOOKING AT THE SUN
WITH A KALEIDOSCOPE

With tears in a jar
and stars behind glass
What happened here I cannot say
Watching television with sunglasses on
Basking in the moon
looking at the sun
with a kaleidoscope

Look past these eyes
Wouldn't you like to see?

Time takes its toll
but stops at a red light
It's always on yellow
Don't move too fast
But speed up
I'm lost in the sea
but found in the desert

Look past these eyes
Wouldn't you like to see?

Warmed by a baseball hat
chilled by a smoothie
Walking up to a stranger
and become friends
Hey you,
pass the cigarette
I'm quitting

Look past these eyes
Wouldn't you like to see?

Michael M. Mehlan
Poetry found in a notebook, March 2003

"With tears in a jar
and stars behind glass
What happened here I cannot say
Watching television with sunglasses on
Basking in the moon
looking at the sun
with a kaleidoscope"

Michael M. Mehlan

Gail

CHAPTER 11—KALEIDOSCOPE

2003

June 8, 2003

Lord, I want more time with Mike before I watch him fall deeper into the muck of addiction. I want to find places of healing for me, my family, and our son. I believe that time away from this place I call home—with no connection to this life of schoolwork or friends—will be a place of healing for our family. Being a continent away and in Spain, with only those who love us the most, can, I believe, bring us all to a place of love, acceptance, respect, and yes, even forgiveness. Being away from these silent, deadly triggers will be a time of nourishment for our souls, draw us together, and give us time and the closeness we so desperately need for healing to happen. Even if it doesn't create miracles in Mike's life, it will make memories.

I want it to bring us back to the center, to our family, to joy—to hope.

Before Mike dies on the couch from an overdose on cough medicine—I want him to know how I feel—that this drug problem has frozen me. It has rendered my mouth incapable of speaking. It has overwhelmed me and obsessed me. Lord, I pray it is not time for Mike to go—but he is on a deadly path. I pray that we are wise. I pray for discernment. Show us what to do.

I can use these words to justify what I want. Ultimately I am asked to follow your plans for me.

I completely surrender my heart to you, Lord, awaiting your answer.

The day after I wrote this desperate prayer, Mike had an appointment with the eye doctor in the afternoon. After the visit, he said, "I want to stop at the library."

"That's not a good idea right now, Mike. You have a bass lesson at 6:00 PM and an appointment with Dr. J at 7:30 PM. We have less than an hour to get home and get it all done."

"I want to go to the library NOW," he shouted, squinting due to the sunlight in his dilated eyes from the exam. Tears were streaming down his face, making him uncomfortable and edgy. Unexpectedly, he jerked up on the emergency brake, and my car came to a dead stop in the middle of the road. Thankfully there was no one behind me.

"Mike! We could have had an accident! What are you doing?" I released the brake and started driving again.

"Just take me to the library!" My mind started questioning: *What was at the library?*

"Mike, what do you need at the library?" I asked him.

"Mom—just take me there!" He yanked the emergency brake *again*. Then he leaned over and took the keys out of the ignition! We were stopped right in the middle of a neighborhood street. Luckily.

"Why can't we just go to the library? I want to go to the library NOW," he yelled at me. I took a deep breath and thought: *NO, Gail, stay calm, don't react in anger. Ground yourself. Think!*

How can you de-escalate? I took a very deep breath.

"No. We are going home. We have things to do. We'll go tomorrow. Give me the keys, Mike." I glared at him. He gave me the keys, and we continued driving.

When we stopped at a corner near the library for a red light, he opened the door and jumped out of the car.

"I'll walk to the library," he said, slamming the door as he left.

The only thing I could think to do was call the therapist from his outpatient program.

He told me to get Mike back in the car and bring him in for another assessment. I felt defeated. There was no way I could even catch up to Mike.

So, I drove to the library, went inside, and waited for Mike to arrive on foot. When he got there, he entered, saw me, and stopped.

"What are *you* doing here, Mom?"

"I came to pick you up so we could go home. Let's go find what you need from the library."

"Why are you *following* me?"

"I'm not following you. I'm just trying to help you find your books so we can get out of here quickly and get home."

"Stop following me!" he said, angry that I was even there. He took off.

I chased him around the library, past the books and video section. He dipped in and out of the bookcases, sneakily slipped out another door, and straight across the street towards Dominick's, a local grocery store. I tried to catch up to him, but he moved very quickly. He headed directly to the pharmacy section, and from down the aisle, I *saw* my son steal something right off the shelves, stick it inside his jacket and walk calmly out of the store.

The manager of Dominick's rushed out of the door after Mike and shouted, "Hey! Stop that man!"

I approached the manager and told him that it was my son and that he should call the police. He thanked me and made the call. The police car arrived in minutes, and the two officers began searching for Mike. I gave them an accurate description, and they found him a few moments later in the library. The police officers ordered him to leave the library, and when confronted, he resisted. The officers restrained him, took his wallet, and escorted an angry, distraught boy to the police car in handcuffs. One of the officers found 40 Coricidin HPB tablets in Mike's wallet.

I went back to Dominick's with one of the officers to speak with the store manager. He was so kind and declined to press charges under the circumstances. I thanked them both, and as we walked back toward the police car, I told the officer that Mike was in an outpatient program at the behavioral health hospital. He told me they would take him directly to the emergency room. I was left watching my child carried off in a squad car, lights flashing. The scene felt eerily familiar.

I called Doug, and he met me at the hospital. We walked into the room and encountered our frantic and desperate son. He became hysterical when he saw us and clung to his father, crying, "Don't leave me here! Please, Dad!"

I stood in the background, scared and angry until the security guard intervened. Mike didn't calm down and resisted until the nurse managed to inject him with a tranquilizer, and as she withdrew the needle slowly from his arm, he finally stopped fighting. I watched as he began to relax into a stupor as they restrained him to a stretcher and began preparing to transport him to the behavioral health hospital via ambulance. There, they admitted him into the hospital as an inpatient. Again.

June 10, 2003
Lord, Lord—he is so sick and needy! He is out of control, and the
relapse seems severe. Now he is inpatient, restrained, angry, desperate,
and sedated with even more drugs. I don't know how I could even
think about traveling out of the country with Mike. Give me what I
need today, Lord, because I don't even know what it is anymore.
Breathe, breathe, calmly accept a safety net, however temporary.
Accept relief for today. He is safe. I love him so much!

The therapists at the program continued to warn us that we should not take Mike on a trip to Europe with us in his condition. I knew this was true. Even though, in my heart, I wanted him to come with us. After only a few days in the hospital, he was back in the outpatient program again.

One of the counselors asked Doug and me one evening, "What are your goals for Mike in the future?"

"We hope he'll go on to college." I'd answered.

His reply was hurtful but had a truth to it that I refused to accept.

"If he doesn't get more help, you won't be visiting Mike in college. You'll be visiting him in the state prison."

I was on summer break and scrambled to find a 30-day residential drug treatment program for Mike that would have an opening at the end of his current treatment and would keep him for the duration of our trip. At the time, there were no beds available in any of the adolescent programs in our area. I set up a phone intake assessment with a treatment program in Minnesota that I knew had a good reputation. Mike reluctantly spoke with them, and they told me they would accept him, but we could not get a placement there for a few weeks either. I scheduled another phone assessment for him the day after we were to return from our trip.

A few short days after Mike's six-week program ended, we left on our family trip to Spain together.

I LOVE YOU

"I should have seen the omens
I should have seen the problem
But I couldn't stop the avalanche
But now I take a stance
I'll take a chance
    I love you
     I love you
      I love you
      I love you
       I love you
       I love you
       I love you
        I love you

          I love you
           I love you
            I love you

           I love you

I love you
  I love you

    I'll say it a hundred times
      It doesn't mean what it did before."

Jolly Jackson
Excerpt from *I Love You*

"Wherever you go, there you are"
Attributed to Confucius

Gail

CHAPTER 12—ESCAPING TO EUROPE

2003

Traveling with two kids and meeting up with the third was challenging, but somehow it worked out. We visited beautiful sights, ate delicious meals together, and reconnected again with my dear Spanish family.

My daughter had to return home to go back to work after two weeks, as did my husband. Matt went on to travel with his girlfriend. So, Mike and I stayed another week in Segovia, where I'd lived in 1973, just the two of us.

Each day we visited with my Spanish *mamá* and *papá*. *Papá* was an artist; he painted beautiful scenes from Segovia and other nearby places. He and Mike painted together on several occasions. We took day trips to local villages, and they would set up the easel, get out the watercolors, and paint what they saw. It was so funny to watch them try to communicate! I had to laugh so many times at the miscommunication.

I have several of Mike's paintings from Spain hanging with love in our home alongside the pictures my *papá* made for me.

My Spanish brothers, who had all been little children when I lived with the family, are all very musical, and one of them, in particular, spent several hours teaching Mike to play the Spanish guitar. Mike picked it up amazingly well. Even though he spoke not a word of Spanish, the music and the demonstration of how to do it worked well.

One day, on our way home from Sepulveda, a small-town north of Madrid, we spotted a field of sunflowers mixed with wheat growing on the side of the road. I insisted we stop and take a picture of me among the sunflowers. Mike was impatient with me, tired from a long day, but he snapped a nice photo of me there. It was one of those moments you don't forget. I was in Spain, standing with my son in a field of such beautiful flowers. It was extraordinary. We were spending quality time together.

That night, Mike asked me, "Mom, why don't you write a book about what life would be like if you didn't have kids and had just stayed in Spain when you were here the first time? You could call it 'Among the Sunflowers'."

I told him I wouldn't have done anything differently. There was nothing I wanted more at that moment than to be in Spain with my beloved Spanish family *and* with him, to walk in the sunflower fields together, and to stay far away from all of our problems and concerns about life back home. He smiled and said, "Yeah, me, too."

As the last week of our trip drew to a close, a few incidents concerned me. One thing I've now learned is that *wherever you go, there you are.* Your problems follow you. Mine followed me way across an ocean.

I woke up in the hotel room one night, and in the dim light coming through the window, I saw Michael wandering around the small room, disorientated. He stopped in front of my suitcase, and I jumped up as I saw him attempting to urinate in my suitcase. "Mike! What are you doing?" I yelled.

He looked up at me with a blank stare. I quickly diverted him to the bathroom just in time. He was sleepwalking, I assumed.

But I lay awake the rest of the night, unable to sleep.

I was on high alert the night he vomited for hours in the bathroom and wouldn't let me come in to talk to him. I sat listening to him gag and regurgitate. I jumped right to the thought that he had gotten his hands on some alcohol or something else, but I wasn't sure. He swore it was food poisoning. I was ready to get him home and into another treatment program.

On the last day of our trip, we made it to the airport, checked in our rental car with no problem, and got on our flight home. We had to stop for several hours in London for a layover, and after we had gone through customs, I looked around for Michael. He'd been walking with me a few moments before but was nowhere in sight. Just like that. Gone.

Now, there I was, alone at an international airport in another country. My sixteen-year-old son was missing, and I didn't know what to do. I panicked. I had his boarding pass, passport, and other information with me, so he had no form of identification on him. If he tried to do something at the airport and got caught, there's no telling what the consequences would be.

I tried to think. I prayed, *"Lord, I am letting go of this situation to YOU right now! I don't know where my son is! I trust that YOU know where he is and that you are watching over him!"* I looked at my watch and walked with determination to the gate to wait for our flight back to Chicago. Could I get on that plane if he didn't show up? Alone? No matter how determined I thought I was, I doubted I could leave him there.

I arrived at the gate and looked for a seat to wait until they called us to board the flight. If Michael didn't show up, I would stay in London and file a report. For the moment, though, I just sat down and put my face into my hands. Breathing in and out to calm down, I repeated my prayer. *"Lord, I am* truly *letting go of this situation to YOU right now! I don't know where my son is! I trust that YOU know where he is and that you are watching over him!"*

"Passengers are now boarding for US Airways Flight 5767 to Chicago. Please report to Gate 5B," came over the loudspeaker. I turned around to look again for my son, and there he was, running towards me in the terminal.

"Where the hell have you been?" I whispered so no one else would hear me.

"I just wanted to look around."

"But, Mike, I couldn't find you! Why didn't you tell me where you were going? I've been sick with worry!"

"It's no big deal, Mom. I'm here now. Let's go."

He looked a little flushed and antsy, but I was relieved. We boarded the plane with no incidents and began our flight home. Mike slept most of the eight-hour flight. When he got off the plane, he realized that he had accidentally left his old, tattered jacket with holes in the pocket on the plane. I was glad. He was not.

Mike did not, however, forget his backpack. The next day, after we arrived home, I checked his bag from the trip. In it, there was a huge bottle of absinthe. I knew it was alcohol and that he had probably stolen it at the airport. I remembered we had to do a phone assessment the next day for the treatment facility in Minnesota. No matter what Mike told them, I would have to let them know about this.

Absinthe is a potent alcoholic beverage. I was unfamiliar with it and was curious to learn more about it. I discovered that it is often used as a hallucinogen by young people. It is debatable whether that's true, but its alcohol content can be as high as 45-50%.

EMPTY VESSELS

The wine it calls to me from the holiest of golden bottles
How can I wait to drink, to sing you songs of sorrow?
A sorrow of a song that laughs loudly
to empty vessels in my soul
The sadness, it comes as lush gardens
and streams of flowing water—
To drown the parish of joy,
the end of our joyous singing
Just as the heavens are blue,
so shall my heart be again standing tall and true
Blossoming like the tulips again in the springtime
So, tell me now, keeper of the tavern,
is your cellar full of all the golden ales?
With silent guitars and lutes ready to strike,
our cups have run dry
For these two horned things go together better
With the sweet fragrance of life
Bring us the cask and fill up my cup
Drink it down to the last drop,
for dark is this life, *dark is our death.*

Jolly Jackson

"Two are better than one because
they have a good return for their labor:
If either of them falls down,
one can help the other up.
But pity anyone who falls and
has no one to help them up."

Ecclesiastes 4:9-11 (NIV)

Gail

CHAPTER 13—YOU'VE GOT TO HAVE FRIENDS

2003

One morning, I drove into the school parking lot and saw a large pine tree in front of me. The tree was obscured by heavy fog, but at the very moment I arrived and pulled into my parking spot, the sun began to shine in the east and light up the tree. It was glowing. The image was breathtaking. I imagined it was the spirit of God sending me a message of hope. My despair dissipated as I gathered my things to face another day.

It had been a rainy, miserable week. I'd been in a funk after I dropped Michael off at a treatment program in Minnesota. My son was making slow progress. I received phone calls almost daily from the staff about how defiant he was. At least it wasn't only with me. He had disconnected the alarm on his door to the outside so he could sneak out for a cigarette. He refused to participate in the group sessions when he didn't feel like it. I was disappointed but so thankful that he was *not* at home. This time of treatment gave us a slight reprieve from the day-to-day ups and downs of his presence.

My job *was* a distraction from what was happening with my son, which was a good thing, but at the same time, I didn't feel like I was doing well in my teaching position. I had been there for over a year, and the job still felt new and challenging. I had always been very comfortable and confident working with young preschoolers in my previous job. I found it difficult to teach various grade levels of students with limited English proficiency who needed so many different things.

I missed sneaking into the church sanctuary during the day to pray alone. I yearned for my teacher friends from the church preschool, who knew my story and understood how it affected me. I began fantasizing about quitting my job at the end of the school year. I took a lot of deep breaths and kept doing my best, but with a heavy heart and an edge of sadness.

Immediately after school, an announcement came over the loudspeaker for the staff to go to the teacher's lounge. There was tension in the room as we all gathered, not knowing what was happening.

The principal, new to the school that year, stood and said, "I'm so sorry to be informing you all of this, but our second-grade teacher has had a recurrence of her cancer and is not doing well. Now, things are critical for her, and they are discontinuing her cancer treatment. She is being admitted into hospice in the next few days. Please keep her in your thoughts and prayers."

I didn't know this teacher well, but I knew she was loved and respected. I felt ashamed of myself for being overwhelmed with my job and home situation. I vowed to keep the teacher in my prayers during the upcoming days. I also promised God I would stop feeling sorry for myself and think about others for a change. I needed to make a conscious effort because my own thoughts and concerns always seemed to barge toward the top of my personal prayer list. I felt like I was very selfish in my time alone with God.

After school, I walked down to the first-grade hallway to talk to one of the teachers about a few of my bilingual students in her class. I was trying to find out what they were working on so I had a better idea of what to plan for them. She was a new teacher in our building, a substitute for a few years before getting hired to work full time. She smiled at me and warmly invited me into her room. In an instant, I felt so welcomed there. It was as if we had been friends for a long time. She had been talking to one of the other teachers and showing her some pictures on the computer. The other teacher needed to leave to get things done. For teachers, there's usually not much time for chitchat.

"See you later, Tami!" the other teacher said as she walked out of the room.

"See you later!" Tami smiled.

"Come over here, Gail. I want to show you some pictures of my son," Tami said to me in the sweetest voice.

I walked over to look at the computer where she had displayed a website of pictures of a group of well-dressed young men, shirts tucked in, all smiling and laughing together in the sun. To me, it appeared as if they were on vacation in a tropical paradise.

"My son is away at a boarding school in the Dominican Republic. I haven't seen pictures of him for three months. Oh! He looks so good. He looks so happy. Oh, my gosh! I've got to tell you about this."

She told me, hanging her head as if she was ashamed,

"My husband and I had to send our son away because he started to get into too much trouble. We wanted to do something before things got out of hand."

"I sent my son away, too," I said with chagrin, sighing deeply.
"You did?" she asked.

"Yes, he's at a treatment program in Minnesota right now."

I smiled back at her, and I felt my heartbeat accelerate. I felt anxious and ashamed about sharing my story. No one here at school knew much about my struggles. I'd been silent about them.

"Tell me about it," she said, no judgment. I could feel love radiate from her as she listened. When I stopped and sighed with resignation, she began telling me her story.

"We need to support one another. You can come and talk to me at any time. I totally understand what you're going through. Believe me. It's not easy."

Somehow, after visiting with her for only a few minutes, I didn't feel so alone.

I couldn't get the images of her son out of my mind, dressed in a shirt and tie, looking happy and healthy. I imagined *my* son, with his long, greasy hair, ragged clothes, pale skin, and deep dark circles under his eyes. I would love to see him healthy. What a stark contrast!

I wrote down the school's name, so I could check it out on the Internet when I got home. She confided that it was a Christian boarding school, and her husband had worked there as a young man. I was curious.

One day the next week, we were again summoned into one of the classrooms for a meeting. We learned that the sick second-grade teacher had declined, and the principal asked us to pray for her if we were so inspired.

"Let's pray for her together now if you're so inclined; you can stay and join us," I said.

Those that wanted to, which was almost everyone, joined hands, and somehow, I managed to pray for this teacher who was in the last few days of her life. Others prayed aloud for her as well. It was very moving. After that day, I knew I was no longer alone at this school. I knew then that several teachers shared my faith. Tami was one of the teachers who stayed to pray with us that day, and I knew that there would be something special about our friendship.

My son's situation continued to be a daily struggle, and several times, I had to take calls from the counselors in Minnesota, which disrupted my school days. I seemed unable to get a handle on myself. I was so distraught over my situation that I always felt on the verge of tears. Some days I doubted I would be able to carry on without the newly found connection with Tami.

As Tami and I spent more time together and got to know each other better, our friendship grew. There was a sense of safety with her. She identified with my sorrow and I with hers. The temporary separation of our families for similar causes united us in a bond that grew steadily. When things got out of control with my son in treatment, and he came home before he completed the program for a suicide threat, she simply said, "We have to pray!"

We would stop in the middle of the school day and say a quick prayer together in the hallway. I was desperate for another alternative for Mike, so Tami invited me to a parent meeting for her son's school. I went with her one evening, learned more about their program, and met some staff.

We prayed together almost every morning. I have clear, strong memories of how we must have looked through the closed classroom doors. Odd to others—our heads bowed, united in prayer for our lost children, tears flowing of the spirit, emotions always at the surface, searching for wisdom. I resisted thinking I might have to do something more. My son was home again, and I feared what was coming. Yet, Tami continued to encourage me. I embraced the growth of our friendship from the bond of shared experience. We were two teachers and *mothers*, united and steadfast in seeking help from each other and the spirit of God. We kept on doing our jobs even when our hearts were breaking.

I had found a friend. Our genuine love for each other blossomed. I believed without a doubt that I was called to be at this school for a reason.

"But do not forget this one thing, dear friends:
With the Lord, a day is like a thousand years,
and a thousand years are like a day.
The Lord is not slow in keeping his promise,
as some understand slowness.
Instead, he is patient with you, not wanting anyone to perish,
but everyone to come to repentance."

2 Peter 3:8-9 (NIV)

Gail

CHAPTER 14—GOD NEEDS MORE TIME

2003

I took a good hard look around our now empty nest when I returned home after the trip to drop Mike off at a treatment center in Minnesota. I was alone. Before Mike got into treatment, I believed I couldn't look at *my* character while dealing with the chaos of his addiction every day. Now that he was gone, I had the freedom to start a much-needed time of learning and growing. Was I ready to tackle and absorb all the ideas, thoughts, and concepts I was *supposed* to have learned along the way in my Twelve-Step program?

This precious time provided me with the perfect opportunity to begin. I was reluctant to start the step requiring me to look at *myself* deeply and find the areas *I* was responsible for changing. I could only change myself, but could I? Did I genuinely want to change?

A casual friend from my Monday night meeting said she would be happy to be my *temporary* sponsor until I found the right one. She was willing to sit with me and walk me through working the steps. So, we began a journey together that I desperately needed. I started with the drive of an addict. I was anxious to get through this and be *done!*

I began the arduous task of looking back on my life and taking an inventory of what and where I had slipped up as a parent and human being. I used printed materials and answered questions about my life in my journal. I took a long, hard look at everything I could have done wrong. I was determined to find my *defects of character.* My sponsor challenged me every step of the way, chastising me every time we met to look not only for the *shortcomings* of my personality but also for the many vital *assets* that I also brought to my family. One of the main things I learned was that *working the steps* was a lifelong process, not a quick "once and done." At a meeting, someone said, "It's not a microwave program, but more of a crockpot—slow and steady."

You never *graduate.*

I found helpful ideas and new teachings as I opened my heart to *my* well-being. I learned that I am who I am, and that was good enough. I could be *authentic*, know myself, accept that, and grow. I began to forgive myself for my real and perceived shortcomings. I stopped my earnest attempts to change into something I *wasn't* or consider ideas I didn't believe.

Around the end of November, Mike came home right before his 17th birthday after spending four months in treatment. When his group from the treatment center was at an evening Twelve-Step meeting in town, he decided he'd had enough and walked out. He was caught down the street trying to steal cough medicine from a local convenience store. When the counselor found him, he called and wanted us to make arrangements to pick up Mike as soon as possible. The staff told us that we should watch him for potential suicidal intentions.

Our son had walked away from many opportunities for counseling, treatment, and sobriety. I took it personally. He had also walked out on *himself* and our *family*. My attempts to focus on the steps and my journey towards *my* recovery were interrupted the day he set foot back in our home.

The counselors advised us to get him into another local out-patient treatment program. We had set that all up and tried to get Mike on board, but he did not cooperate. Instead, he stayed home, waiting until the second semester to begin his classes again at an alternative high school.

With my mind on my son and fear in my heart, I struggled to do my job at school. Getting ready for the holidays seemed impossible. My thoughts were on high alert all the time. My intuitions told me something was happening, and they were often correct. I suspected drug or alcohol use, but I kept telling myself I could not change this. I couldn't change anything.

Sleep avoided me, and I laid in bed many nights praying and willing my mind to let go, let go, let go! I would ask God, "Are you there? I believe you are! Take this burden from me!"

I think God already knew that Mike had relapsed.

Mike came home one evening and was acting strange. I questioned him, but he retreated to his room. I went upstairs to check on him a little later and discovered he had locked himself in the bathroom. I could hear him in there, vomiting over and over again. It reminded me of the horrible night at the hotel in Spain.

He was so out of it. I can't even remember what he said. None of it made any sense. Doug came upstairs, and when Mike wouldn't respond to us, he broke the lock and pushed himself into the bathroom. We found a 7-Up can on the bathroom counter filled with vodka. Mike was so sick and belligerent. Doug turned around and began to remove the door off its hinges so that Mike couldn't lock himself in there again. When Mike tried to get out, Doug tackled him in the hallway, holding him down, trying to get him to settle down and make some sense. Mike was hysterical. "I don't want to be an addict," he sobbed repeatedly.

We noticed a metal box had fallen to the floor, and a handful of red gel caps rolled away, spreading out onto the carpet. Maybe we should call 911 again? I froze. I could not make myself pick up the phone. I started praying and handed my concerns over to God in my head on repeat until I thought I would explode from the tension and pain of the moment. Doug managed to get Mike into bed, and he proceeded to pass out. We went back and forth about whether we should take him in for alcohol poisoning or not, but we did *not* act. I prayed that he would be okay, that he would wake up in the morning. I knew we would have to confront the issue the next day. In a whisper, I asked God one final question, "What will we do tomorrow, Lord? There *will* be a tomorrow, right? What should we do?"

I was tired of trying to figure things out. I was waiting for a response to the prayers that never seemed to get answered.

December 18, 2003
Gail, my child, my heart goes out to you in sympathy for your loving mother's heart is breaking and fragile. I am still here. I am working on this issue in your family, although it may not seem that way at this moment. TRUST. Recovery is a process, and I will watch over Mike as he lives his own life and makes his own choices—many of which I cannot control. I will be here for Mike when he is ready. There is little more you can do at this time. Give up the struggle with the addiction. You will not win over it—for it is powerful and can be overcome only with the hard work and willingness on the part of the addict. The solution to come home from treatment was another way for Mike to

GAIL MEHLAN | M. M. MEHLAN

avoid facing his reality—and he has not hit his absolute bottom yet.

Gail, dear, I know this is difficult for you to stand by and accept as a mom—trust the process—continue to let go and detach in love. I am here for you! Do not lose your own power and will to live to any person's addictions, not even your son's. Live your own life today—as if it were the only gift given to you now. Live, and be strong, patient, and understanding. I will answer your questions if you give me the time.

I am here. Choose peace and serenity—if only for a moment. I am with you.

Surprised, I must have recognized that there was inside of me a place where God existed, and the message that came through me as I wrote in my journal to myself calmed me. It was as if God *did* answer my prayer for tomorrow. The sun came up the next day and the next. Mike was alive. We celebrated Christmas as a family in the next few days and had some wonderful holiday moments, even with the persistent presence of an addict at home.

One night, I was lying in bed, winding down and reading. Like a little child, Michael came into our room and gave me a great big hug and said in a sweet voice, "Goodnight, Mom. I love you."

I couldn't respond as the lump in my throat grew. I reached out and took Mike's hand, squeezing it hard, conveying all the love and concern I had for him.

In that brief moment, I found a way to carry on, to move forward. I felt that the spirit of God had come to me, taken hold of my soul, and moved in me. I was thankful.

97

A MOTHER'S PRAYER

As I sat and watched you sleeping the other night
I was taken back in time
to when you were small

You were so peaceful, calm
and unbothered
by any cares

Your mind was resting
no fighting
no frustration
no aggravation
with me
or your dad
or school
or life itself
You appeared to me
as a child
as a boy
who just wants peace

I am afraid that I am powerless
to give you anything but love
Sometimes even that is a struggle for me

When the awake-ness of
addiction consumes you

But when you are sleeping
　　　I see the real you
　　　　　and I pray to my God
　　　　　　　for you, for your spirit
　　　　　　　　　to open to all of the good
　　　　　　　　　　　and wonderful

Moments that are
　　　grace and forgiveness and hope

In that moment of peace
　　　　　for me

Your mother rests,
　　　trusts,
　　　　　tries to let go of control

Knowing that her prayers will someday be answered
　　　and God is listening

(Even though extra time is needed)
　　　God's time is not our time.

　　　　　Gail Mehlan
　　　　　January 7, 2004

PRAYER #1

Starting at the beginning
Pulled up by the roots
Terror at prospected sinning
If I screw up these blessings
I'll have to accept this life sentence
With wire and land mines, I'll be messing
Oh! Please, GOD! ACCEPT MY REPENTANCE.

Jolly Jackson

Gail

CHAPTER 15—ARRESTED

2004

One Sunday morning, I gave my testimony at our church. The story of what was happening in our family was still a living, breathing part of my life. I gave it my all.

"God has always been close to me, even as a young child. I always felt that God was watching over me. I tried to do the right things and make the right choices. He seemed to be tugging at my heart as I grew. I felt God's presence was moving me along. I wanted to be a "good girl" and prided myself on being right. I felt very naïve when I went away to college. I held myself to specific high standards of conduct. I attended church in town, and at a candlelight service, there was a cross at the front of the church, and many heavy-duty nails were around the communion railing. The pastor invited us to come forward, accept Christ as our Savior, and take one of those nails. I

remember hesitating for a moment, then being brave enough to move forward and make a profession of my faith by the physical act of taking a nail. It was my first public moment of accepting my Savior. After that service, I felt a more profound call, a deeper understanding of my faith.

When I traveled to a foreign country, I experienced a deeper faith. Being aware of God's presence in the large cathedrals and seeing the passion of Christ displayed in the artwork and statues there had a significant impact on me. God's presence and support were there as I moved forward in life.

God has a way of letting us know when we need to listen up. We sometimes don't realize it when things are going well—then "ZAP"! Something happens that jars us back into reality. We get a wake-up call.

~ a parent dies unexpectedly
~ a baby is born prematurely and hangs onto life
~ a child has an accident
~ money is tight

These things humble us before God. All have happened to me. I've been through those times and shed many tears. Yet through all those things, I felt the still, quiet voice telling me it was okay. God was there. I have been humbled and grateful for God's continued presence in my life.

Still—

I have the embedded feeling that life should be a certain way. I could have and be all that God wants me to be. And, of course, I thought I was fulfilling God's call in my life and receiving God's blessings because of my faithfulness. I can be a bit self-righteous.

But then, something rocked me to the core, something I could not have imagined and couldn't fathom. This thing shocks me in a way I cannot understand, and I cry out—

"NO! NO! NO! Not THAT!"

Not ANOTHER wake-up call!

"This is for YOU, Gail! Don't be so self-righteous! MY will, NOT yours! You must surrender it all to me. Life becomes unmanageable without me! You WILL get through this!"

I can't imagine why these things keep coming at us. I know I must surrender all of myself to God, but I am still unfolding here. How can I NOT see that I'm still holding on?

I imagine the disciples felt much the same way when they gathered together in secret after Jesus had died. They must have felt such grief, full of fear for themselves. They did not have confidence in what they knew had happened. The death of Jesus had rocked the disciples to their very core. And then what does the risen Christ ask of them? And bring to them? I believe he gave them a tremendous gift—and it was only a breath away.

It's not about me anymore. It can't be. Although I must confess, I struggle with that daily. When you let go of yourself, when I let go of myself, and allow the Holy Spirit to enter me with each and every breath I take—even when I cannot think about it, I am receiving the breath of life.

Afterward

I am not the same.

I will never be the same again.

We will never be the same again.

You will never be the same again.

Some situations don't change

> *~ our sons and daughters are still in Iraq*
> *~ our loved ones may still be addicts*
> *~ our illnesses may not be cured*
> *~ our marriages may still be over*
> *~ money may still be tight*

Whatever it is, you cannot be the same after receiving the Holy Spirit in you.

You change your perspective.
You keep on keeping on.
You pray, even when you can't find the words.
We get through it because of the Spirit in us.
Here is my interpretation of today's Gospel:
(John 20:19-23)

Jesus appeared to them and said,
"Peace be with you!"
Then he breathed on them and said to them,
"Receive the Holy Spirit!"
And they took a breath—It was only a breath away.
So, I ask you now to take a few deep breaths. It's not just magic,
It's just there when you breathe. Simply inhale—
PEACE.
In other words, surrender to God. and let go—
Then breathe in the Holy Spirit;
the breath of God will be upon you and receive his PEACE."

"On the evening of that first day of the week, when the disciples were together, with the doors locked for fear of the Jewish leaders, Jesus came and stood among them and said, 'Peace be with you!' After he said this, he showed them his hands and side. The disciples were overjoyed when they saw the Lord.

Again, Jesus said, 'Peace be with you! As the Father has sent me, I am sending you.' And with that, he breathed on them and said, 'Receive the Holy Spirit. If you forgive anyone's sins, their sins are forgiven; if you do not forgive them, they are not forgiven.'"

John 20:19-23 (NIV)

After church, I was exhausted and emotionally drained. I had shared my soul that morning, but, I still couldn't say the simple words "my son is a drug addict." Even though I hadn't said it, many of the people there were friends who *knew*. After the service, several of them spoke to me, thanking me. My closest friends hugged me and vowed to pray for our family.

On Sundays, I spent time preparing for the upcoming week. I needed to go down into the basement to do some work for school the next day on the computer. I found Mike sitting there playing the guitar. His hair was long and hanging over his eyes.

"What're you up to, Mike?" I asked, extending a friendly greeting.

He looked up at me with a disconnected look in his eyes. He was shaky or nervous or something. I sighed and turned back to the computer to get started on my work.

"Mom, I've got something to tell you."

I turned around to face him again and asked, "What's up, honey?"

"I got arrested yesterday."

I took a deep breath, trying to regain that peace from God I had earlier in church.

"I got arrested yesterday at Target. I stole a couple of video games."

I supposed he thought it'd be easier to tell me first, not his father. I took a few minutes to come up with a response.

"Mike, why? Why would you do something like that?"

He admitted he owed money to someone who had threatened him with something *terrible* to get back at him if he didn't pay him right away. He told me the store had pressed charges and that he had to go to court to face a judge in a week. The officer that arrested him said he'd be there in court too.

"Well, we will have to talk to your father about this."

"I don't want to, Mom. I don't know what to say."

"I don't know what to say either! God, Mike, what were you thinking?"

"I was afraid, Mom."

"I'm afraid too." I sighed as I looked away.

I turned my back to him and began the work I needed to do on the computer. He sighed and slammed the wall as he headed to his room. I knew Doug wouldn't be happy, but he would know what to do.

TRAVESTY

Travesty is a word I fear
The thoughts they wrinkle and twist
Scratching the fool; footsteps
Back and forth...
Back and forth...
Swarming like chandeliers of worry
Swinging Back and forth...
Back and forth...
What shall I do? Lay myself bare?
Abandon what I feel, to find, a silent sun?
Is it a dead son or daughter?
You say we're going
The future, it seems
All and along
With it too, and down the drain
Without coming in out or down the hall
Full feeling absent in the danger
Break the siphon, Break it all
But ice, the ice
Jingles now in all the broken glass
My feet are tired, and my knees, they ache
I've slammed the door I'm left to crawl
I cannot keep the curtains open
For every fraught and thoughtless and angry notion
Still, I shake in all perceived and perpetual motion
Back and forth...Back and forth...
Swelling oceans of endless, timeless worry
I pace...
Back and forth...
Back and forth...

Jolly Jackson

"OOOOH child, you got a bad case of the big ideas
you cryin' when we don't need that
it's a sickness."

Matthew D. Mehlan
Excerpt from *Sickness*

Gail

CHAPTER 16—BEING JUDGED

2004

I could tell something was not right with my son that morning. It
was the day he was to go to court to face the judge. Shoplifting.
This crime he committed brought up so many feelings for me on
so many levels. We planned to stop on the way to the courthouse
to get a drug test. I felt *contempt* for this child of mine. I looked at
him, sitting uncomfortably beside me in the car. He was wearing
a long-sleeved shirt and a tie per his father's request. He refused
to get a haircut, but his hair was clean and brushed away from
his face. He still didn't look well. His skin tone was grayish, and
beads of sweat kept forming on his forehead. He sat there mop-
ping up the drips with a dirty bandana. It was warm out, but
he was anxious. *When was the last time I washed those jeans?* We
stopped and went into the clinic for the drug test. He did not put
up a fight.

As I waited for Mike, a memory of a bright-eyed five-year-old
on Christmas morning popped into my head. He was opening up
some of his gifts and was excited and happy. Realizing it was a new
Lego building kit, Mike immediately tore open the package and

began constructing it. He laughed as he completed the project quickly.

"See, Mommy? See? I can make this without looking at the *destructions!*" he'd said.

My heart still held onto that intelligent and funny little guy. Following the directions was never his strong suit. He always had his own particular way of doing things. I missed that little one.

The quiet between us on the drive to the courthouse was painful. We hadn't had any conversations about things since his arrest. It was so uncomfortable talking to him. He felt like a stranger. He *was* a stranger to me, this thief, this criminal. Could he indeed be my son? That was such a paradox, my *son*, the *criminal.*

"How do you feel about what's going to happen today?" I asked, trying to break the uncomfortable silence.

"I don't know. I don't care."

"It's obvious you *do* care! Look at you! You're a wreck."

"I am not. Leave me alone!"

"We haven't talked about this much, but you do *realize* that shoplifting is a crime. You broke the law, Mike."

"Geez, Mom, let it go—I don't give a f**k about any of this. I'm gonna keep stealing things as long as there are things to steal."

I shook my head in disgust. All I could do at this point was sigh. There was nothing left to say. I could not believe this had happened and that this trip to the courthouse defined my day. I was experiencing a new low. I never in a million years would have imagined I'd be taking a child of mine to court. I kept going over this in my mind, and it was true; I couldn't let it go. My thoughts were a hamster running on the wheel in its cage. Our story just seemed to take one awful turn after another. It hurt me and haunted me. I told myself to breathe, breathe, and breathe again.

We arrived at the courthouse and met his father. We had

agreed that we would not do anything special as he faced the judge today. We did not want to rescue him from his misdeeds. He would face the consequences as they came. As I entered the courtroom, I sat down on the hard bench. I was too emotional to stay with my husband and son. Instead, I waited for them to be called in by the bailiff. I was just a spectator.

"All rise."

I stood as the judge entered the courtroom. I sat back down, uneasy. I listened as, one by one, cases were called to the front. The judge heard each case, then made a decision, and moved right on to the next one. Finally, they announced my son's case. I watched, my heart doing flip-flops inside my chest, as he and my husband walked to the front of the courtroom. He was charged with misdemeanor shoplifting. The judge looked at both of them and spoke directly to Michael.

"Where is your attorney, young man?"

"I don't have one."

"So, you *don't* have an attorney?" There was a sharp, sarcastic edge to the judge's question.

"No, we were told we didn't need one, that the court would appoint one for him." My husband interrupted, trying to be respectful.

"Excuse me. Who are you? Are you this boy's father?"

"Yes, sir."

"Who told you that he didn't need an attorney?"

"I spoke with an attorney I know over the phone, and he told me it would not be necessary. We wanted our son to face the consequences of his actions, Sir."

"So, you expect *me* to rehabilitate *your* son? Sir, do *you* have a job?"

"Yes, sir."

"Do you own a house? Do you have money? An income?"

"Yes, sir. What does that have to do with this situation? I was told I didn't need to hire an attorney."

"So, you are telling me that you *can afford* to get an attorney for your son, but you decided not to?"

"Yes, sir, but I was told we didn't *need* to get an attorney. This has nothing to do with me or how much money I have. I didn't do anything wrong. I didn't break the law. I'm just here to support my son."

"Don't speak back to me, Mr. Mehlan. You should have *supported* your son by *hiring* an attorney. I will not *tolerate* disrespect in my court, nor will I appoint this boy an attorney."

"I was told, sir, that I did not *need* to get an attorney, that one would be appointed if necessary." My husband was trying to maintain his respectful demeanor.

"Sir, if you speak out of turn again, I will hold YOU in contempt of court, and YOU will be breaking the law, and YOU will be arrested!"

The judge was finished with this case.

"Come bring your son back to court when you have found a *good* attorney for him. This case is adjourned." My husband and son both walked out of the courtroom with their heads down and slightly bewildered. I had a large pit in my stomach. It was over, but it was not. We were given a date to return to court *with* an attorney.

My husband and son drove home together, and I made my way home alone. I sat in the car listening to music and cried. The tears seemed to come from a bottomless fountain inside of me. My husband told me later that our son bawled like a baby all the way home, inconsolable. This news made me feel the slightest bit of compassion for him. He *was* sick.

I discovered the next day that Mike had been high on cocaine while we were in court.

LET GO!

Today I feel this deep sense of despair.
My life has not changed~
All I asked God for a year ago
was
HOPE
Hope that somehow—we
would be able to
fulfill
the American "dream."
be able to pull ourselves, all of us,
out of the muck
and make a turn
for the better~
But, with drugs, "it" just
keeps pulling us back down
Not only him
but for me as well~
ALL of us
and I
bristle
get angry
because I don't want to
keep going back down~
and he's pulling me
"It's" pulling me
Don't let it.
Don't let it keep
pulling you down~
Let go!
Give up the constant struggle.

Gail Mehlan
April 2004

THE KILLER

The walls are closing in on me now. I can't breathe
They said if I just said I'm sorry, they'd set me free
But instead, I'll plead guilty,
And they'll take my life away from me
But they caught me red-handed,
Tonight, I'll be branded, reprimanded
Then taken to the
Yard!

I'll tell you it was worth it.
I can see who you are in the mirror
But now I know I'm the man they say I am.
I feed off that fear
But I can see how deep it can go,
My conscience is clear
I sent the mad kings to Valhalla
Because they ate my sons and daughters
But now their screams have left me violent and cold
In the night, I'll be beaten at random
And be left to die all alone
Because I tried to build a place, I called IT
"Home"

Jolly Jackson

"It's where me and my brother
Pretended we could
Walk on water

And out on this lake
Where we escaped
We played in its wake

And on the ice
We skated around
Each other's advice

We played on this beach
The sandy way
On a sunny day

And if these walls could talk
They'd tell a story of my family
So candidly

And if these trees could see
They wouldn't understand
What they mean to me

But the water will rise
But the water will rise
The water will rise
The water will rise."

Michael M. Mehlan
*Excerpt from a song called "Clear Lake" about
the family home of his grandparents.*

"And if these walls could talk
They'd tell a story of my family
So candidly
And if these trees could see
They wouldn't understand
What they mean to me"

Michael M. Mehlan

Gail

CHAPTER 17—STOLEN LOVE

2004

It was a dreary, cloudy, and rainy week when we spent a few days at my mother's lake house for a weekend during spring break. We all needed to get out of the house and the usual school-day routine. Mike was very reticent about doing anything with us, let alone spending a weekend at the lake with his parents and his grandmother. Somehow, we convinced him to come with us.

One day, we decided to go to the shopping mall in town so Mike and Doug could look at fishing equipment and archery supplies at the local sporting goods/outdoor store. My mom and I decided to look at the clothing store next door while the guys did their own thing. We enjoyed a little shopping and then checked on the boys at the sporting goods store. They were still busy looking at something, so Mom and I told them we'd meet them at the local Mexican restaurant a few doors down. They caught up with us a few minutes later, and we had a delicious meal together. Mike was talkative and interacted with us as if everything was normal. He seemed excited to use his new archery equipment to target shoot back at the lake.

It was a lovely, relaxing, and fun weekend. Mike appeared to be happy that he had come with us. It was an interlude from the persistent fear of the upcoming court date and the unknown consequences Mike faced.

Doug and I had been at odds with each other. I was still so unsettled about the drugs, the alternative school situation, and the failure at treatment. It was too much, and I was tired of living with constant fear. I wanted to *do* something, but now we had this additional burden of a court date. Mike's presence in our home was a wedge between us. Doug sided with Mike about things and didn't hold him accountable for his behavior. He acted like the stolen video games were no big deal. It *was* a big deal.

After arriving home from Clear Lake, I wandered into Mike's room one evening when he wasn't home. I can't even remember where Mike was, maybe at a meeting. Doug was downstairs working on his notes for the day. I quickly scanned Mike's room because I was on high alert for something to be amiss. I noticed an old suitcase under the bed that I hadn't seen before. Curious, I pulled it out and opened it. Inside was a gun.

I let out a gasp, ran downstairs, and confronted Doug with the news. Doug and I rushed upstairs, and I stood there in shock as he carefully took the gun out of the suitcase. He turned it over in his hands and looked at it carefully. "It's no big deal, Gail—it's *only* a pellet gun!"

"I don't care *what* kind of gun it is! Where the hell did he get that? I don't want *any* guns in this house! Especially in Mike's possession!" Then I remembered. Mike had been at a sporting goods store a few days ago, and he somehow stole the gun when we stopped there to shop and eat dinner with my mother. I was furious. I was angry at Doug for his casual attitude, mad at myself for letting Mike stay in a store shopping by himself while Doug looked at fishing gear.

"We have to call the store and let them know that Mike stole that gun!" I started looking for the phone number to make the call. I was going to do it right then.

"You are *not* going to call the store," Doug said. "I'm taking care of this myself. I don't want to get the store or the police involved! Are you crazy? With all we're dealing with now? I'll take care of it."

"I don't care that it's *only* a pellet gun. It's a gun! We can't let him get away with this!"

"I said, I'll take care of it!" Doug took the gun and put it somewhere while I stood in the kitchen, fuming with anger and disbelief. I couldn't believe my husband would let this slide and *not* turn Mike in. We needed to do the right thing! How could I live with this? My son had stolen a *gun.* How was I supposed to know it was *only* a pellet gun? If he had pulled that on me in one of his moments of anger or frustration, I don't know what I would've done. Worse yet, if he took it somewhere to try negotiating with the dealers he owed money to, he'd be *dead.* What if he got caught with a gun by the police?

If.

I couldn't go there. This whole situation was too much. I didn't want to be there anymore. I was scared of my son and disgusted with my husband. I made a decision.

Downstairs I found my husband calmly finishing up his paperwork. I stood confident in front of him and said, "I'm leaving. I can't take it anymore. This is *it.* I can't be in this house with you and Mike and a gun he stole. I'm *done!*"

I turned away from my stunned husband and went upstairs to pack my bag. I had been considering leaving for a while. The constant presence of fear of what was going to happen had me

GAIL MEHLAN | M. M. MEHLAN

fantasizing about an escape. I knew of a short-stay hotel not too far from work where I could stay for a few days. The need to catch my breath and get away from the situation was a force rising in me. I turned away from my stunned husband and went upstairs to pack my bag. *I was done.*

I was so distraught over what was happening with Mike that I wasn't putting much energy, compassion, or understanding into our marriage. We would try to work things out over our evening meals, but it was difficult. I looked to Doug for the strength and leadership I couldn't find in myself. When he didn't make the decisions or take charge, I stood back and boiled over with anxiety and resentment. I was *ready* to leave the marriage and let Doug handle *everything.*

So, I took my cell phone to my room as I began throwing a few things together. I called my sponsor because I knew I was about to go over the edge and needed her calm advice. She gently reminded me that one of the traditions of the program is *unity.* She said that Mike needed his parents to be a *united front* if he were ever to recover. We *needed* to be a team. I hung up the phone and walked downstairs with my bag. Even after all the talk about unity, I *still* needed to get away for a while.

I looked at Doug, sitting at the table with his head in his hands. He looked up at me, and saw my overnight bag, stood up, and moved toward me with tears in his eyes, "Please, Gail, don't go—"

No words came out of my mouth, but *I knew* I couldn't leave. I walked towards Doug, and he pulled me in close, wrapped his arms around me tightly, and whispered, "I can't do this alone." My face was wet with tears as I melted into him. His warm, strong body calmed me. The hug made it seem possible. We needed each other. We needed to be a team.

As we stood in the kitchen together, we heard the garage door open, and we knew Mike had come home.

"Let me handle this," Doug said.

I turned and went upstairs with my packed bag, set it down on the floor, closed the bedroom door, and sobbed.

"And everything I see
And all I believe deep down
so whole-heartedly
is an illusion."

Michael M. Mehlan
Date unknown, found in a notebook

Gail

CHAPTER 18—REARVIEW MIRROR

2004

The station is busy, and disgruntled people are all around me. Everyone seems to have someplace to go. It appears that everyone's destination is more important than where I am going.

"Hurry up!"

"Step this way! Get in this line. Buy a ticket!"

"Get out of the way!"

Today is an important day. Something big is about to happen. No one else can know or understand the absolute truth of the matter. I feel a sense of urgency. I *need* to get *somewhere*, but where is not clear. I *must* make it.

I sling my purse and another heavy duffle bag over my shoulders and pull a suitcase with each hand. My suitcases both feel like they are full of rocks or books. They have roller wheels, but they will not move. Ugh! I look behind me and see that I have one more bag to grab. I try to slip it somehow over the other suitcase handle so I can proceed in line, but it keeps falling off and making the suitcase uneven, so it continues tipping over. Feeling frustrated, I inch forward slowly. Someone rudely bumps my arm, and my heavy purse drops off my shoulder. Struggling, I get it back up on my shoulder. I look around me and realize I am alone. The carrying of these enormous bags is all my responsibility.

As I approach the front of the line, I glance up at the sign. I don't understand exactly what it says but realize with discouragement that this is not the station where I should be. I cannot get to where I need to go from here. I begin working my way around the crowd and down to the next block, dragging my heavy luggage with me. The weight of my bags increases with each step. The effort to continue seems impossible. Feeling the pressure of people pushing in on me, I am desperate.

Then in the corner of my eye, I see a cab. I decide to step out to the curb, dragging the bags, and hail a cab. *Perhaps I will make it if I get a taxi*, I think.

One by one, different cabs fly by me, *occupied* or *not for hire*. I stand on the corner, feeling the frustration rise within me. I have that hopeless sense that this situation is futile. I won't make it. Suddenly a cab stops in front of me. It takes all of my strength to lift the burden of my bags into the trunk and stuff a few into the cab itself. We take off—perhaps I will make it after all. My heart feels a glimmer of possibility.

Riding in the cab is not the answer to my problem. We seem to be going too fast for how far we have to go. The cabbie appears to be lost. I look out the window, and it is pitch black outside. Rain and sleet are pelting down on the windshield. There is no way the driver can see ahead of us. I try to look forward, evaluating if I can see anything at all. Are my eyes working? Black. It is nothing but darkness ahead of us, completely black. A sense of sadness overcomes me. My eyes brim over with tears, and my head starts to pound.

Then I notice the rearview mirror. I find myself straining up over the front seat to see the mirror. As I'm looking in the rearview mirror, I see myself.

In the mirror, I can see the road *behind* me. I see images of the life I have lived. The images flash in the mirror before me, but I see only things that *have* happened. I keep struggling to look up at the mirror, wanting to see more and return to those familiar times. Suddenly the frantic attempts to find the station dissolve. I look up and discover that I'm already *at* the station. I don't have to go anywhere else to get where I need to go. I will make it. I sigh with relief as tears of gratitude slowly roll down my cheeks.

Then I woke up.

The dream left me with a horrible headache, still-in-my-brain fogginess, and a sense of immense sadness. When I was finally fully up, the dream still on my mind, I began to think. Sometimes I allow myself to *over*think, but I *wanted* to understand. This dream had meaning. Someone, something, had spoken to me.

I asked myself some serious questions.

What was I so afraid of?
Why the overwhelming feeling of sadness?
What was all this baggage I was trying to carry?
Was I fearful and sad for an unknown future?
Why all the searching, working, reaching, and striving to get somewhere different?
Why the struggle when so much was right here, at this moment, this place, this time?
Was it normal to feel this inexplicable sadness?
Was it a letting go of my perfect "image" of life?
Was I grieving expectations, my unfulfilled expectations?

I worked at it, trying to find answers and shake the foggy feelings. I convinced myself to go about my day, breathing, letting God be in charge. I asked God to take the heavy baggage. I suspected I knew just *what* that might be in the light of day.

I knew God was showing me that the station was right where I already *was*. Home.

GLUE

Big pieces
Small pieces
Shards of perspective
Lost to the cracks, there
lost in the floor
I was delicate and glass
and you swung a hammer at me
a hard swing of betrayal
that left me weak
Quite a long wait for the spidering fissures to shatter
In an explosive game of despair, of what does it matter?
It is all your fault
I reflected up at your trust
as you stomped all of the fragments tiny into dust
I swept up the pieces
And I'm taking my time
To place them back together with glue
But a few of the pieces I've left them with you
Stuck in the crevices to the bottom of your boot
I may not be able to fix them all
Missing all the pieces wedged into your shoe
Perhaps tomorrow,
I'll get a little more glue

Jolly Jackson

"I reflected up at your trust
as you stomped all of the fragments
tiny into dust
I swept up the pieces
And I'm taking my time"

Jolly Jackson
Excerpt from *Glue*

Gail

CHAPTER 19—TOUGH DECISIONS

2004

July 2004

He was just a little child, a baby, trying on a lifestyle that sucked him in and spat him out—lost, alone, and addicted. I grieve for the loss of the innocence of my child. I know he wanted me to write a book about how my life might have been different, "Among the Sunflowers." I wonder—was he thinking of MY life, or was he speculating that HE could somehow be something different himself? (–Or not exist?) If I had my life to live over, did he think I did NOT want him to be a part of it?

There was never a doubt in my mind that his life was valuable. I gave him my all and would do it again. Now, I give him over to my Lord to care for and love him and break down these walls of addiction. As his mom, I am entirely powerless—I NEVER had any power. I cannot go back and live a different life—nor would I want to. My life IS good. I can just pray that Mike will find a NEW life—some-way, someday—a miracle, perhaps.

After our first experience in court, I felt a need to explain all we had done for our son. I wanted to defend our parenting to the judge who made *us* feel judged. We *were* good parents.

I imagined us sitting on a famous talk show and having the good doctor look at us with a judgmental glare, saying with a *snark,* "What kinds of parents don't know that their twelve-year-old child is smoking marijuana? How can a *young child* get involved in such a thing? Where *were* you?"

One morning, I was sitting at the dining room table. I stared at the mess in front of me. It hadn't been cleared off for months, at least since Easter. The table was piled high with all sorts of brochures and leaflets from programs I researched as possible placements for Mike. Some of them we *had* already tried, but I was looking for something that would *work.*

My husband and I had insisted that Mike attend several rounds at the local *inpatient* behavioral health hospital. When he was released, we tried to get him into a residential program before our trip to Europe, but no beds were available.

Our trip, and the events that happened there, solidified the need for him to get additional help. Upon our return, we pushed to get him accepted into residential treatment in Minnesota. I looked over the colorful brochure with all the positive reviews. We had been so hopeful. When he came home, we faced multiple outstanding medical bills. The insurance company would *not* pay for the treatment unless it occurred over a continuous time period. We had to argue with them to cover the subsequent treatment because it was interrupted by our vacation to Europe. We were still fighting that financial battle. I tossed the brochure aside and picked up another.

The counselors at the 30-day program in Minnesota rec-ommended that Mike go live in a follow-up halfway house for teens on the West Coast in the state of Washington. Again, the brochures were beautiful, and the website made the place look idyllic. This follow-up treatment for Mike was unsuccessful. Even though the facility was in a beautiful part of the country and well renowned, our son couldn't make it that far away from home. He had threatened to kill himself after one long and stressful phone call home. The counselors felt he was not ready to live a sober lifestyle. Mike returned to the same youth treatment program in Minnesota for an extended stay until the day he walked out of the meeting in town. I tossed that brochure aside as well. It felt like we were tossing money into a giant garbage disposal.

Although we were *cautiously* optimistic with each new or dif-ferent treatment plan, these programs were expensive, and the ups and downs were getting to us. I was devastated when he walked out of treatment in Minnesota. The whole situation brought our *entire* family down. We had no alternatives, and he ended up back at home. The options had come to an end.

The judge in court that day knew nothing of all of this. It's not like we hadn't tried to *help* or *support* our child.

It wasn't too long after the first experience in court that Mike and his father returned for the second scheduled appearance. My husband had done his homework this time and went well-pre-pared with the best attorney he could find.

This attorney was no beginner at dealing with troubled teens. He was wise to the court system and managed to help my hus-band and son appear before a much more sympathetic judge. Grace was bestowed upon them as the day approached. I chose not to go with them to the courthouse that day. I was too entan-gled and tied up in knots to go. I went to work, trying to finish things up for the end of the school year, business as usual. My job as a teacher was a temporary distraction.

This time, Mike *did* get a haircut and cleaned up before heading out for his day in court. I didn't question the state of his drug use at this point. I was tired of fighting that battle. Once they got there, the court proceeded without much ado. They called his case. My son was convicted of a misdemeanor and issued a fine. As part of his sentence, he was required to do 24 hours of community service. My husband and son left the courthouse with some paperwork and a charge on Mike's record.

I sat at the table and looked at all those brochures and piles of paper in front of me. I didn't know what to do. I prayed for wisdom in sorting through these options for Michael. I wanted him to continue with his schooling. He had not been in school while he was away in treatment. When he returned, the high school enrolled him in an alternative high school at the district level. At the time, that was the plan for him again in the fall. Going to the alternative high school was not the best solution for Mike. I knew it, but I didn't know what *would* work. I could *not* imagine or accept just letting him drop out of school. Once he turned 18, there would be nothing I could do if Mike chose that option.

I vividly remember the day I searched for New Horizons Youth Ministries on the web. This program had three options for troubled teens. Escuela Caribe was one of them. I had just seen the images of Tami's son on their website with a smile on his face, enjoying a field trip in a tropical paradise. I didn't know Tami's son before he left, but her emotional response to the photos was of disbelief and hope. It appeared that a transformational change had happened for her son. I longed for a transformation for Mike too.

What popped up on my computer screen when I got home from school that day was a list of questions:

Do you have an adolescent who...
- *has low self-image?*
- *rejects your love?*
- *is unmotivated and failing in school?*
- *rejects your family's Christian values?*
- *is out of control?*
- *shows lack of character?*
- *is irresponsible or disrespectful?*
- *runs with a negative crowd or has no friends?*

"YES, YES, YES, YES, YES, YES, YES, YES!" I answered each question aloud to no one. Hope began to grow in me as I read the rest of the promo information on that website.

"...serving as a place of Christian refuge for spiritual growth and character building."

"We are dedicated to assisting parents with their high-potential, yet underachieving youth..."

"...our successful history in therapeutic Christian character building and education is due to the untiring efforts of our staff...They have been willing to share their lives and love with...teens and their parents for over thirty-five years."

I dreamed of *all* of these things for *my* child.

While I was off for the summer, I looked into Escuela Caribe in the Dominican Republic. As I held that brochure in my hand again, I still wasn't sure it was the best solution. The words used to describe the school when I'd called were that it was *blatantly* and *unapologetically* Christian. I knew that they believed in corporal punishment. Tami and I had talked about it. Part of me wasn't sure that the strict discipline would sit well with Mike, but I was desperate for *any* solution. I was *more* intrigued by something else they said about their ministry. *They promised they would never give up on a child in their program.*

My husband continued to be reluctant to move forward with these plans or do *anything* more for Mike. We had already put out a lot of money to try to help Mike, but it wasn't about the money. Doug and I both worried about keeping Mike alive. I continued to do all the research required for his admission to this Christian school. I kept thinking about how healthy and happy Tami's son had looked in the pictures. I had also kept up with her son's progress there. He seemed to be doing well and was getting close to returning to the states. I held back and didn't force my thoughts or opinions on anyone. I was waiting for Doug or even Mike to move in one direction or another. I did, however, send in the required deposit and the paperwork I'd completed. I didn't tell my husband *or* Mike. I just prayed that they would come around. I prayed that God would speak to me in some way and provide an answer. Deep inside, I continued to have unrelenting doubts about all of it.

Being 17, about to turn 18 in November, and almost an adult, I felt Mike ought to have a say in deciding what his future might hold. I tried not to think about the fact that he would typically be looking at colleges, not reform schools, at this point in his life. Even still, I wanted him to know that we hadn't given up on him and wanted his input. I wanted him to have hope for his *own* future.

Of course, he was not interested in any of it, but I persisted. As I looked at all the information from many types of alternative schools and camps, boot camps, and wilderness treatment programs spread out all over the table, I thought some options might be *fun*. Of course, *all* of them would take our son for a large sum.

I left all of the brochures strewn out across the dining room table. "Have you looked at any of this stuff, Mike?" I prodded. "Are you sure you don't want to think about doing something different in the fall?"

"No."

Nothing further was said. Mike always walked out of the room when I tried to talk to him. I left all the brochures on the table, hoping he would look through them at some point. I hoped my husband would look at them as well.

In the meantime, Doug set up a community service project for Mike at the local park district. He had 24 hours of work to do before school started. Mike was supposed to call them and set up a schedule to complete his sentence before the next court date. Day after day, he struggled to get out of bed, shower, eat, or do anything. Occasionally I could get him to help with some chores around the house for a small amount of cash.

"Did you call the park district yet?" I asked him daily.

The answer was always, "No."

Most days, I let him be. He spent most of the summer isolated and at home.

I would catch myself looking back over our lives and wondering if there was something, *anything*, that I could have done differently to prevent this horrible addiction from taking its toll. I realized that I was looking at the rearview mirror again, and it only revealed what I know now to be true. I could not have done anything. I *was* powerless.

Even though I knew I was looking back, I couldn't help myself. I love my children so much. God blessed me with three healthy children and a husband who supported us while I stayed home and cared for the family. I was involved in many volunteer activities and was an active mom. When I was pregnant with Michael, our world turned upside down with a problematic pregnancy and many days, weeks, and months of bed rest. He was born one month early after a high-risk pregnancy and was on a respirator in the Newborn Intensive Care Unit for ten days.

When we came home after those ten days, it was a joyful celebration of life with his older sister, brother, grandmother, and grandfather. He was a beautiful baby and truly one of the miracles of my life. God answered our prayers, and he was healthy and developed typically. Michael was a charming child, creative, active, and intelligent. He was so cute, with his blond hair and a ready smile. He was a joy to everyone! During that time with big sister and brother's activities, we had such a busy life that we used to call Mike the "Schlep-along Kid" because we always dragged this poor baby to events here and there.

When he was about two years old, I would have to gate him into the kitchen so that I could take a shower or use the bathroom when he was awake. He slept very little. One day I got out of the shower and went into the kitchen to check on him. I found him on top of the counter, reaching up to the top of the refrigerator, saying in his sweet little toddler voice,

"I get cookie? Mommy? I get cookie?"

I should have known better! I had put the cookie jar up on top of the refrigerator on purpose to keep it out of his reach. He pushed a kitchen chair over to the counter and climbed up to try to get it anyway. He was my little climber. The next time I tried to shower, I took all the chairs out of the kitchen first.

I don't know how all this joy and sweetness turned and went downhill, but realizing that my beautiful baby boy began experimenting with drugs and alcohol when he was barely twelve still makes my heart ache. No parent gives birth to a baby, holds them in their arms, and thinks about raising a child to grow up and become a drug addict. When I tried to figure out what led to these events, there were no answers.

Prayers for Mike were always on my mind, even when they were unspoken and seemed unanswered. I knew that loving grandmothers and other family members also prayed for him. It seemed there was no end to the heartache for all of us. My well of faith had begun to run dry.

We had some tough decisions to make. I wanted us to make them *together*. So, I listened and prayed that answers would come. I prayed that we would *all* know what to do when the answers appeared.

PETER PAN

I never grew up
I'll never get old
My brain didn't mature beyond the last star to the left
I'm stern; I'm stoic
I'm angry all the time
But it's just because
I wanted a little more time
To play...
Imagining me as an explorer
Sailing the oceans wide
A pirate perhaps waiting in the tides
For fairies and crocodiles
I waited, for adventures and mummies and spaceships
    to the stars
I waited, for love and loss and giants and kings I waited,
But then I looked in the mirror
And suddenly I saw wrinkles and gray hairs
Where there was once excitement,
I only found sad and lonely stares
And just between where you're asleep and awake
In the place where you remember your dreams
You said you'd be waiting

Well, I wait there too
And someday I'll remember I can fly and close my eyes
And count to three and remember all the happiness
    I'll ever have.
But now I see they've all grown up, and well,
I never had

Jolly Jackson

"Love is patient, love is kind. It does not envy,
it does not boast, it is not proud.
It does not dishonor others, it is not self-seeking,
it is not easily angered, it keeps no record of wrongs.
Love does not delight in evil but rejoices with the truth.
It always protects, always trusts,
always hopes, always perseveres."

1 Corinthians 13: 4-7 (NIV)

Gail

CHAPTER 20—TIME OUT

July 20, 2004

On the night of our 30th wedding anniversary, Doug and I were still at odds because of Mike's ever-worsening behavior. I had resigned myself to the thought that Doug would keep allowing the behavior we had seen from Mike as a way of life. I couldn't stomach that. I was ready to decide what *action* was needed. We hadn't seen eye to eye about this for quite a while. I was hoping to spend a little *time out* with my husband without the *drama* of Mike. I wasn't going to be so lucky.

Doug and I planned to go out to eat at our favorite restaurant. Over the last few weeks, I'd spent time thinking about our life together. I made a photo album for him with beautiful pictures of our family, travels, and love over the last thirty years. I was anxious to share those happy memories with him, trying to bridge the ever-widening gap between us. I got all dressed up and felt beautiful. Doug also cleaned up well. As he walked down the stairs sporting a new shirt with his white hair and beard all trimmed up, I wondered, who is this handsome man? We could both feel the anticipation of an evening of reconnection.

As we were about ready to go out the door, an old car pulled up in front of the house and honked the horn. Doug went outside to see what was going on, and a young man named Kyle was sitting in the front seat of the car. He would often pick up Mike to take him to meetings. Doug didn't think he was going to a meeting that night, though, as sitting in the front seat cup holder was a half-full bottle of whiskey. Doug chatted with Kyle as Mike bulldozed his way past me on the stairs,

"Where the heck do you think you're going?" I asked.

"To a meeting with Kyle," he said as he ran outside and hopped in the car. Before we could even respond, they drove out of our driveway, spinning the wheels and burning rubber.

Doug wrote down the license plate number, make, and color of the car as we closed the door and looked at each other.

"What do you think we should do now?" I asked, always being the one who wanted to take some action.

"What do *you* think we should do?" Doug redirected the question, a habit that I found infuriating. *He* was the father. *He* needed to find the courage and make some decisions about this problem. Despite my angry thoughts, I picked up the phone and reported to the police, saying there may be a car of the make and color I described with an impaired driver. After the call, I turned to Doug and said, "Let's just go. I'm not going to let this ruin our anniversary." And it did not.

We shared a delicious steak meal and a glass of wine. We spent much-needed time talking and reminiscing about our dating years, looking at the pictures of our family in the album I had made, trying a little too hard to put the earlier event out of our minds. Still, it did come up in the conversation once or twice.

A few weeks earlier, amid all the ups and downs of having

Mike at home, Doug had asked me if I wanted to redo my engagement ring for our 30th anniversary. I agreed, of course. He had been treating a patient who was a jeweler, and he had been working with her to design a ring using my original diamond and working in two other diamonds. I hadn't heard a word about it since I gave up my old engagement ring to him over a month before, and I hadn't thought about it with all that had been going on.

That evening after we came home, Doug had me sit at the kitchen table. He drew a little picture of a house on a piece of cardboard and said to me, "My house is now full of love. Will you marry me again? Close your eyes!"

I closed my eyes, and he placed my *new* ring on my finger! It was just gorgeous, and the diamond was huge. My eyes brimmed over with tears. Unbeknownst to me, Doug had found two letters in my old Bible from childhood that we had written to each other on the day we got engaged, August 31, 1973. In Doug's letter to me, he had written about how we were building a life with a family in a *house full of love*. At that moment, it just seemed to be true.

The diamond was not what made me feel special on that day. It was the love and romance this gesture had sparked. I *was* recovering too. I needed to remember to be gentle with our relationship. We needed to be better *together* as parents, partners, and *ourselves*. My sponsor had been right. Unity was so essential.

July 20, 2004
It has been a long time since I have felt so romantic, loved, and special!

I'm so grateful, Lord, for our wonderful times together, your constant presence with us in life, and the reaffirmation of our commitment to each other and our family.

Much later that night, Mike popped his head into our room, saying only, "I'm home, and I'm safe. Goodnight."

"Since we live by the Spirit,
let us keep in step with the Spirit."

Galatians 5:25 (NIV)

Gail

CHAPTER 21—A PRESENCE TO WALK WITH

2004

It was a humid night at the end of July. We had the air conditioner on to cool things off, but it was stifling in our home. Our son was up in his room. At least we knew where he was. Doug and I decided to go up to bed at about 10:30 PM.

Sometime during the night, my husband awoke to the cat meowing on his side of the bed. He got up, rubbed his eyes, and went to check the house. Suddenly, I woke to the sound of the thud, thud, thud of someone falling down the stairs. In my sleepy haze, I heard my husband call to me.

"Gail, Gail—wake up! Hurry! Call 911!"

I grabbed the phone and dialed 911, and as I waited to speak to the dispatcher, I grabbed a robe and went into the hallway. There I found my husband bent over Mike lying at the bottom of the stairs.

"What's going on?" I asked as I listened to the 911 dispatcher's questions.

"I don't know! I found him on the floor in his room, and then he got up, and when he tried to run down the stairs, he stumbled and fell. He's not responding!"

My husband tried to get him to stand or even sit. But with each attempt, Michael's legs buckled under him.

"Mike, Mike!" Pleaded my husband. "How much did you take?"

He looked back at his dad with glassy eyes that registered nothing. As the minutes passed, he slipped deeper and deeper into incoherence.

I reported to the dispatcher what was happening, and he said they would send out an ambulance right away.

I automatically said a prayer, but I wondered who would hear it. With dread in my heart, I knew that Mike had taken something that caused this reaction, too much of it this time. We stood at the door in terror as the paramedics strapped Mike to the stretcher and started an IV. As they loaded him into the ambulance, I reached for Doug's hand and wrapped his arm around my waist. I felt numb. Watching the ambulance drive away with the lights flashing and no siren, I felt a horrific sense of *deja vu*.

I went back up to Mike's room and looked on his bed, and sure enough, I found a metal cough-drop box with several green pills inside it. There were pills all over the floor. I scooped them up and went into my room to get dressed to head to the hospital with Doug. In my room, I fell to my knees and screamed from the bottom of my heart and soul: "God damn it! NO! NO! NO!"

I felt abandoned. My sobs echoed throughout the quiet house. My husband gently called up to me, "Gail, are you all right?"

"Yeah, I'll be right there."

I knew it was probably not a street drug or prescription painkiller that had put Mike into a coma. My son had overdosed on common over-the-counter cough and cold medicine before.

Once we got to the emergency room, we sat on cold, hard chairs as the life support machines beeped and hissed. The nurse placed a tube down my son's throat and connected him to a heart and breathing monitor. They closely monitored his oxygen levels.

The doctor told me they were treating him for an overdose of DXM, dextromethorphan, a cough suppressant in many cold remedies. He suspected other drugs were also in his system. I knew that in large doses, DXM could cause *death*.

I sat and stared at my son lying there. I kept thinking I should pray for him to get better, but I felt empty. A tear ran down my cheek as I saw this young man before me, clinging to life, gray, sick, and unresponsive. He was once a young, vibrant child. The thought made me feel so sad. How had we come to this?

I had prayed for this child so many times. I was tired. God was so far from me that he wouldn't hear me, hadn't heard me before, and didn't even care. I wasn't sure that prayer was worth it. I felt ashamed to be Mike's parent. The overdose had happened in *our* home while we were *there*, and this wasn't the first time or even the second. Good grief, we were *not* very good parents! Why didn't we *do* something? We had to answer many questions and make difficult decisions, and I didn't know what else to do. I had given up hope. I *knew* what the outcome could be. I was preparing for the worst.

After many hours in the ER, Mike started to come around a little. He was *not* happy to be there. He was belligerent and used physical force to try to escape the nurses. They called in a security guard who held him down and tied him to the bed with restraints. I fell deeper into self-pity and despair. Why did this keep happening? There seemed to be no easy solution. *At least he was alive!* I kept thinking. But, somehow, that positive thought didn't help.

The next day, they held Mike in a guarded room in the ICU to wait until all drugs were out of his system. When he was stable, they moved him to the behavioral health hospital for inpatient treatment. After being transported by ambulance, I met them there. I asked Mike,

"Mike, *why*, why did you do this? You almost died!"

His sarcastic response was, "It was fun."

You, asshole, I thought but didn't say. *You have no idea. None. Whatsoever.*

I went home and couldn't sleep. After trying for several hours, I gave up and got out of bed. The sun hadn't come up yet, and it was too early to return to the hospital. I told my husband that I was going to go for a walk, and I did.

The air was cool, and it was drizzling. I took my iPod and listened to music, pounding the pavement, hoping that a good walk would ease my sense of stress and hopelessness. The rain began to fall as one of the songs played something about the rain healing us. Over and over, the words, "Healing rain is raining down—down—down..." played on repeat. It became a mantra as I walked. Somehow the rain was healing me—blessing me—washing me—baptizing me.

I kept walking and playing the same music over and over again. I felt like my body was on autopilot, and my mind was along for the ride, one foot in front of the other. I wasn't thinking. I was simply trying to let go—I was trying to let the light rain wash away my guilt, pain, and sorrow.

As I was walking, I sensed that someone was walking with me. Of course, no one was there, in reality, but I felt a presence. After a while, as the rain continued and I kept walking, I felt a slight pressure on my hand, so I held it out. I could feel someone gently holding my hand and pulling me forward. The presence felt so close and was right there with me, guiding me.

After walking a few more yards like this, the rain began to stop, and the sky started to lighten with the new day. I felt the presence dissipate and began to think that now I ought to head home again.

The sky continued to lighten, and some of my sadness lifted with the new day. I felt that there was something, *someone* that was walking through this dark and challenging time *with* me. I believe God had taken my hand—indicating that I could step forward into this scary situation and that God would be there with me. I began to let go and let the Spirit direct my path then, little by little. I began to believe once again that a presence was there to walk with me.

For the first time in many weeks, I felt a sense of *hope*.

"No one has seen God; if we love one another, God lives in us, and his love is perfected in us."

1 John 4 (NRSV)

PART TWO:

A Long Reach of Hopes

GRACE

Sweet words among strangers
Once familiar dangers gone
Who were we when the curtains opened?
When the face and masks had boiled over?
"I knew you once."
I said in my mind
"You knew me too."
The response to myself was not kindly omitted
Who can feel the ghost of your breath in my ears?
As a sweet "I love you" falls silently dead
Glittering flakes peeled off a colorless world
A faint sparkle shining bright in the iris of confident stares

None have had your lovers embrace
But I've felt your soft, harmless hands
A long reach of hopes amending "Grace."

Jolly Jackson

"As the silence fades
I see myself,
but I can't say "Hello."
My empty eyes staring back—
"Look at me!" I screamed!
But the clouds looked like
my memories.
The clouds looked like
my family.
The clouds looked like
heaven.
I remember:
I was five—
I remember:
I was happy."

Michael M. Mehlan
Date unknown, found in a notebook

Michael

CHAPTER 22—AMONG THE SUNFLOWERS

2004

As a man, I am three things now in my life: a Christian, an artist, and a son. But I would not be these three things now, as I am, without the first, second, or third. These thoughts take me back to three years ago, to a hospital, a conversation, and a boy who was hurting, an addict.

HEY, W' HAPPENS?!!

"Take away the heat and leave the sunlight?
Take away the dope and give you hurricanes?
They find a hole in your body to squeeze God in!

You think they're on your side,
long arms and heavy hands tattooed to look
like they're wearing gloves.
They give you the biggest hugs, and OH! It hurts!

I got pockets full of gravel,
my knuckles are skinned,
I got a wall made outta marbles
and you're not allowed in!
I got a suit made a drugs, a mind of tin,
and I know you got a plan, but mine's gonna win!

Find your target
look down to the ground
Every dirt road's got a million stones—"

Matthew D. Mehlan

It was visiting time at the behavioral health hospital, a Wednesday, I believe. It's so hard to remember the details. My parents were visiting me. Seven days earlier, I had overdosed on cough medicine, heroin, and cocaine. The doctors were surprised I had even made it through the night. The following days were some of the most painful I've ever experienced. Between the vomiting and the cold sweats, the last people I wanted to see were my parents. I couldn't face them. They had been the ones that had found me unconscious and unresponsive, and I didn't want to feel those judging eyes pressing my heart into my chest. But I swallowed the rock I had lingering in my throat and gave my mom a hug. It was the coldest hug I had ever received from her. She was scared, and a tear welled up in her eye. I loved her even then, even after all our arguments and fights. I may have said I hated her to her face, but deep down, I hated myself.

Our conversation went well to the best of my memories. My dad spoke first as always, being the proud father and husband he is, and asked, "How are you?"

"I'm fine," I replied. "How are you?" I hated answering my father's questions. Each one seemed loaded and threatening, so I would always try to avoid answering him by turning it around on him.

"Worried," he said.

"Oh yeah," I said.

"Yeah, Mike, I don't know what to do with you. This is the third time this has happened, and I'm done with it."

"Whatever," I said in disgust.

"Whatever? Mike, is that all you can say is 'Whatever?' You almost died, and your father and I have been going crazy, and all you can say is 'Whatever?'" my mother asked.

"Yes, that's all I can say. I'm not happy. I'm not sad. I don't feel anything anymore, and I'm sick of it. I'm sick of not feeling anything."

"Well—what do you want us to do about it?" My mom cut in.

"Nothing. I don't want you to do anything. I just don't want to feel like this anymore, so I'm going to California with Kyle and his girlfriend." I got a little quieter and said softly,

"Then I'll be out of your hair, and you can just forget about me."

"Mike," my dad said sternly, "You can't go to California. You're sick. You'll die!"

"I'll be fine. I just need to get away from you guys for a while 'cuz I'm losing it."

"Were you ever happy, Mike?" My mom asked, off-topic.

"Of course, I was."

"When?" she asked.

The last time I was truly happy was when I was in Spain, standing among the endless fields of sunflowers. It was one of the few times my mother and I actually got along for more than a few minutes. I took a picture of my mom there, and she was smiling so wide. She was happy. Spain was her Eden. She had studied there in college and talked about it constantly when I was a child. It made me happy to be there with her. I couldn't tell her this, of course, so I said the next thing that came into my head.

"I don't know. When I was five."

My mother rolled her eyes. My dad stood up and said, "We should be going; our time is up." There was a long pause. No one said a word until my dad said with contempt, "Goodbye, Mike."

"Goodbye, Dad." I began feeling a little sheepish.

"I love you," he said.

"Love you too, Dad."

"Mom—" I whispered as I gave her a hug. She hugged me so tightly I couldn't maintain my composure, and I began to cry.

"Goodbye, Mike. I love you," she said. I knew she was crying too.

"Love you too."

That afternoon would be the last time I would see or speak to my parents for seven or eight months.

That night two men came for me. One was an ex-cop, the other a marine. They were taking me far away, and no, not to California, but to the Dominican Republic. I was going to boarding school. The next three days were very tense; I must admit, they were not my best moments. To sum it up in three parts, I was tackled by a U.S. Marshall and handcuffed to a pillar at O'Hare International Airport. I ran from the police and assaulted a Chicago police officer. I was finally shackled and driven to Atlanta to catch a flight from there. They don't let crazy people on airplanes in Chicago. My lovely escorts told a few fibs here and there to get me to cooperate. Don't get me wrong; I was asking for it. It's not worth going into detail. No. These were not my best moments.

WALKING AWAY

If there's something more painful than walking away
Walking away from the ones you love
I do not want to know how that feels

For this is the feeling of burning at the stake
If the smoke had not killed you first
This is the feeling of drowning at sea
If you're stranded and do not die of thirst
This is the rock that is unmovable
In the pit of your guts
This is the cold you feel before the warm drip
Of first blood

This is the feeling of walking away
Walking away from the ones you love

Jolly Jackson

"What you decide on will be done,
and light will shine on your ways.
When men are brought low, and you say,
"Lift them up!" then, he will save the downcast.
He will deliver even one who is not innocent,
who will be delivered through the cleanness of your hands."

Job 22:28-30 (NIV)

Gail

CHAPTER 23—THE BEDS WERE EMPTY

2004

"Gail, we need to do something," Doug said to me one evening while Mike was still in the hospital. "We can't go on like this."

These words brought me enormous relief, and I quickly realized that this was an answer to my prayers. I had prayed daily for Doug to recognize that we, as parents, needed to *do something*! I felt like this was our last chance to have an influence on our son and try to get him out of the cycle of addiction. I wanted a different future for him. Doug understood the gravity of the situation and was ready to talk. We discussed the options available, pouring over the brochures that littered our dining room table. Neither of us wanted to give up on Mike and do *nothing*. We talked long and hard about what we *should* do.

Finally, we decided to go ahead and send him to the Christian therapeutic boarding school in the Dominican Republic, where

Tami's son attended. Her son was still there but would soon return to the states to graduate from high school in the spring.

Relief and distress coexisted for me. We made a decision, but there were *so* many unknowns. I constantly went over each possibility in my thoughts. Mike would be less likely to walk out of the program because the legal age of adulthood in the Dominican Republic is 21, not 18. The staff would keep all of his documents and medications, so he would be less likely to try to escape. Lying and trying to get drugs in a foreign country would be difficult since he didn't speak the language. The school was rigorous, and Mike would have to comply to earn freedom and gain independence. He would be enrolled in high school classes and on target to graduate the following June. I felt more secure with him there, even though it was so far away, in a foreign country. Tami told me they had an armed guard at the entrance gate to the school.

An advisor from Escuela Caribe suggested we hire an escort service to pick Mike up at the behavioral health hospital during the middle of the night. It would be a legal *kidnapping*. After receiving the school's recommendations, we met with the men who would provide the service. One was ex-military, and one was an off-duty law enforcement officer who were both very professional in their interactions with us. They reassured us he would be taken there safely and answered our questions. I was shocked that these two had so much experience escorting troubled teens to treatment. Reluctantly, we signed away our guardianship of Mike to them. We said goodbye to Mike on that last day at the hospital during visiting hours. After our goodbyes, we went home and waited.

The trip to the Dominican Republic was *not* smooth, but Michael arrived safely. Every possible obstacle occurred, but communication was limited. We knew we had to wait several months for the first parent phone call with Mike. This waiting made me anxious, but I reminded myself that the school had agreed to work with Mike for however long it took and that they would not give up on him. I believed the staff was committed to our situation. They kept us updated on Mike's activities via email and sent us pictures on the school's website, much like those I had seen on Tami's computer. My first email from them included a story of how much Mike loved getting to know one of the counselors' pet monkeys.

August 5, 2004
My burden seems to be lifting as I go from day to day, knowing that Mike is safe and able to move forward—now, he must turn to the "end of himself," as they say at the parent meetings.
Things are better with Doug; it has been freeing and joyful. I cannot go back to the way things were!

I would wait anxiously every day to see if there was an email with news about Mike. Doug and I prayed for him often, and the constant turmoil in our home stopped. With each passing day, we began to relax, and our marriage began to heal. The empty beds in our house symbolized that *all* our children were off living their own lives. That felt like a *good* thing.

The date crept up on us quickly for Mike's scheduled court date after completing his community service. My husband called the courthouse to inform them of Michael's situation and tell them that he was not at home and wouldn't be able to appear in court. The court secretary's response shook Doug up,

"Mr. Mehlan, Michael is not *allowed* to leave the State of Illinois until he completes the terms of his sentence from the court and appears before the judge."

"Excuse me. I was not aware of this." My husband hesitated and asked with dread, "What do I need to do now?"

"You will have to appear in court on his behalf. By sending him out of the country, you have acted in contempt of court and could also be convicted."

"Wow, I guess I'd better call my attorney."

"Yes, and you will need to appear again in court on the date listed in the directives from the sentencing."

Our attorney was disturbed that we had sent Mike away *before* discussing it with him. "We were in a crisis!" Doug told him, frustrated.

With the court date quickly approaching, the attorney instructed us to gather all sorts of paperwork to present to the judge. We needed signed letters from the pediatrician, the psychiatrist, the high school counselor, and the psychologist. The court also required a written statement from New Horizon's Youth Ministries and the school in the Dominican Republic describing their program in detail. We needed to demonstrate that our decision to send Mike away was in our son's best interest and that the professionals agreed with us. We prayed that at our hearing, we would have a compassionate judge.

"I knew this father,
left notes for his children
before he cut the lawn
He forgot that the beds
in his house were empty
He forgot that the rooms
had been cleaned."

Matthew D. Mehlan
Excerpt from *Don't Worry*

"The steadfast love of the LORD never ceases,
his mercies never come to an end;
they are new every morning;
great is your faithfulness."

Lamentations 3:22-23 (NRSV)

Gail

CHAPTER 24—NEW EVERY MORNING

2004

Doug and I were both facing a potential contempt of court charge. Early that morning, as I sat preparing to begin my devotions and feeling the anxiety of what our day could bring, I flipped through my Bible, and a story in John popped out at me about the adulteress. She was brought before a group to be judged and then stoned to death for her infidelities. Jesus spoke to her accusers,

"'If anyone of you is without sin, let him be the first
to throw a stone at her.'
Not one of them approached to throw a stone at her.
'Woman, where are they? Has no one condemned you?'
'No one, sir,' she said.
'Then neither do I condemn you.' Jesus declared.
'Go now and leave your life of sin.'"

John 8:7-11(NIV)

August 24, 2004
We face the judge today—to defend our decision to send Mike out of
the country. I ask you, Lord, to stand beside us this morning as we
make our position known to the judge. I know in my soul that you
guided us to make this decision. Stand by us. Help him see our actions
not as defiance of the law but as an act of mercy for Mike. I praise you
for your continued support, love, and encouragement. May the judge
say, in mercy, "Go, you made the right decision. May your son leave
the life of sin behind and have a fresh start."

We didn't say much that morning in court as I stood beside
Doug with our attorney. The printed information we had pro-
vided about the school, along with letters from the high school
and physicians, made the judge's decision easy, or so it seemed.
He granted us mercy, saying almost word for word what God had
promised me.

"Go, you made the right decision."

Doug and I walked away free of a contempt conviction with
a sense of relief and a deep sigh. We *did* have a compassionate
judge.

August 26, 2004
And so, he did even as YOU promised. Thank you!

After our day in court, our house seemed empty and quiet
once again. I was still trying to figure things out. I continued
working on my Twelve-Steps and spent hours of prayer and re-
flection after each parent meeting with the program staff from the
Dominican Republic.

Staff members would fly up monthly to the Chicago area to
meet with all the parents who had children in their program from
throughout the Midwest. Anxiety was always present at the parent

meetings. It was the one time we could get feedback on what was happening with Mike. Sometimes the news was good; sometimes, it was difficult to hear. We couldn't intervene, and that was hard. We had to let go. For the first few months, Mike had to write us handwritten letters weekly. We began to have occasional phone calls after his birthday in November. The letters and calls were monitored, but when we met with the staff at meetings, they seemed honest about the real struggles. They explained their philosophy to us and how they handled each situation.

At the parent meetings, I tried to blend their very conservative teachings with my *own* faith and the principles of the Twelve-Step programs. I spent hours scouring my notes from the parent sessions and comparing them to what I learned in my meetings. There *were* many similarities, but I discovered that mixing and matching two completely different things is difficult. Even when we learned similar ideas, only some of the lessons applied to *our* situation. I studied my devotionals, and I tried to be open about everything. I maintained the attitude that was always shared at Twelve-Step meetings. *Listen and learn.*

Our empty nest became a reality. I was free from dealing with any children in our home. So, I began to switch my focus to all of the little irritating things about my *husband*. Every quirk in his personality and behavior popped out at me as if a magnifying glass was on each detail. Each week, there seemed to be something new bothering me, and although I tried to look for *my* part in the problem, it seemed like we were still out of sync.

I was trying to change myself to be a better person, but in doing that, I didn't want to accept *someone else's* character defects, especially if *they* weren't attempting to change. If I could see the log in my *own* eye, I wasn't going to let *his* log remain unnoticed! With no Mike there to look at with my hovering microscope, my husband became the only one to bear the brunt of my scrutiny.

I was not a very nice person. I should have given Doug the same grace I *craved*.

Looking back now, I realize that Doug was going through many of the same emotions and self-reflection I was. He was short with me because he suffered the same guilt and grief that I did, only it manifested itself in different ways. I wasn't being entirely fair to him. It seemed like the situation was a mess, but we kept trying. Tami was my sounding board, experiencing similar concerns in her family. It felt so good to have someone with whom I could confide.

At our first parent meeting, there was a lot of talk about family dynamics. Fathers were supposed to be strong, make the decisions, provide for, and stand up to the child causing trouble. The mother was to accept the father's decisions without question. These gender-biased roles were not exactly how our family had worked all these thirty years of marriage and family life. We had always worked out the difficult things in our family *together* as partners.

The leader frequently said one line at our meetings that was difficult for me to grasp. "*If Momma ain't happy, ain't no one happy.*" The theory was that the mother was the family's pillar of emotional and spiritual strength. If she were unhappy, everyone in the family would suffer this emotional pain and unhappiness. Because of this, it was the *family's* responsibility to ensure that the mother was happy. Still, I didn't like being solely responsible for the spiritual and emotional health of the family. I have never believed it was someone else's job to make *me* happy. I realized that my distress in dealing with an addict had taken its toll on us. My sadness, frustration, and emotional pain spread from me to my husband, to the other children, and even to our friends.

Though I was trying to work on the Twelve Steps and making progress, relieved that Mike was not there, I was enveloped in grief. I didn't know how deeply my misery had affected Michelle and Matt. I was impatient for Doug to step it up and be the leader, yet I could not accept the idea that Mike's addiction had also drained my husband's strength. He could not be a strong family leader while grieving. We had so much to learn and sort out *together*.

Through the time spent in prayer and study, I realized that our marriage wasn't based on Old Testament rules. No one blamed me, the mother, for my grief surrounding the situation. I was making space for healing and finding my way. I needed to discern what I believed.

It was also unfair to attach the word *weakness* to my husband or blame him for not leading the family. The only thing that made sense was that our shared emotional pain went back and forth between us in ways we didn't see and came back through to the children and affected all of us.

"Take what you like and leave the rest" was the slogan that helped me get through these meetings. I listened and took in any information or suggestions that seemed helpful. I realized and saw how we needed to make *each other* happy. Our marriage was unique, and we were learning to discern what would be *our* way.

During this time, our friendship with Tami and her husband grew. We were in this together and knew we could share similar situations with them. Tami and I often spoke about what we were hearing from Escuela Caribe about our boys and often looked at the pictures on the web together. We would frequently go out to dinner with Tami and her husband and commiserate. Knowing others involved with the school had advantages that helped us make the difficult choice. Sharing the experience made it so much easier.

Tami and I decided it would be fun to take a ballroom dancing class through the local park district, and we signed our husbands up to join us. It was so much fun, and we still have fond memories of laughing together as we tried to learn swing dance (my favorite) and tango, the most romantic and complex dance by far. Tami's husband was a pro, Doug was a bit clumsy, but he tried. When I hear certain music, I recall an image of Tami and her husband shaking their hips as they danced, making me smile. We needed the lighthearted challenge of dancing to keep us going. One night we all went to a dancing event with a live band. We'd never laughed as hard as we did that night, trying to remember all the steps and applying them to an actual dance. We grew closer through these shared times while the boys were down in the Dominican Republic, and we've become lifelong friends.

September 10, 2004
Lord, I sit here thinking, praying, and grateful that you always listen and respond to my prayers and concerns. One year ago, I was desperate for YOU to intervene in Mike's life and bring him some peace. With this time to reflect, study and just be me—I feel like I am becoming a happier Momma! I am becoming me.

My devotion today says, "I've learned to stop managing other people's lives and to take care of myself.—If he ever does get into recovery, he will have a healthier, happier parent."

So, Lord, I face my day again, "Among the Sunflowers," those beautiful flowers that open their faces to the sun each day. You, Lord, are my sun—and the soil I am rooted in is God's earthly world. Planted here, I am trying to find a place for myself, doing what I can to fulfill your will for me on this earth. I know I have so much yet to learn about life! So, to be a happier, healthier parent, I must live my life according to your will. I long to know what that is.

I am opening my face to seek your light today as a sunflower opens to face the sun. I thank you for your Divine light and understanding. AMEN

"I'll be there waiting to sweep away the ashes
And I'll pick the last speck of debris off your eyelashes—
Gently pull it away
And blow it into the wind—Like a wish
And I'll embrace you with all the power of the rejected demons
Haunting the ruins of our lives and whisper—Let's go
Is it time to start over?
I am the devil on your shoulder.
I heard when you said, "I'm not miserable."
But I never heard you say,
'I am happy—'"

Jolly Jackson
Excerpt from *I Just Might be the Devil Part II*

Gail

CHAPTER 25—ALWAYS SECOND CHANCES

December 2004

It usually brought me joy to play holiday music as I decorated the tree or baked sugar cookies in preparation for Christmas. This year, I didn't have the energy to listen to music or bake. The prospect of waking up on Christmas morning and seeing the excitement on my young children's faces always made all the hard work worth it. Now that my children were adults, my enthusiasm had disappeared, and this year would be especially strange. One of them was missing.

Early on the first morning of my winter break, I sat looking out the window, sipping a cup of coffee, unmotivated. A beautiful red cardinal flew in close and perched on the dark branch of a tree. Its red feathers were a bright contrast against the blue sky and white snow. As I looked at the bird, I felt the power of the Holy Spirit settle over me. I needed that inspiration to keep going as I put up a few decorations here and there, shopped for my daughter and son, who would both be home, and wrote a letter to Mike. I would send a package to the Dominican Republic with some of his favorite things.

I had already received several lengthy newsletters from friends and couldn't stomach the thought of writing such a letter. I couldn't find any cute family photos to include—the last one was taken at Matt's graduation and wasn't the reflection of my family that I wanted to put out in the world. All I felt was pain and sadness. I was missing Mike, but I also *wasn't*. This distance between us was doing me some good.

We had a good laugh at one of my support meetings as we discussed sending out the usual holiday cards. One of my friends quipped, "Those braggy Christmas letters are the *worst* for us to get! I hate them. Like we're really going to tell the whole sad story to all our friends in a cheery, upbeat letter! Hah! Ri-i-i-i-ght."

"Yeah, like we're going to write about our *wonderful* child in drug rehab! He's doing well, working on his fourth step inventory! Hah!"

We all laughed at the absurdity of the situation.

Christmas morning was uneventful, almost dull. It was the four of us, Michelle, Matt, my husband, and myself. We leaned into one another and talked. In the quietness, we discussed our decision to send Mike away. We talked about what we knew from his emails, letters, and infrequent phone calls. He had made it clear it wasn't easy. The school was rigorous, and there were different levels from one to five for the teens to work through. I knew they used swats to deal with confrontational behavior, and Mike would hate this type of discipline. He had moved up to the first level and seemed slightly motivated to move through more of the levels. It was so hard for me, knowing Mike as I did, to imagine him cooperating, working on, and celebrating small successes. His underlying frustration came through with every letter and phone call.

When we explained what was going on with their brother, Matt questioned why we decided to send him so far away and to a program that was so strict. He was concerned we'd overreacted, but Doug and I used this quiet opportunity to explain our drastic decision.

"Other treatment programs didn't work. Mike walked out of two of them and continued to overdose. We're thankful he's still alive." Doug told him.

As I listened, I realized that in my heart, I had been second-guessing the decision to send Mike away every day since we'd made it.

"The counselors and staff come to Chicago monthly for meetings and tell us that Mike seems happy and well-liked. He's made lots of friends," I said. Instead of sharing my doubts, I spoke of the positives. "They make sure he's safe and feed him well. He's getting exercise every day and learning to care for his physical body. They give him opportunities to be a leader and a role model for other students," I continued, *not* talking much about the strong Christian values or the strict discipline.

We looked at the photos Escuela Caribe posted on their website. The pictures showed a child we hardly recognized. Michelle commented, "He looks so cute!"

We all missed Mike. That was easy to acknowledge.

The serenity of sitting in the quiet with our two children and my husband that morning brought me joy. There seemed to be genuine affection between us. We were able to have conversations without drama, and I felt loved. We were healing our hurts and missteps. I believe I finally *celebrated* Christmas then.

A reading from one of my devotionals struck me that day as I wrote in my journal, *"I have a perfectly imperfect family, and I love them."* I could accept that we all didn't have to be *perfect.* We could just be ourselves.

This brief visit from my daughter and spending time with my other son allowed me to listen and hear what was happening in *their* lives. Michelle was teaching health and physical education at a middle school near Indianapolis and coaching cheerleading. She had recently reconnected with a former boyfriend and was happy. She was enjoying her single life with friends who lived in her apartment complex. I spent time shopping with her, taking her out to lunch, and doing some baking together. Several times, our visits to see her in Indiana had been disappointing. Her brother's behavior had thwarted things. One time, we canceled a planned trip after Mike had a meltdown on our way. I put those worries to rest and *enjoyed,* for the first time in a long time, just spending time with *her.*

Matt was also at home, and we shared this time with his girlfriend, who we knew and loved. Her folks lived nearby, so he was in and out. Nevertheless, it was *so* good to have him home for Christmas morning and to listen to him talk about his adventures with his bandmates as Matt delved into the recording business. He was working hard to find a way to make a living doing what he loved. We were so proud of his graduation from college in May, and he was about to release some new music in the New Year. He was excited and anticipatory about that. It seemed like an exciting time for all of them.

We talked about the possibility of trying to all go down to the Dominican Republic to see Mike for a family visit in March during spring break if Michelle and I had our breaks at the same time. Each of them wanted to make that happen. It had been a long time since we *all* took a trip together. I was happy and excited.

Because Christmas had been so wonderful, the idea of what I'd write in a braggy Mehlan "after Christmas" letter began to creep into my head. I gathered all my courage and wrote.

As I reread the letter, I realized that there *were* many blessings for us that Christmas. We had a few misunderstandings, but in reality, we responded to the situation with our love intact and our family strong. We had the best Christmas possible.

The days after the holidays were quiet, and I made a list of resolutions, something I hadn't done for a long time. I had almost forgotten what it felt like to make my own goals for the future. I was healing and moving forward rather than standing still in constant fear for the next shoe to drop.

One morning I woke up from a restless night and a horrible nightmare. In the dream, I was walking along the beach with Mike enjoying the ocean paradise. Suddenly he bolted on ahead of me and disappeared into an alligator-infested swamp. All I saw was an alligator's head and its enormous jaws chomping down, chewing, and swallowing, and no sign of Michael. The following morning, I cried out to God in my journal:

I just give him to you, Lord; I know I cannot control or keep him safe! He is my son, and we have an indescribable bond. However, he is not mine to hover over or control any longer. I ask for your help putting these crazy thoughts and dreams into perspective. I know my subconscious mind is worried and disturbed by all that has happened. I also know how important it is for me to let you show me YOUR will for Mike and for Mike to discover YOUR will for him on his own.

I still had so much healing to do. Was it possible to be at ease when the future seemed scary and unsure? I have always struggled with that uncertainty. It's hard to live life with questions that linger, and this was something that only the passage of time and my faith could bring. I wanted the *good* future to be here now. I wanted my child to have a second chance at life. As if to answer my prayers, I received a poem written by Michael on a small piece of lined paper a few days later.

AMONG THE SUNFLOWERS

With sun above
and sun below
We looked out
with longing to be
Among the Sunflowers
A mother who's tired
A son who is restless
Find a solemn peace together
Among the Sunflowers

Michael M. Mehlan

Even in my dreams, I longed for that solemn peace together. I waited for that second chance.

*"Trust in the Lord with all your heart and lean not
on your own understanding;
in all your ways, submit to him, and he will
make your paths straight."*

Proverbs 3: 5-6 (NIV)

Gail

CHAPTER 26—FIRST LETTERS

2004-2005

Dear Mom and Dad,
*I'm trying to get used to it here, but I really hate it, and I want to
come home, but you prob'ly won't let me. There are cockroaches here,
and I hate cockroaches. I really miss all of you very much, and I'm
tearing up just writing this letter. I really need a hug. Also, they made
me shave off my mop, and that pissed me off, but if I didn't, I'd have
gotten "units of concern," which are swats on the butt with a paddle.*

This first letter was exactly what I was expecting. Mike had
complained, whined, and made a fuss from each residential
treatment program he attended. I knew he wouldn't like it in
the Dominican Republic. The staff had warned us and prepared
us to hear these types of comments. It was hard, though, to lis-
ten to your child be unhappy. I knew Mike was tugging on my
mother's heart to see if I would cave in again and rescue him. I
couldn't. Honestly, after the third overdose on heroin and other
drugs, I was thankful he was *alive*. There wasn't much life left in
him when we said goodbye at the behavioral health hospital. But
somehow, slowly, we began to witness some changes.

I realize now that I was lucky to have a personal connection with a friend who had a child enrolled in New Horizons Youth Ministries. Tami's husband had worked for them as a camp leader when he was a recent college graduate. Before we decided to enroll Mike, he took the time to explain the philosophy and beliefs of New Horizons Youth Ministries (NHYM) and their discipline methods. New Horizons had several different sites for therapeutic services for youth. One was a summer camp in Canada, another was a residential high school in Indiana, and the farthest was Escuela Caribe in the Dominican Republic.

I truly believed that God had answered my prayers when things fell into place for us to send Michael to Escuela Caribe, and I could *not* lean on *my own* understanding of what the future would hold.

Tami told me that when Mike arrived at Escuela Caribe, they introduced him to the other kids on campus, and when her son heard that Mike was from Schaumburg, he began asking a few questions. He told Mike his mom was a teacher in that school district, and Mike said, "My mom teaches there too!" A light bulb went on—both of their moms worked at the same school.

"Sorry, Bro. I'm probably the reason you're here."

There was a connection.

The second letter from Mike was a blow.

Dear Mom and Dad,
They won't let me play my guitar or draw or write until I'm on second level, which won't be until a minimum of three weeks, but some kids have been here for nine months and are still on zero level, which is the level I am on.

I knew the discipline would be harsh at Escuela Caribe, but realizing that Mike had all his coping skills, such as listening to music, playing the guitar, and writing, taken away from him was a shock. I was under the impression that *love* would be the strategy they would use to facilitate positive change. All I could hear between each line of Mike's letter was the frustration and futility he felt. His dad and I had made this decision, and I prayed every day that he would ultimately forgive *us* for putting him through that. Again, the words that always calmed me and echoed what I knew to be true were, *choose life*. We sent him off. We had *chosen* to save his *life*.

As the weeks went by, I began to choose *life* for myself, too. I needed this distinct boundary and distance between us to help untangle the web of my enmeshed relationship with Mike. It seemed like I still felt his pain and wanted my *baby* to be okay. But he *was*. I could see it and feel it in his letters. He began to adjust to the program's structure as he slowly moved up the levels. He learned how to *work* the system and liked getting positive feedback. Within a few months after his arrival, his letters were much more upbeat. I knew the staff monitored his letters, but I don't believe the staff withheld vital information from us either. I sent chatty, newsy letters about home life to Mike. I monitored his photos on the website, and he appeared happy and healthy.

Dear Mom and Dad,

I'm dealing okay here. Granted, I still don't like it, but I'm here, and you won't let me come home, so whatever—a month and a half have gone by, and it seems to have gone by fast. The days are long, but the weeks are fast, so it doesn't make any sense. If we pass inspection, we are going to this place called 27 Waterfalls. It's like a park of natural waterfalls where you go swimming, jump from high rocks into the water, and stuff. It sounds like fun, and we get to eat at McDonald's. There are a lot of cool things to do on the island.

   Love, your son, Mike

Mike's letters continued to come weekly, and we saw progress in his attitude as his writing became more mature. We began to hear about all the exciting and fun things he was doing, and he shared his hopes and plans for the future. He talked with his counselor about college and what options might be available for the next school year. By January, we heard a much different tone in his letters.

Dear Mom and Dad,
Mr. B told me to start talking to you about where to go to college, what I'm going to do in college, rules that I'll have to follow (Well, "expectations") if I have to move home before college—as of right now I have a 2.3 grade-point average, so it's hard. So, tell me what I need to do!
Your youngest, Mike.

By the end of January, we could have our first scheduled phone call since his birthday in November, and although it was short and sweet, it was great to hear Mike's voice. He sounded good. He sounded strong. In his letters, he sent recommendations of Bible verses to read that had special meaning for him. We scheduled our Parent Visit (PV) for March, and he started to sign his letters with the Greek word *Agathon* (the good servant). I began to feel reassured that we had made a wise decision.

Dear Mom and Dad,
I was so glad to hear about our phone call and that when I have a PV, Matt and Michelle will come. That is awesome. I'm keeping second level, and I made 382 last week and 382 this week. I thought that was funny. Mr. B says I can start playing praise music on Sundays at the service. I'm writing journals on stuff. I'm going to write you guys a letter about stuff you didn't know. It's going to be pretty long. But

*it will clear my conscience. It's Step Nine to its fullest, so it goes. I'm
making amends the best I know how. So, I love you all so very much
that I must make amends. With love, your youngest, Mike*

Agathon, The Good

"I know it isn't fair
It isn't much better for me
The wind, you know, it does decree
That every minute hurts
Every second is a winch to my heart
But those who love you don't seem to care."

—*Jolly Jackson*
Excerpt from *With You Soon*

Michael

CHAPTER 27— THE GOOD SERVANT

2004

They took me and flew me 1,000 miles to an island I could not escape. The thoughts now are mangled, the memory depersonalized so I could cope. The first thing they did was degrade my sense of self. They shaved my head of the long mop top I had grown over the last few years. They made me ask to enter every room, begin eating, and use the bathroom—I had two minutes to do my business. They forced us to clean every room in the house under threat of calisthenic exercises in an amount more than I was even physically capable of doing. I wasn't allowed to listen to music or play my instrument or allowed to read anything that wasn't pre-approved. Hard labor such as moving rocks, building cinder block houses, or digging in hard clay were daily tasks. If I refused or rebelled, I was given swats with a leather paddle, then taken to a concrete cell where I was left to piss and shit in a bucket in a room with no windows and only the light from underneath the door. I was left inside in 90-degree heat and fed only what was brought to me, usually in the form of broth or oatmeal gruel.

To free myself from the Quiet Room, I had to do hard physical labor in the heat for 14-16 hours a day. On one occasion, they made me dig my own grave in some faulty attempt to get me to understand my own mortality. I already wanted to die. I wasn't me anymore. I had no sense of self and formed a new identity out of the suffering. I became Agathos Doulos, The Good Servant. I was gonna do everything that they asked of me. I was gonna give in and lock away the person I was for later. I was gonna become the thing they wanted, so I would never have to be in this kind of pain again.

But the pain never left. It just changed and morphed into despair. Those in charge would complete the nightmare over and over and over to me, my friends, and the weak. I don't know if I will ever recover from it. As a boy, I got it easy. The girls got it worse. I will never forgive myself for doing nothing. But I wasn't me anymore. I wasn't even a person. I was a robot, a servant. I did what my masters required of me.

Thinking back on my time at Escuela Caribe now, it feels like a dystopian nightmare, like someone describing the concentration camps from the Holocaust. In my reflections, it was certainly not that. Still, it was brainwashing, and it was indoctrination. They told me, "Become a good Christian servant, be a man." The values were not the values of love and egalitarian poverty that are at the heart of Christianity. I was abused, taken advantage of, and my parents paid for them to do this. My parents didn't know how bad it was.

The first nine months at Escuela Caribe were very hard for me, and even now, it's hard for me to talk about the physical, mental, emotional, and sexual abuse I experienced there at the hands of people I had no choice but to trust.

I wrote letters to my parents, and those letters were censored and read, and I was forced to rewrite many of them if they didn't fit the narrative they were feeding my parents. When I was finally allowed to see my family, I cried at the music I could now hear, and it unlocked the cell in which I had hidden and locked my true self, the self I wanted to protect, the little boy who was full of love, the real me, not the GOOD SERVANT.

THE GIRLS FROM SANTIAGO

When you think you're escaping,
You find the longest way round is the shortest way home
But we've slain giants and seen the ghosts of old men
Who have found their way back to the start again
When love learns to love, we've learned to love, love

I wanna take ya down to the fountains of truth
So, we can bathe in the fountains of youth once again
When love learns to love, we've learned to love, love

I see our ambitions flying away
Like the pictures in the scrapbooks of our yesterday
Because my love learned to love when love was just a fool

When love learns to love, it learns to love, love

I remember the mountain air and putting flowers in your hair
Just like the girls in Santiago used to do
On our way to the oceans of many days,
we pass them through all of ourselves
So, hold fast to now
To which the future plunges through
Like an arrow straight through me, and you
Let me be who you would be

When love learned to love, it learned to love, love

Jolly Jackson

THIS IS MY DREAMS COME TRUE

I had my cereal for breakfast
I fell asleep on the train
There's always rivers
to throw things into
I think that I'll do the same
Let's do the gas mask
gas mask
Let's lock the door
This is my dreams come true
This is my dreams come true
I'm in love…
This is my dreams come true
Gonna f**k it up.

Matthew D. Mehlan

Michael

CHAPTER 28—AMONG THE SUNFLOWERS 2

2005

Seven months passed, and it was finally time for my parents to visit me. I was ecstatic. I was waiting at my house for the call that my parents had arrived.

When the phone rang, I ran out of the house and down the hill. Standing there was my mom, my dad, my brother, and my sister. I greeted them all with a smile and hugs. We all got into a cab to go back to the hotel so I could stay with them for five days. In the cab, my brother handed me his iPod and played me a song. It was one of his originals entitled, "This is My Dreams Come True." I had heard the song hundreds of times before, but something hit me so hard at that moment that I began bawling my eyes out uncontrollably.

"What's wrong, Bro?" my brother asked.

The only thing I could say was, "It's so beautiful."

He hugged me and said, "It's okay, Bro. It's good to see you."

It was the first song I had heard in seven months. We weren't allowed to listen to music at school. As a musician, music is my life, and at that moment, the song was the most beautiful thing I had ever heard. This was the first time I had spent with my family since I could remember; where I got along with them, I was clean, and I was happy.

However, there wasn't much talk about me coming home. I would spend another eleven months at the boarding school.

"…but while he was still a long way off,
his father saw him and was filled with compassion for him;
he ran to his son, threw his arms around him, and kissed him.
The son said to him, 'Father, I have sinned against heaven
and against you.
I am no longer worthy of being called your son.'
But the father said to his servants,
'Quick! Bring the best robe and put it on him.
Put a ring on his finger and sandals on his feet.
Bring the fattened calf and kill it.
Let's have a feast and celebrate.
For this son of mine was dead and is alive again;
he was lost and is found.'"
So, they began to celebrate."

Luke 15:20-24 (NIV)

Gail

CHAPTER 29—SEEING THE PRODIGAL

2005

March 22, 2005
Thank you, Lord—for watching over my son, Mike, helping us see more clearly where we needed to be as parents and resolving some financial issues, so we have enough to cover all the costs.

It's hard to trust, but we have been blessed and are grateful for your presence in our lives and for keeping your hand on Mike.

Stay with me as I prepare for our trip—bring us safely together. Be present in our time—in the love we share and the bonds of family. Move all of us, Lord, to be aware of your presence in our lives, Matt, Michelle, Mike, my children, now adults. Help me give them to you daily, for their lives are not my own, and I must let go. And I do—I go now to face the day! Thank you! AMEN

The day had come. We were leaving to head to Santiago, Dominican Republic, for our family vacation and our scheduled parent visit. As we prepared to go, it was the four of us, Michelle and Matt, Doug and me. We would meet up with Michael on the island at Escuela Caribe. All the arrangements were made, tickets in hand, luggage packed. Anxiety flowed through me that morning and the days before our leaving. As was typical for me, I was full of excitement for our visit and our time together. I tried so hard not to put any expectations on it. Still, with five different people traveling, weather, time, physical needs, and wants, vacations always brought out the best and the worst in our family.

Invariably things were never simple. I wanted to mother *all* my kids on this trip, to be a person, a friend, and a parent. I was desperate to *let go* of my concern for their comings and goings. I couldn't control any of them. I said a prayer thanking God in advance to help me avoid holding negative and unnecessary thoughts in my mind. Despite my prayers and longing to do things right, the tension grew in my shoulders and neck and presented itself as pain. I kept repeating the mantra *"whatever, whatever, Lord, whatever."* I wanted to focus on the small gifts of this special time.

The day after we arrived, the sun was shining brightly, and the air was cool as I sat on the balcony at our hotel in Jarabacoa. I felt a bit out of sync that morning. I wanted to be present and aware, not guarded when I saw my son that day. I wrote in my journal: *"I don't feel the sick dread of seeing Mike—I am anticipating it with joy!"* Writing it made it possible. All of my *chicks were in the nest*, and I was about to see a son I thought I had lost, and even though my neck and shoulder were still acting up, an impending celebration was definitely on my mind.

The prearranged drive into town and to the school in the taxi was interesting. Although I speak Spanish and consider myself fluent, the particular accent in the Dominican Republic was different from what I was used to. The taxi driver understood me completely, but I sat there guessing at half of what he was saying to me. There was a rifle sitting right between us on the center console of the van that was quite unsettling to me, although perhaps I ought to have been thankful to be protected. We drove down and around winding gravel roads and up hills until we came upon a gated area with an armed guard. They were expecting us.

The taxi pulled forward and stopped in front of one of the buildings. We got out of the car and looked around at the school grounds, blooming with flowering trees and bushes. The school's campus was beautiful, with a large central building, the chapel, adorned with blue stained-glass windows. The bright sun was streaming down upon us as I looked around.

Suddenly I heard a voice calling, "Hey, Mom! Hey, Dad!" Mike ran faster than I'd ever seen him run down the hill from his house, arms spread out wide, straight into my arms for the biggest hug I'd ever received. I broke away from him, briefly, to look into his eyes, and I saw a young man that I hardly recognized! It felt so good to see in his face the joy he had in reuniting with us and hugging his dad and siblings. There were tears in my eyes at that moment, and they stayed close to the surface all that day. It felt surreal and beautiful, and I knew my son was truly *with* us.

We briefly met with Mike's housefather and a couple of the Escuela Caribe staff members. They gave us a few restrictions about what Mike was allowed to do on our visit, but it was pretty simple. The school secretary gave us all the information we needed about the resort where we would spend our time. After a short tour of the grounds, the staff permitted us to take Mike and enjoy our time together. The taxi driver had waited for us as he was to take us back to our hotel in Jarabacoa. Mike had a different plan.

Mike wanted to show us the beautiful waterfalls near the school, so I asked the driver if he could take us there and wait as we hiked up to see them. He agreed and walked with us that afternoon; perhaps he felt responsible for us. I was uneasy about leaving my bag in the car unsupervised, so I headed off on this hike carrying a heavy duffel, which wasn't helping my sore, tension-riddled shoulder and neck, but I persevered.

The cool morning had turned quickly into a hot, muggy afternoon. We followed Mike up a questionable path, pushing back branches and watching our steps to avoid tripping on roots beneath large green leaves on the ground. The trail we were climbing went up and up quite steeply as we continued. Mike kept promising that it wasn't much further, and I cursed the heavy bag I repeatedly switched from one sore shoulder to the other. Doug carried my bag for a while to give me a break. Finally, we began to hear the sound of rushing water in the background.

"We're almost there!" Mike yelled.

The breeze from the cascading water cooled me. We turned onto a worn path, and directly in front of us was an opening in the trees. The rocks jutted up from the ground, and a giant cliff with clear, powerful water spilling down from the top appeared. We had arrived, and it was awe-inspiring!

Walking carefully across large stones and smaller rocks, with water swirling all around and underneath us, we finally landed on a group of large boulders that were in the middle of all that rushing cold water. Matt and Mike wasted no time taking off their shirts and shoes and jumping into the frigid mountain water. Michelle, Doug, and I were more tentative, taking off our shoes and cautiously dipping our toes into the water, slowly tolerating it. Michelle finally jumped into the cold water, too, going in only waist-deep and staying clear of her splashing brothers. I finally began to relax as I watched my boys playing in the water. Their laughter and screeching at each other made me giggle with joy. As they waded closer to the waterfall, they happily teased each other with splashes of the frigid water. The water was cold, but my heart warmed as I watched them. I reminded myself that this was what I longed for. I witnessed a baptism of sorts in that cold mountain stream.

A decent amount of time passed before we headed back down the mountainside towards the taxi. The driver had walked with us the whole way and laughed with me at my children's antics. He would receive a good tip for staying with us that entire time. Once in the car, damp but happy, we headed back into town.

In the morning, we were greeted early by the hotel office, calling to let us know that our ride was there for our trip to Puerta Plata—an all-inclusive resort. The drive was about three hours along rough roads. We had a different taxi driver that day, one who had taken many students and their families across the island to the resort.

Motorcycles and scooters honked and zigzagged around us as we drove through the towns and the countryside. I was shell-shocked to see how poor this country was. Colorful shacks were all around near the road where the Dominicans lived and worked. Mike told us that the workers in the sugar cane fields were only paid about one dollar per day for their hard work. You could see a shack where one TV was sitting outside on a front porch with a hand-painted sign that said, *El Cine,* The Movie Theater. That was where the neighbors would all congregate to watch television.

Chickens and goats were running about, and we could see shops selling beverages or snacks along the way. I listened to the driver's Spanish, slowly figuring it out and translating for my husband. After the three-hour trip, I finally got the hang of his accent and understood most of what he was saying.

The all-inclusive hotel was extraordinary. Everything was beautiful inside and out. There were multiple restaurants, manicured grounds, swimming pools, and a long stretch of private beach. Palm trees and flowers were everywhere. There was luxury all around us, yet I was still on edge. It was stressful having Mike with us after all those months. Trying too hard to be relaxed felt forced and uncomfortable. That was how I felt the majority of the time. I still carried all the doubts and fears in my shoulders. I had tried hard to let go of them during the eight months we'd been apart, but my trust in Mike was low, and I felt that constant need to be super-vigilant.

One day our son, Matt, returned from making a phone call and said that some Dominican woman had stopped him on the sidewalk and said in Spanish, "*Jesucristo, salve mi vida!*" (Jesus Christ, save my life!) Matt had shoulder-length brown hair and a full beard and mustache. When we thought about it, it made perfect sense. He *did* look like a potential Jesus. We all had a good laugh about it, and the very next day, the beard and mustache were gone. I remembered the image of the boys splashing each other in the waterfall. I *had* thought of it as a *baptism* when it happened.

Our time together had beautiful moments of laughter and joy in each other's company. When those moments came, I was acutely aware of them. I was able to loosen my grip and let go cautiously. We played board games together some afternoons, and the kids were competitive at every turn. One night at dinner, we began making "Mehlan" music by squeaking the rims of our water glasses in the restaurant. The music was eerie and other-worldly, but it was, in its way, beautiful and memorable.

The staff had asked Mike if he wanted to bring his guitar on the trip so he could play and practice a little. He would serenade us on the guitar every evening, enjoying the chance to play. I hoped it would motivate him to continue working hard to move up the levels after this trip. As soon as I had that thought, I realized it *wasn't* up to me.

The days on the beach were glorious, and there was so much to do. Michelle and I enjoyed the bright sun and sandy beach. The boys took a Hobie-Cat out on the water and sailed. We snorkeled around the reef and enjoyed a fabulous Caribbean meal at one of the included restaurants. It was hard to believe that we were in a country with such extreme poverty on the other side of a large stone wall.

Mike and I had a long talk on the last evening of our trip. The truth came out about how much he was still struggling.

"I really hate it at Escuela Caribe, Mom. I want to come home, please!" Mike said, looking me straight in the eye, sober, present.

"Oh, honey, I know you do." I'd responded, unsure *I* was ready for him to come home. "What's going on that's so awful?" I asked.

"I can't play my guitar, and that sucks. They only let me listen to the music *they* choose. I wish I had more time to talk to my friends. We're always working. I've had a great time with you guys this week. It's been more relaxed."

"Me too. It *has* been a fun week, hasn't it? So, you wish you had more time to socialize? I get that."

"I hate my housefather," he said.

"Why is that?"

"He's so mean—I'm afraid of him."

"I'm sorry, Mike. That's not what I want to hear. I thought things were going fairly well for you. You're moving up the levels and getting your schoolwork done. Is there anything good about it at all?" I was hoping to stay focused on the positives.

"I just wanna come home, Mom, please? Can you talk to Dad about it? I can't take it much longer. I wanna come home with you guys now. Please? At least give me a time, so I know."

"I *don't* know, Mike. Dad and I still have to talk things over with the staff to see what they think. We both want you to finish school first. We don't know when that will be."

I knew that the open-ended time frame of his return was bothering him. We hadn't set a final date yet. We valued the advice the counselors were giving us monthly. I encouraged him to work hard, follow the rules, move up in the leveled system, and wait and see.

"Geez, Mom, I need a break. Tell me when I can come home!"

"It is what it is," I said firmly. Mike wasn't too happy with my response.

Later, I reflected on our talk in my journal and remarked on how much progress he had made. I was very thankful for that. Mike grappled with the program's intense structure and the lack of free time to meditate, reflect and relate on an emotional level to other kids and adults he cared about in the program. He was my little boy, the authentic Mike, opening up his heart to his mom, wanting control and still unsure about his faith. I thanked God for the small positive changes and asked God to keep a close eye on my son.

April 3, 2005
I cannot sleep anymore today, God! I am full of love, peace, and joy at the gifts you gave us. This is a beautiful place—this has been an amazing trip.

I understand the story of the prodigal son, and I rejoice that my son is alive! He once was gone to me, and I grieved for him—the loss and the pain were great! But you are faithful in your promises, and now I have hope for the future.

I see Lord, too, that the future is in your hands, not mine—and that you will complete your work in him—In your time and your ways.

All I can say is THANK YOU!

I LOVED YOU FIRST

You know I said once before, you know I'll say it again.
I know they're just words, but I'll say it again.
But you know I loved you first.
For what it's worth, I never left, but I heard, I've tried so hard,
So, I say it again, every day.
But I don't know if it's true, but I'll say it again.
I loved you first.
I see the secrets on your face; I want you to learn as I've learned.
As you get older, I see it in your bones, but I loved you first.
And I know the world. It hurts.
I throw down while you nurse.
But even though, even though while I wait.
The dream of the moment has burst.
And I hope beyond hopes that you learn just to thirst.
But remember, I loved you first.

Jolly Jackson

"You…if you scrub, the dirt might come off.
You're wrong,
you can do backflips and break your neck
and do backflips again.

There are people with perfect vision.
There are seagulls who live in parking lots.

You…you can start over
You…you can burn things that are flammable
You…you can start over."

Matthew D. Mehlan
Excerpt from *There are Seagulls who Live in Parking Lots*

Gail

CHAPTER 30—THOUGHTS

2005

Sent: May 22, 2005

Mike Mehlan, parent letter

Dear Mom and Dad,

*I'M DONE WITH HIGH SCHOOL! I'M DONE WITH HIGH
SCHOOL!*
    I'M DONE WITH HIGH SCHOOL!

I ACTUALLY FINISHED IT! I ACTUALLY FINISHED IT! I ACTUALLY FINISHED IT, MOM!!!

I ALMOST CRIED. I ACTUALLY FINISHED IT. IT'S ALL OVER. I'M STARTING OVER!!!

I'm giving my testimony today, and it's pretty tough for me to talk in front of people. But I'm a living sermon that has to be preached, so I'm gonna do it. They are actually gonna let me play one of Matt's tunes about starting over for it, and it's gonna be good. I leave out to Angosto, the summer program, tomorrow morning, so I have to pack tonight. Tell Michelle happy birthday, and I love her. I'm constantly praying for her and Matt, you, Dad, and all of our family. I love how God is working in our lives. Pray for me. I love all of you so much.

Love your youngest son, Mike, AGATHON

The tears streamed down my face when I read the news. I could feel Michael's pride and sense of accomplishment. Finally, after all he had been through, he would graduate from high school! After our parent visit (PV) in March, Mike was allowed to send and receive emails from us, and our communication was much more consistent.

Doug and I decided to make the trip again to the Dominican Republic for Mike's graduation. Being there for his graduation that June was such a blessing. Everything I witnessed at Escuela Caribe on that visit appeared positive and hopeful. He had done well in school. He was healthy and happy. We met many of Mike's friends, including students and adults. The mutual affection and respect between them seemed authentic. NHYM had delivered precisely what the brochures and website had promised, *"It is our mission to provide promising youth with a combination of learning experiences designed to raise potential through character enrichment and cultivate a lifetime desire for excellence."*

The program's philosophy expounded on the advantages of

distance and *culture shock* to help the students realize the depth of their problems. As a parent, I, too, experienced the benefit of the *distance* between us for my own healing and growth. I learned to live my *own* life and allowed the knots in my soul from the trauma of addiction and fears for my son's life to unwind. Doug and I needed the time to reconnect and become stronger as a couple, as parents. Mike gained an enhanced appreciation for Mom and Dad and his siblings after this time of separation. We *all* shared the dream of *"being a united family again."*

The culture shock of being in a new and distinct environment positively affected Michael. It helped him realize the enormity of the world and the stark differences in economics between what he had at home and what was available to the residents of the Dominican Republic. The program encouraged mission work to inspire the students to think of and care for others. The climate differences, such as the constant heat and humidity and the different food and language barriers, created many opportunities for growth, communication, and healing of old habits. My experiences in a foreign country (Spain) had been very formative for me as a young woman, and I wanted this for Michael. The experience in the Dominican Republic seemed to have a positive impact on him. He still, to this day, loves to cook a Dominican dish, *pollo guisado,* for his friends, more than ten years after returning home.

Mike's impatience to get on with life came through loud and clear in his letters and phone calls. When the staff informed Mike that he would stay at Escuela Caribe in their *Work Force* (a supervised job program where the students received pay for their work) the fall after graduating, he was extremely disappointed. He often complained about being there and having to work after deciding to go to Trinity University in Deerfield, Illinois, upon his return in January.

The counselors and psychiatrist decided to reduce some of

Michael's medications to see how he functioned without prescription psychotropics. He had been on several medicines when he got to Escuela Caribe for mental health, focus, and mood swings. The staff worked with a psychiatrist to wean him off these medications, but I could see subtle changes in his attitude and focus even from afar that were concerning. He would often complain about being disciplined for being unable to stay focused. I waited patiently to see what would happen. I wanted to give Mike time to adjust to the change knowing that it takes time for the body to readjust after being medicated. I encouraged Mike to give it a chance.

Sent: September 25, 2005

Subject: Mike Mehlan, parent letter

Dear Mom and Dad,

We talk tomorrow, which is really good. Got a letter from this girl I like, which is cool, so hey, that made me feel good! I'm really tired of working. I still love it, but it's just exhausting altogether. I get paid 1003 pesos tomorrow, which is like 40 bucks. That's more than teachers make here in a week for spending money anyway, so I might go out for a steak dinner or something with my group leader or something that will be fun. I'm so excited to go to Trinity, but it feels so far away, and it's hard to stay patient. I just want to come home and work till then, but I know that's probably not an option right now, which sucks. Because it's not reasonable. But I think I know what I want to study, film. It's everything I love; music, art, imagination, and good writing. It all wraps into one category. I have been thinking about that possibility for a long time. I even tried to write a screenplay. Do you remember? I just think it would keep my attention and I would enjoy it very much. I could make some really awesome Christian movies that will rock the boat a little and stir some ideas in people. Dad asked me about my dreams, and well, I want to do something to change the world, a thought, an idea, a concept, and share it with the world, and movies would be a good forum. But, I only want to be happy and have fun and have a family. I want to go skydiving, hunting for bears, ride a motorcycle all over the US, visit Europe, go to Palestine, visit China, and climb a really tall mountain. Those are just ideas. I would like to play more music and record and someday maybe with Matt. I think he underestimates my guitar-playing skills. I'm writing him right now, and I'll send out his letter soon. I'm trying to make an effort. You know, if I never did any of those things I mentioned, I would be just as joyful as if I did. As long as whatever I am doing is glorifying to God. Well, I'll talk to ya'll tomorrow. Love your youngest son, Mike AGATHON

PS Her name is Kara. in case you were wondering.

Reading this letter convinced me that my son *was* maturing. He was thinking about his future and could consider his strengths and weaknesses. He was proud of working hard and earning some money. He had achieved the highest level allowed, which was *off-level*, and meant that he could come and go as he chose. He could go into town and make plans with friends or play music. He often spent time with his teachers and their families off-campus. I could see in him the desire to go and do things and be part of the larger world. I noticed *positive* changes in my son.

The counselors encouraged the students to develop a sense of *humble repentance* for their actions. After more than a year there, we did receive a letter from Mike asking for forgiveness and offering his sincere apologies and an account of all he had done to himself and our family. I hated reading the details but appreciated that he owned them.

"Time is but slowly passing,
the drop of single grains of sand
The journey has been hard in these
harsh and empty lands"

Jolly Jackson
Excerpt from *Unrelenting Joy*

Michael

CHAPTER 31—REFLECTIONS

2006

*It was NOT all abuse and hatred that I experienced at Escuela Cari-
be. I was immensely influenced in positive ways by the GOOD people
who worked at the school. It was not all constant and continuous
suffering, but when some of the experiences stunted my development,
it took years for me to deprogram my brain. I do not want to labor
extensively or chronicle the horror of what I suffered. It took me al-
most fifteen years to tell anyone about the bad stuff. I locked it away
and pretended it didn't matter, but it did.*

*I was just a kid, a 17-year-old neurodivergent kid with a ma-
jor depressive disorder. Some staff members used my greatest fears to
force me to comply with their standards. Their solution was systematic
abuse and Orwellian brainwashing. Forcing me to dig in garbage
pits filled with cockroaches, to which I have a terrible phobia, to
convince me to love their God as my big brother only left me with the
question: If God truly LOVES ME! WHY WOULD HE WANT ME
TO ENDURE THIS?*

Trauma doesn't just dissipate. We internalize it. It becomes a cancer. You try to mask it the best you can, but that monster rears its ugly head, and until you cut it out, it leads to depression, relapse, and poor communication with your partners and friends. It also opens you up to feeling okay about being abused by others. I cannot express how small I felt and how small I still feel. Processing this trauma became my internal struggle for many years, and it took me a long time to develop a sense of self again.

I have always been tuned in to the situations of others, sometimes to a fault. I remember my friend, Drew. I think of him every day. He is currently serving a long sentence in northern California for armed robbery. He was a student at Escuela Caribe, and if anyone got it the hardest, it was Drew, an adoptee with two conservative white parents. Being a black child, he experienced the abuse of the program worse than most. He was on zero level for almost the entirety of his time there. He spent weeks in the Quiet Room and hundreds of hours doing hard labor. Drew endured hundreds of swats and verbal blastings yet refused to comply. Even until the day he left the program, he said to me, "Jesus wouldn't do this to his children. God wouldn't do this to those that he loved. This is the Devil. These people are monsters." He would spend his limited free time punching a punching bag 'til his knuckles split, and I would ask him, "Drew, why?"

"'Cuz the pain I cause myself is my own. They didn't give it to me." He was tortured beyond belief, and I hold the program responsible for his desperate attempts at life afterward. He is now spending 18 years in a government prison. He was a victim upon a victim.

I wish I could tell him, "I love you, Drew. I'm sorry this happened. But you never broke. You never gave in. You remained yourself throughout the arduous torture, and I'll never forget you."

Thankfully, someone found out about the abuse, and my house situation changed. Things got better, less harsh. Our new house parents were loving and fun people. The discipline was less cruel, and I achieved higher ranks with my efforts. I was still required to be a

Gestapo in the house and turned in my friends for punishment in exchange for a reward. I did what I had to do as long as I was comfortable, and it still haunts me that I was so selfish.

Solemn peace together
Mother—Son
separate beings
yet united by a bond
unexplainable
connected
Life separates us
challenges us
directs us
It is good

Still
the memories
of time spent
Among the Sunflowers
remains.
It is good.

Gail Mehlan 2005

Michael

CHAPTER 32—AMONG THE SUNFLOWERS 3

January 2006

There's a song by the Steve Miller Band, that played on repeat in my head in the days before I was going home. I'd sing out loud to myself, "I'm going on a big 'ole jet airliner—Gonna carry me to my home." It went something like that. I was excited. But when it came time for me to go home, it occurred to me that I'd have more freedom, which scared me. I couldn't go back to the way my life was. I just couldn't. I was stronger. I believed in something greater than myself. I was determined to make a new life. I was sorry that I had wasted so much time and money thus far. But I was ready.

I got off the plane and walked down those stairs at O'Hare International Airport and saw my parents standing there, greeting me with open arms. I hugged my father, and he said,

"Welcome home, son." He hugged me like I was the prodigal son returning to his home and forgiven. I then turned to my mother and hugged her so tightly that she almost couldn't breathe.

"I missed you, Mom."

"I missed my son, and now you're home," she said. It was then that I knew my life had changed forever. I was happy. I was there again, standing "Among the Sunflowers."

SUNFLOWERS AND SAGE

Perhaps loving glares
And simply smiling stares
Are exactly as they appear
I don't want to ruin the moment
With my words, so, I say nothing
But hurting hearts
And our defective parts
Wired up in our sacred scars
Leave us speechless
I don't want to ruin the moment
With the lines on my face, so, I say nothing
But I see the truth in your sunflower eyes
Turned to fire red in the darkness
Made alive by the prismatic light
Turned as green as the sacred sage
That cleanses the demons that live inside
It's the broken ones that need it the most
The shimmering sunlight that two people can share
In primitive moments showing how much we can care
Let me turn your sunflowers to sage and
Let me clean off the past performance from the stage
I don't want to ruin the moment
With my words, so, I say nothing

Jolly Jackson
Excerpt from Sunflowers and Sage

"But hurting hearts
And our defective parts
Wired up in our sacred scars
Leave us speechless."

Jolly Jackson
Excerpt from *Sunflowers and Sage*

Gail

CHAPTER 33—POSSIBILITIES

2006-2007

It's tough to put into words the feelings that erupted inside my soul on the afternoon we arrived at the airport to pick up Mike. It was a cold day in early January as Doug and I walked from the parking garage at O'Hare International Airport to meet him in the baggage claim area. We entered the building and watched anxiously for him to descend on the escalator. I could feel the anticipation in my stomach as familiar butterflies did flips and twirls inside of me. I was ready to see him again. He was finally coming home!

Based on the staff and counselors' recommendations, Mike stayed after graduation and through the summer for an additional camp-like experience in a rural town in the Dominican Republic's mountains near Jarabacoa in a town called Angosto. The camp was very primitive. Mike and his campmates had to rough it out with no running water, no TV, and many responsibilities for cooking and cleaning the house. They all had fun bathing themselves in the mountain waterfalls. Mike's group of young men volunteered in the town doing mission work projects for the residents and continued with some additional coursework. It wasn't an easy summer for Mike. The decision to postpone his return home left him disappointed. He had hoped to come home in the fall after the summer program.

Mike stayed an additional four months following the summer camp to work on leadership skills, mission work, and physical labor. He gained more and more freedom and opportunities as he succeeded each step of the way.

That fall, Mike was accepted at Trinity International University in Deerfield, Illinois, into the music department to play in the orchestra. He would be preparing to head to Trinity within a week of coming home. The possibilities ahead of him seemed to grow, and we were excited for him. Even with all the opportunities in front of him, I could feel my anxiety increase. It seemed I could never quiet the thoughts. Before I could even finish the thoughts feeding my anxiety, I heard Mike's voice calling us from the top of the escalator,

"Hey, Mom! Hey, Dad! I'm HOME!" He stumbled awkwardly in a rush down the escalator steps and straight into our arms. I looked into his bright, green eyes and saw a few tears brimming just as I felt them creep into my own eyes. Doug gave him a big hug with a brief, nervous pat on the back. My voice was silent, not having any words worthy of speech. Our hug was intense and heartfelt, and I could feel the love moving between us even as we kept our words at bay. My prodigal son was home.

We stopped to eat at a local hot dog restaurant. Mike couldn't wait to get his hands on a good, original Chicago-style hot dog. He asked to say a blessing before eating, which surprised me. This simple moment was intensely spiritual. To pray together at a fast-food restaurant had never been a habit in our family. After Mike prayed, I just sighed and studied him, thinking, who is this young man sitting in front of me? Had he changed? Is he *really* Mike?

Soon I was back in the swing of having an energetic and busy young man living in our house, running up and down the stairs laughing on the brand-new cell phone we had gotten him with some old friends and helping me organize his clothing and needs for heading off to college. There were still moments of doubt that crossed my mind and clouded my confidence. But I wasn't going to look back. Looking back was not productive. I was ready to move on and let Mike move to the next chapter of his life.

It was exciting and bittersweet as we dropped our youngest child at college. I had done this before, and it was emotional for me each time. We were launching their lives into the unknown future. We had just gotten past the *welcome home*, and Mike was about to *blast off*. I wanted to let the past be in the past, so I focused on and treasured every little moment. We took lots of pictures. It was fun to meet his roommate and others on his floor, set up his bed and study space, and help him unpack his clothing. We walked around the campus and had lunch with him at a local restaurant. Another young man Mike knew from Escuela Caribe was also starting at Trinity. We left Mike that day with his friend and returned to our quiet house. I was doing a lot of sighing again, trying to let go, needing to let go.

The first semester at Trinity went well for Mike, and before too long, he was home again for the summer. He chose to return to the Dominican Republic for a six-week mission trip during that time, building latrines for the workers in the sugar cane fields. He was happy to return and spend time with friends he knew from Escuela Caribe.

The following fall, Mike returned to Trinity, auditioned for, and made it into the Jazz Ensemble, playing the bass for them. He loved jazz.

Fortunately, Mike is extremely smart intellectually. Unfortunately, he always struggled with time management and study skills. His grades plummeted that fall until he could not return to Trinity the following spring semester. Mike did not give up on his education, however. On his own, he found a new doctor who evaluated and treated him for ADHD (attention deficit and hyperactivity disorder) and bipolar disorder. Mike decided to enroll in the local community college for the second semester. With very little parental involvement, he completed the second semester at Harper College with passing grades. His love of music continued as Mike joined the local community orchestra that performed in the college auditorium. We attended the spring concert, and it was rewarding to see Mike participating. The affection he had for the other orchestra members was visible. He was moving forward with the possibilities in front of him.

In the spring of 2006, our daughter, Michelle, got engaged. We were so excited and happy for her. Michelle and Brian planned to be married on a lucky day, 07-07-07. The mad rush began to plan a wedding, find the best venue, and pick out a dress for the bride and me. There was much work ahead of us.

One day at school, right before the end of the school year, I had an interesting conversation with one of my students.

"There are so many books about *nice* families—I don't see many books about *messed up* families," he said.

We talked for a few minutes about how no family is perfect and how much love is still to be shared, even in families with problems. I told him we'd had some issues in my family too, but we kept working on them until they got better.

He smiled at me and seemed okay with that answer.

As I reflected on that conversation, I felt a tug on my heart to write the story of my son's addiction and the recovery process. He was doing well at the moment. The possibilities for Mike seemed endless, and the answers to prayers were evident. But I wasn't quite ready yet.

May 25, 2006
So, can I be a writer, Lord? Could that brief encounter with a student be a call to write? I felt it once with Mike's idea for the book "Among the Sunflowers." I felt the call to write while listening to an author I heard at a conference say that his students often inspired him—perhaps my book should be about imperfect families. I could start now while I feel inspired. Thank you, Lord, for moving the days forward with moments. Moments are all that we have. Do we gain anything from the future? Do we take anything from the past? If I focus on the past, I am resentful, ashamed, and full of regret, yet if I focus on the future, I am full of impending doom. So, I ask you, Lord, to guide me in all this—am I a writer? I don't know—but could I write something good? With your help, maybe. Oh! The possibilities!

And now—the current problem, so many decisions about a wedding!

ON CHILDREN

Your children are not your children.
They are the sons and daughters of Life's longing for itself.
They come through you but not from you,
And though they are with you yet, they belong not to you.

Kahlil Gibran
Excerpt from *On Children*

Gail

CHAPTER 34—IT'S NOT YOUR LIFE

2007

I always set aside summertime to get a lot accomplished, and this was a very busy one for us. Mike was home, trying to get a job but not *really* trying. There were moments of concern, but I was so preoccupied with the upcoming wedding that worries only crept into my consciousness late at night. In the days and weeks surrounding the wedding, I wrote in my journal to vent and check myself. I had no time to get enmeshed in Michael's shenanigans.

June 29, 2007
I hate to start a brand-new journal on a low, frustrated, anxiety-ridden day.

So, I am using up pages of an old one to vent my despair and fears! I give them all to you, Lord! I am trying—so many worries, and you then tell me, "Do not worry"!

"Therefore, I tell you, do not worry about your life,
what you will eat or drink, or about your body, what you will wear.
Is not life more important than clothes?...
Who of you, by worrying, can add a single hour to his life?"

Matthew 6:25-27 (NIV)

I went to bed one night and fell asleep. No worries—I slept well for the first few hours of the night. I awoke with a start at 3:18 AM and looked to see if Mike had come home. He had not—a rush of adrenaline surged through me. Mike had been so good lately about being home before midnight. I had relaxed, assuming he would be home. The early wake-up signaled that something was *wrong*. Doug and I both reacted in a big way, fearing he had an accident. We called Mike's cell multiple times to try and reach him, but he wasn't picking up his calls. Doug wanted to call the police to see if someone had reported an accident.

I knew something was up. I also knew that I was overreacting. Mike was an adult, and he could make his own decisions. He could legally stay out all night if he chose to, but I felt disrespected and disregarded when he didn't answer the phone—anger set in.

When we hadn't heard from Mike for an hour, Doug called the parents of the girl Mike was supposed to be with, a friend from Escuela Caribe, Kara. Her parents did not answer, so he left a message. Calling them was ridiculous. Mike told us where he was going, and I secretly hoped he had simply fallen asleep and forgotten to let us know.

Finally, at about 4:30 AM, I called Mike again. He answered this time and was "So sorry"—said he was "inebriated" and would get home as soon as possible. He came in the door at about 6:15 AM and promptly fell asleep.

June 30, 2007
Lord, I want Mike to live a life that means something! I want him to
live a productive life—But at this moment, I almost want to let him
go indeed—to let him leave home, give him his car, pay for his cell
phone so we can at least call him—and just tell him to go—far away
from here—to find himself and seek your will for him.

Others have always swayed Mike, and he gets sucked into unhealthy choices. His new therapist called it an *addictive personality*. I feared Kara was using him, but again, I was being judgmental, failing to realize that they shared a bond of common experience from their time in the Dominican Republic that I did not understand.

Michelle's wedding was days away, and with all that, I was genuinely and desperately in need of God's calm and peace. As I flipped through my Bible, I found a verse perfect for a mother of the bride with less than a week until the wedding!

"Lift up your eyes and look about you; All assemble and come to you;
your sons come from afar, and daughters are carried on the hip.
Then you will look and be radiant,
and your heart will throb and swell with joy."

Isaiah 60:4 (NIV)

Venting on paper helped me make it from one day to the next. I'm not sure that my sanity was intact, though. Things were building in me that I couldn't let go of as much as I tried. The next night, I also had trouble sleeping and started hyper-focusing on what Mike was doing with his life. I think I knew in my mind that it was *his* life, yet I wanted him to go about it *my* way. In my warped way of thinking, I wanted him to go to school and be successful. But he wasn't *in* school. I tried to control the situation and reign him in by imposing my high expectations. Was it so wrong to have these expectations for your children? My mind spun out of control.

I realize now that I was *not* attending meetings during those weeks around the wedding, which was a big mistake. There was a great wave of change coming in our family. My daughter was to be married in a few days to her groom. They would begin to create their own new life together. Our family would never be the same again. I don't think I considered the impact that this wedding was having on my heart. I had no answers for myself. I continued channeling my stress and insomnia by writing it to God on paper.

July 1, 2007, 1:15 AM
I am again feeling that knot of anxiousness in the depths of my soul. I long for that peace that eludes me. I watched a woman speaker on TV today, and she said that if you are having trouble letting go, you should just hold on even tighter and examine the holding on to see what you learn from it and what its hold is on you. Am I holding on to Mike harder because he is my youngest child, and I am afraid to move forward from my role as a parent of all adults? Am I afraid to move on to the next call on my own life? What does this looking hard at my attachment to Mike mean for me? How can I understand my heart, where it is, and what I need to do to become free of my obsessions and dysfunctions and allow my man-child to be free from me?

THE LET'S GO

"Come. Follow me."
A man once said.
He didn't say pray
He didn't say ponder
He didn't say worry
He said, "Let's go."
And when you let go
And let's go
You find you can get everything
Malaise, Blasé
Stop your suffered thinking and go
Go—get what you need
Don't steal it
Earn it
Learn it
And go
Let go and let's go!

Jolly Jackson

"Go, eat your food with gladness,
and drink your wine with a joyful heart,
for God has already approved what you do.
Always be clothed in white,
and always anoint your head with oil.
Enjoy life with your wife, whom you love,
all the days of this meaningless life that
God has given you under the sun—
all your meaningless days.
For this is your lot in life
and in your toilsome labor under the sun.
Whatever your hand finds to do,
do it with all your might, for in the realm of the dead,
where you are going,
there is neither working nor planning
nor knowledge nor wisdom."

Ecclesiastes 9:7-10 (NIV)

Gail

CHAPTER 35—NO SLEEP AND A WEDDING

2007

The days right before Michelle's wedding were a whirlwind of activity, and I had no time to think. The chaos of having all three children at home was wearing on me. We had Michelle and Brian's Boston terrier, Kozmo, and the cat, Louie, chasing each other around. We needed to make it to several spa and nail appointments, and there was food to buy for the post-wedding picnic. Guest gifts, cards, table decorating items, and paraphernalia for the wedding were lining the hallway and cluttering the dining room table. The window company came and washed our windows, and the cleaning lady was there to make our whole house immaculate. Michelle and her bridesmaids were to spend the night before the wedding at our home, so we changed sheets and put out new towels. When night came, I laid down, assuming I would have no trouble falling asleep, but it eluded me.

Mike was restless and worried about his friend, Kara, who lived nearby. He was going out every night and staying out late. Mike had a history of always trying to *save* some girl from herself. Resentments built as he kept running off when I wanted him to be *home*, helping *me*. I wanted him to be present with the *family* and his sister before the wedding. Maybe I was being selfish. Writing out my frustrations barely seemed to help.

July 6, 2007, 12:30 AM
Again, I am not able to sleep. Mike still hasn't come home, and I am so full of anxiety. My stomach is all in knots, and I cannot relax into sleep. What is going on with me? I don't know if it's the wedding, Mike, Matt, or my silliness. I do not even have dreams these days, just the constant battle with sleep. I want to blame someone or something, but there is no one to blame but myself! I am hopelessly enmeshed with concern for Mike. Again.

Each time this crops up in me, I don't know what to do. What is my part in this?

Why am I struggling so much with this? All I ask for, Lord, is your peace.

I DON'T CARE ANYMORE WHAT HAPPENS TO MIKE!
But that's a lie! I do care, and I think I'm crazy, and I'm going to bed!

I know I am anxious because of the wedding, the pets in the house, and the thunderstorm that is dirtying my newly cleaned windows. I am trying to be strong and organized for Michelle, and she doesn't feel well, complaining, wanting to feel good, yet fighting the effects of too much partying. Doug was so talkative tonight, telling one story after another. Maybe HE should write the book! Sitting and talking with all the children at home was fun, but now I still cannot relax. Sleep evades me again for some reason.

"I lie awake; I have become like a bird alone on a roof."

Psalms 102:7 (NIV)

That's how I feel. I am a lonely bird sitting on a roof, waiting for her baby chicks to come home. In reality, my baby chicks are one by one, leaving the nest, and this has me both proud and terrified at the same time.

Wedding day arrived. The hustle and bustle of all the girls getting ready in our home felt chaotic. I wanted a special moment alone with Michelle, but time was racing. Finally, as my daughter carefully slipped her magical white dress over her head and I zipped it up for her, I had the chance.

"Are you ready, honey?" I asked.

She looked at me with her big brown eyes, smiled, and said, "Yes, Mom, I'm ready."

"This day will be special, you know, but your marriage will be so much *more* than just this party." I hugged her gently, not wanting to mess up her hair or make-up.

"I know that Mom, we love each other, everything's going to be fine. I'm so excited!" She was reassuring *me*.

"I know," I said. "*I* love you too. Let's go have a wedding," I stepped down the stairs and greeted the photographer waiting for her to come down.

I turned and looked back at my beautiful daughter, a bride. I watched her slowly walk down the stairs holding her dress up in her hand. She looked just like a princess, ready to meet her prince. Emotion rose within me, and the love I felt for her almost hurt. A tear or two came into my eyes, but I kept it together. My heart *was* going to open and grow to accept this new version of our *family*. I was adjusting slowly to the idea with a tinge of sadness at the swift passage of time.

Everything about the wedding was perfect. I couldn't think of anything I would have done differently. Michael and Matt showed up looking handsome and ready to party. Brian's face said so much as I watched him look Michelle in the eye as he took her hand. I couldn't have been prouder of my growing family. It was an unforgettable day.

Any anxiety I felt in the days around the wedding was related to this change, these shifts. Our children were growing up and moving on with their own lives. Maybe I *wasn't* ready. I just needed to be the stable bow.

"You are the bows from which your children
as living arrows are sent forth.
The archer sees the mark upon the path of the infinite,
And He bends you with His might
That His arrows may go swift and far.
Let your bending in the archer's hand be for gladness;
For even as He loves the arrow that flies,
So, *He also loves the bow that is stable.*"

Kahlil Gibran
Excerpt from *On Children*

NAUGHTY

Protecting your virtues
—All but illusions
You've said, "I'll sell them off no more."
I saw that look
I know what moves you
I've seen those eyes before
If you'd like? I can take you on this floor
You don't want to be sold off
For what was that kind pleasure
You wanted the "it feels so good!!" kind of roar
You don't want to be "Naughty"
But? The fire feels warm!
Until its flames, they burn you
You're afraid to show love
For fear in the shadows
That—perhaps
It's the only love that's true

Jolly Jackson

THE PRICE

I would've traversed the heavens
I would've killed any dragon
I would've gone to Tartarus and back
To spend a smile on you

But when I beckoned the gods,
And they summoned a mighty witch of passion
Whose storms have trapped me asunder
Damn it to you, Witch of the Cold Night
I told you this would be the final straw!!
I cannot stop your shivering curse
For alas even great heroes
Cannot possess the power of gods
As the skies shake away the moans of the lost
I will be found
To spend a smile

Jolly Jackson

"The maddest of all is to see life as it is
and not as it should be."

Miguel de Cervantes

Gail

CHAPTER 36—HONORABLE INTENTIONS

2007-2008

Mike tried hard to provide a haven for troubled girls. He was a *Don Quixote*, fighting for his *Dulcinea*, fighting for the lives and love of each one he met. His intentions were honorable in every instance. Rescuing was not a good pattern for Mike because he often got hurt, but it continued in one relationship after another.

A couple of weeks after Michelle's wedding, Mike came to me and asked if Kara could stay at our house for a night. She had been fighting with her parents off and on for weeks, and though I was curious, her problems were none of my business. I didn't want to allow her to stay, but I tried to understand why he wanted to support her. Mike told me she was trying to work things out with her family, which I advised him to encourage her to do.

That afternoon I waited on pins and needles, hoping something would resolve with her parents and I wouldn't have to come up with an answer for him. I was still hesitating until the end, and Mike kept pestering me.

"Mom, you always told me to love on the downtrodden and give 'til it hurts! I want to do this. We *have* a room! I don't want her to be homeless." He stormed off in his car to be with Kara, I assumed.

July 19, 2008

I don't know what God's will is for me, Mike, Kara, or her family in this situation. I ask you, Lord, to come quickly and show me how to have compassion without *judging. I am doing precisely the thing I don't want to do. I am convicting Kara—casting her as untrustworthy, and I don't even know her. I don't, so who am I to judge her or her parents? I wish I could speak to them and get their side of the story before reacting to her and Mike. I just got off the phone with Mike, and he believes he is helping her. I know all too well the trappings of that form of helping and loving too much. I need to find that inner peace of knowing that when I set healthy boundaries for my family, they will be respected. Rereading a support group's pamphlet has calmed me, and I will not get riled up again. Why did I get so worked up over this whole Kara thing? I felt like there were issues to be concerned about, and her situation did not seem to be getting better. Could I bring her into my home and trust that she's not bringing in something we don't want in our house? Will my serenity be intact at the end of this situation?*

HELPING

My role as helper is not to do things for the people I am trying to help, but to be things; not to try to control and change their actions, but through understanding and awareness, to change my reactions. I will change my negatives to positives; fear to faith; contempt for what they do to respect for the potential within them; hostility to understanding; and manipulation or overprotectiveness to release with love, not trying to make them fit a standard or image, but giving them an opportunity to pursue their own destiny, regardless of what their choice may be.

I will change my dominance to encouragement; panic to serenity; the inertia of despair to the energy of my own personal growth; and self-justification to self-understanding.

Self-pity blocks effective action. The more I indulge in it, the more I feel that the answer to my problems is a change in others and in society, not in myself. Thus, I become a hopeless case.

Exhaustion is the result when I use my energy in mulling over the past with regret or in trying to figure ways to escape a future that has yet to arrive. Projecting an image of the future— and anxiously hovering over it for fear that it will or it won't come true—uses all my energy and leaves me unable to live today. Yet living today is the only way to have a life.

I will have no thought for the future actions of others, neither expecting them to be better or worse as time goes on, for in such expectations, I am really trying to create or control. I will love and let be.

All people are always changing. If I try to judge them, I do so only on what I think I know of them, failing to realize that there is much I do not know. I will give others credit for attempts at progress and for having had many victories that are unknown.

I, too, am always changing, and I can make that change a constructive one, if I am willing. I CAN CHANGE MYSELF, others I can only love.

I continued to be conflicted. How could I be so hard-hearted that I would risk allowing this beautiful young girl with lovely brown eyes out on the street or crashing on someone's apartment floor in the city? On the one hand, she looked tough and hardened, but her eyes and smile told a different story. In them, I saw a vulnerable young person who needed to find her way in the world. She needed self-confidence and love. How could I lecture, moralize and scold Mike? It didn't do any good. It just made things worse. I was feeling quite disgusted with my reactions. I knew I needed to make amends, but I was still so full of confusion and misconceptions that I didn't know what to think.

I could only love and let be. All my striving did no good if I felt bad about my decisions. If I said, "Let Kara stay." I might have felt a little uncomfortable. If I said, "NO." Could worse situations have been out there waiting for her? I felt at a loss as to what to do.

Later that very day, Mike called me and told me that things were not working between Kara and her parents. So, they decided she would stay with her grandparents the following day. After listening to his pleas, I decided to speak to Doug and ask him for his opinion on having Kara stay with us. He agreed that it would be all right for her to stay in Michelle's old room for one night. One night evolved into two.

Kara was quite pleasant and appreciative when she came to the house. I didn't see any signs that she was taking advantage of us. Instead, I felt that Kara *was,* in fact, in need. I spoke with Kara's mom the second day, and our conversation helped me find compassion for them. Her parents were upset by the whole situation too. I reminded myself to pray for them and not try to fix anything. It wasn't my business.

Mike continued to hang out with Kara's friends for another week. One night he got into a fight with one of them and had a minor fender bender with his car. Thankfully, he was okay and made it home safely. After that, I didn't hear much more about Kara. Perhaps she *had* gone to live with her grandparents.

One evening not too long after the accident, Mike came home, sat down, and talked with Doug and me for quite a while. He told us he wanted to return to Trinity University in the fall. We told him we would support him, but it was his responsibility to find out if it was even possible. The next day he called the admissions office and was re-accepted. He proceeded to get in touch with his old roommate and some other Trinity friends. He also called some high school friends who had gone to our church and set up times to get together. Just like that, things seemed to flip for him. He seemed much happier and excited about the chance to start again at Trinity.

The rest of the summer went by quickly, as I was busy getting back into the swing of things at school. It was a great deal of work to set up the classroom and prepare for the school year. Perhaps it was the distraction of getting back to work and preparing for my own life the next few weeks, but it felt like I had let go of my preoccupation with Mike.

The fall semester started well for both of us. Mike was living in the dorm at Trinity and seemed happy and involved. We had our house to ourselves again, which helped calm *my* anxiety.

The Trinity Barbecue Cook-Off was an annual match-up between faculty and students. Mike decided to enter the event where they would create barbeque sauces and rubs from their unique recipes and compete for prizes. The competition was fierce. Mike was home all day on the day of the event, using my kitchen to prepare his *special* sauce. After the cook-off, he walked away with the first-place prize and a monogrammed chef's shirt with his name on it.

In November, Mike turned twenty-one, and we celebrated

the milestone with a nice dinner at a German restaurant. I only noticed a few hints at difficulties for Mike. Money seemed to drain out of his checking account, and he'd gotten several tattoos, driving into the city to do so.

In December, I learned that I would become a grandmother and that Michelle and Brian had heard an actual heartbeat! I could hardly wait to hold that newborn baby in my arms and be a grandma. Even a frustrating phone call from my son didn't dampen my spirits.

December 6, 2007
Michael called Tuesday night. He was out of gas and frustrated because he was out of money. He asked me to put money in his account, and I said, "NO." He was very persistent, but I felt convinced to STOP giving him money. He called me later to apologize, and we must address this issue soon. Give me the strength to be firm and hold to the conviction to do the right thing. Help me to have compassion for this son I love, who also causes me frustration.

At the end of that semester, we got word that Michael had failed most of his classes at Trinity and dropped out of college.

"I sing a sad song every time I wake
I feel boney fingers grip the nape
I feel familiar coldness coursing through me
prepare myself to make a new mistake.
I don't know
I can't stand on my two feet"

Michael M. Mehlan
Date unknown, found in a notebook

Gail

CHAPTER 37—I DON'T LIKE FAILURE

2009

I had a vision several years ago. I came across a written copy of it recently amongst some papers that I was cleaning out. It surprised me that God had been trying to speak to me about the state of my heart long before I even knew I had a heart problem.

While at a women's retreat, the leader guided us through a visualization/relaxation exercise to help us learn how to meditate. Soft relaxing music floated through the air, and the teacher's calming voice led me on my journey.

I fight off thoughts of school and home for a few moments, and finally, a sense of peace and calm makes me feel like I am floating. I still feel pain in my shoulder, but I don't fight it and simply accept it as an existing injury. The words "I am not my body" keep coming to me, crossing my mind, and I can detach for a few moments from the physical part of me that often carries pain and anxiety. I feel very relaxed and open.

I imagine sitting in Segovia, Spain, looking over the beautiful landscape from high up on the road. I see the ancient aqueduct, the cathedral, and the mountains in the distance. I walk down a rugged dry dirt path to a small square, patio, or plaza. I am alone. There is no one there. I sit on a small metal chair. I sense beauty and complete peace, yet I do not notice other details. A figure dressed all in white appears, Christ himself, as I recognize him. He approaches me and reaches out to me with a beautiful, whole, bright red heart and gently places it in my hands. He folds his hands over mine around the heart and gives me a reassuring squeeze. As he turns to leave, he looks me squarely in the eyes with confidence. No words are spoken. There is just a feeling of peace, healing, and serenity.

I need to remember this moment, that Christ himself brings me a whole, unbroken, beautiful heart. I want to treasure that moment he reaches out for me with his hands, reassures me, and looks me in the eyes. He gives me confidence without saying a word.

I am prayerful and meditative today. Wanting so much for life to be good instead of taking life on life's terms, realizing that only Christ has the power to heal me, heal my broken heart, and open my eyes that don't seem to see. What a powerful experience!

A little over a year ago, I was diagnosed with heart failure. The official term is *idiopathic cardiomyopathy*, which sounds better to me, more technical and medical than dealing with *any* part of me as a *failure*.

Failure is not an option for me. I am a perfectionist. Maybe it's because I am the daughter of a teacher and a father who also held high expectations for my education. It's part of my personality. I always strived for good grades in school. I felt anxiety about it from time to time, but I managed to find a way to succeed, especially academically.

When dealing with a student who was not doing well, as the teacher, it became my *mission* to help them do better and find success. Failure is *not* an option.

When I heard that I had heart failure, it genuinely took me by surprise. I have taken care of myself and never smoked or drank excessively. I didn't experiment with drugs. I exercised regularly, watched my weight, and saw the doctor as needed, and my heart was still *failing!* I did not take the diagnosis well, almost as if it were a *moral* issue.

I have since had procedures to place a pacemaker, defibrillator, and resynchronization device into my heart to help delay the progression. I'm sure I am no different than any other person diagnosed with a life-threatening disease. There needs to be a time of acceptance and dealing with the immediate medical procedures to help, but having my body fail me has brought up other thoughts about failure that have weighed heavily on my *heart.* Literally.

I received a forwarded email from my sister with the words *Failure Notice* in the subject line because there had been a problem with one of the other group-list emails. I had a gut reaction to that notice, feeling the familiar sense of impending doom in my body when I saw it. My response to *what was nothing* was strong and resonated deep within me. I *knew* this had nothing to do with me, but I reacted to it unnaturally.

The day I learned that Mike had failed almost every class he had taken at college that fall semester, I was down and depressed, feeling like *I,* myself, had failed. I let the feelings flow. Tears dripped from my eyes as I drove along, heading to a meeting. Suddenly in the silence of the car, I heard a voice speak clearly to me.

"Gail, *you* did not fail!"

I did *not* fail. My son's failed coursework was not *my* failure. Somehow, I felt like a failure anyway. I thought that the inability of someone as close to me as my son to complete his requirements was somehow a reflection *of me*. I turned the failure around in my mind, making *me* feel unworthy. I have these crazy deep-seated fears of not succeeding and, through that, losing control. Maybe I was always such a people pleaser that I attempted to control situations as a child by excelling academically. That was my way of being *good*.

"There are no failures, only outcomes." This quote in a Facebook meme resonated with me. Outcomes. That is all. There were just outcomes.

When I heard that voice telling me, "*You* did not fail." It took me back to those painful memories where I *felt* like *I* had failed. I took it personally. Maybe I didn't take care well enough in some situations. Perhaps I *have* been a failure as a mom. If you are a good parent, your child ought to turn out *right*, right? But what is *right*? When I look at my children's lives, I wonder and *judge* them *and* myself on standards that are not mine to set. I feel the guilt. Where did *I* go wrong? How can *I* fix it? How can I help *them* achieve more? *What do I do? Intervene more?*

I battle these feelings every day that some defect in *me* has been the cause of my perceptions of others' failures. I should know better. There are only *outcomes*.

I have cared for my family and will continue to show them love and respect. I must respect Mike for *his* efforts and successes that I don't even know about or understand. God must have a *purpose* for our failures. I may not always see what that purpose is, but it is *something*. I need to stop the nonsensical talk racing through my mind and let the message settle in my soul that the voice, I believed to be God, said clearly to me, "*YOU* DID NOT FAIL!"

Today I accept my heart failure as merely a health problem I probably inherited from those who loved me, and I must learn to deal with it. My heart failure is not a failure to love or care for the people in my life. My heart failure is not a lack of my heart to feel, love, and give the best I have to offer. This broken heart of mine can continue to lift all the people I love in prayer. I can intercede for them today by giving them all to the *one* who loves us all, and when I can *do* that, Christ brings me a beautiful, whole heart and places it firmly in my hand.

"I will give you a new heart and put a new spirit in you;
I will remove from you your heart of stone
and give you a heart of flesh.
And I will put my Spirit in you and move you."

Ezekiel 36:26-27 (NIV)

PART THREE:

*Regards from the
Land of the Living*

THE END #1

The end is only the beginning of the future
The future is only hope until the end
I hope to see you again my friends
When I send you my regards from the land of the living

And if you see me on the other side
Send me home and hope again
To see the pictures of your face
I will make you laugh, and cry tears of wondrous joy
In the end, I'll see you there to make us all brand-new

Jolly Jackson

"Mom, when I grow up
I'm gonna be an astronaut
I'm gonna fly higher than anyone else
I'm gonna make my home in the stars."

"Mom, when I grow up
I'm gonna be an astronaut."

Jolly Jackson
Excerpt from *Astronaut*

Gail

CHAPTER 38—ASTRONAUT

1996

"Hey Mom, I wanna be an astronaut! It'll be so cool! I'm gonna fly so high!" Mike told me one day when we were shuttling his older siblings to their various activities.

"That'd be great, honey. I've always wanted to fly!"

"Yeah! It's gonna be so cool, Mom! I'll get to see the stars!"

"Yep, I know you will, sweetheart. I know you will!" Then the subject quickly changed to the new level he had created in his mind for his *Super Mario Brothers* or *Zelda* video game, and he would chatter on until my mind would wander off to *my* concerns.

"Hey, Mom, are you *even* listening?"

Back then, I never questioned whether Mike would some-day attend college and find a way to have any career he wanted. He was intelligent, verbal, imaginative, and a creative thinker.

It never occurred to me that anything would prevent that from happening. There had also been much talk of becoming an archaeologist, a paleontologist, and even an Egyptologist. His list of interests was vast.

As a young child, Mike was particularly fascinated with all things space. When he was in fifth grade, about ten years old, we took a trip to Huntsville, Alabama, and spent a long weekend attending Parent-Child Space Camp. It was a memorable trip. We flew down and stayed in a room on the U.S. Space and Rocket Center Museum grounds. One of the highlights was a replication of weightlessness in orbit. Our favorite experience was a simulation of a trip on the space shuttle where we acted as the pilot and co-pilot.

After going to Space Camp, Mike told me he wanted to attend the Air Force Academy. We had been talking about college a lot at home. His sister, Michelle, had been looking at different schools, and the whole family spent much of our vacation time traveling to visit various college campuses. I was impressed that his young mind had started thinking about the future.

My dad had passed away several years before, and we found some old military awards that my father inherited from the Civil War era. Amongst all the awards was what looked like an official Medal of Honor from the United States Army. Mike was so excited, and we began to search for information to see where this medal came from and what it stood for. In his search for information in my parent's old version of the *World Book* encyclopedias, Mike discovered that if a family member or a descendant of a Medal of Honor winner wanted to attend the Air Force Academy, the academy would accept them without question. My mother told him that when they had visited Washington D.C. a few years earlier, they had seen an exhibit about the Medal of Honor. They looked for my great-grandfather's name on the official list of award winners, and much to their disappointment, his name was *not* on the list.

Mike was adamant that he would be eligible to attend this prestigious academy without meeting their rigorous admission standards because we had the medal in our possession. He spent hours in the basement reading the encyclopedias and formulating a letter to the Air Force Academy's admissions department. I still have a copy of the letter he typed on my parents' old IBM Selectric typewriter. It was all so sincere. He believed that he *had* the ticket to becoming an astronaut. I never discouraged him. I always believed he could do whatever he set out to do.

After researching my family's history several years later, I discovered that although my great-grandfather, Horace B. Parker, received a Medal of Honor during the Civil War, it was officially rescinded in 1911. The government re-evaluated those medals and why they were assigned. A scandal surrounding them took place. This information came to us long after Mike wrote his letter to the Airforce Academy.

"Mom, I don't think I'm gonna be an astronaut," Mike mumbled one day as we were alone in the car. I was slow to respond, and the moment, so vivid in my memory, still haunts me. I felt his sadness at this admission, and I didn't want him to feel discouraged. I asked him why.

"It's just gonna be too hard for me. I'm not smart enough."

I brushed it off, reassuring him of his keen intelligence. It was the same year he began to struggle with school.

"Mom, when I grow up
I'm gonna be unemployed
I'm only gonna be worth my work
I'm gonna get higher than anyone else
I'm gonna find solace in bottles and pills
I'm gonna find comfort in needles and girls."

Jolly Jackson
Excerpt from *Astronaut*

Gail

CHAPTER 39—HEROIN

April 2009

After the "Amen," I whispered, "You okay, Mike? You seem tired."
"Yeah, I'm fine, Mom. I'm fine."

I had started with a short prayer because I knew it wasn't the boys' thing to get too heavy on the prayer. I glanced at Mike as I prayed. He seemed extraordinarily sleepy and was wavering over the food as if he was about to drop his head down onto the plate.

Easter Sunday was supposed to be a nice quiet day for us. Michelle and Matt were living in other states at the time and had not planned on coming home. I always enjoyed making a nice meal for my family, so I told Michael it would be nice if he would have dinner with us. He asked me if it would be okay if his friend could join us since Jay didn't have family in the area. I responded, "Sure, that would be fine—what time do you think you can be here?" I gave him an approximate time the food would be ready.

The boys were late getting to the house, and I had everything waiting for them when they arrived. I had set the table and used the best dishes, our finest silverware, and real cloth napkins. I was hoping to have a nice meal for us to share. The menu included ham, mashed potatoes, green bean casserole, and corn pudding, all Mike's favorites. When they showed up, I was impatient for the boys to finish having a cigarette outside in the garage before inviting them inside to eat.

After the prayer, as we continued eating, Mike became increasingly drowsy. He shoveled a few bites into his mouth but was not engaged in the conversation around the table. Jay seemed to be holding it together, though, and he, my husband, and I visited and talked about a few random things. At one point, Mike asked to have the potatoes passed, and when Jay handed him the bowl, it crashed down onto his plate, and he slumped over. He lifted his head and, barely opening his eyes, blurted, "I'm going to go lie down for a little bit—Is that all right, Mom?" He got up, left the table, and went to lie down on the couch.

A few minutes later, Jay got up and politely said, "Hey—I've gotta go! Thank you so much for dinner, Mr. and Mrs. Mehlan."

That was it. The boys were gone, and my husband and I were alone at the table. We nibbled on a few more bites of the food still on our plates. Neither one of us felt very hungry. I looked at my husband, and he looked at me, "I found this in Mike's jacket pocket," he said, breaking the silence. "I had a gnawing suspicion that something was going on, so I checked his pockets."

It was a syringe. It was one of the small, orange needles we used to give our diabetic cat insulin. I had never given a second thought to keeping those in the house! In my heart, I *knew* why he had it, but I was afraid to admit it to myself.

Michael slept on the couch for about four hours, and we let him be. At about 10:00 PM, he got up, grabbed his jacket, and stormed out of the house.

April 11, 2009
A Prayer for my son:
Lord God, I know you have already rescued my child from the pit of
addiction and drugs, and I fear that the ugly demon has grabbed hold
of him yet again! PLEASE keep your hand on him tonight, protect
him from evil influences, and dwell in his heart so that he will do
the right thing and come home in one piece to face another day. He is
YOUR child, too, as much as he is mine. My heart is breaking, and
I feel the cracks.
Lord, Help ME!

HEROIN.

My thoughts churned in my brain. My son was using heroin.
Later that evening, we received an apologetic text from Mike.
"Sorry for what happened. Be home in the morning."

April 13, 2009
We were formed in the image of God, right? Then God must have
two hands—one to hold our troubles and the other to hold us. My
devotion today tells me that I should never cast aside my burden but
share that burden with God, that the companionship of God will
lighten the load.
I admit that last night I wanted no more part in the pain this
child has brought me. I wanted to cast him aside! Now, today, I un-
derstand that I cannot do that. I must place my burden, my heavy,
broken heart for Mike, into God's one hand and allow myself to fall
into the other. God will care for Mike, but I cannot, nor should I
cast him off as something I don't want. God is out of the grave and
holding me in the palm of his hand.
We share the burdens of their lives with God when the going gets
rough. He bears our burdens with us.

"Take my yoke upon you and learn from me,
for I am gentle and humble in heart, and
you will find rest for your souls.
For my yoke is easy, and my burden is light."

Matthew 11:29-30 (NIV)

"Into the great wilderness, he goes,
alone and in darkness, his armor still worn
I cannot now save you from the death that you own,
but life has a way of getting me home
This isn't a future of possible lives,
but a symphony of destruction of possible pasts."

Jolly Jackson
Excerpt from *My Sweet Queen Marie*

Gail

CHAPTER 40—DARKNESS CONTINUES

July 2009

"Mom, can I please come home?" Mike sounded desperate, but I hesitated, recalling all that transpired. After a brief pause to catch my breath, all I could say was, "Yes, of course."

I witnessed firsthand the desperation of an addict when I caught Mike in my room, rummaging through my jewelry box. The thought of him stealing from *me*, his own mother, was gut-wrenching. I kicked him out of our house that day, so angry. I had yelled at him, "Get out and don't come back!"

When he took most of his things and walked out the door of our house, it was one of the worst moments of my life. I stood alone at the kitchen counter, devastated. I had cried over this child before, but this was a guttural, heaving cry of betrayal. I couldn't even talk about it when Doug got home from work. I was still weeping when I shared the story with my pastor later that evening at my counseling session. Here we were again, in that uncomfortable space of *not knowing*. The *darkness* seemed to have found us again.

When Mike called a few days later, a sense of relief washed over me. The evening he came home, we had dinner together, the three of us, and talked late into the night. What were we going to do? What was Mike going to do? How were we going to handle this?

Doug and I had given up trying to require treatment or counseling even though we knew there was drug abuse. We had done our part, but we knew we needed some firm boundaries—my idea of what that looked like had changed. I sincerely wanted to know what *Mike* wanted for his own life, and I was resigned to letting go of having any aspirations for him. I found myself listening, trying to have an open mind and heart.

Not long after the moment God had spoken to me that *I* was *not* a failure, I realized something that should not have surprised me. College was not going to be for Mike. Why was I still wrestling with *that expectation*? Why did I want academic success for him? Expectations. They always got in the way of me accepting Mike as he was.

I was about to have surgery to add a second electrode to make my pacemaker more effective. Christ had promised me a new heart, and I was beginning to accept what was going on in multiple areas of life, both physical and emotional. I hoped for *more* healing of my broken heart.

The memory of what had happened on Easter continued to haunt me, and the fear of drug use was constantly present. Somehow, and I believe it was pure grace, we managed to formulate a plan for Mike to stay at home for the rest of that summer. He continued to work for a few short weeks at the restaurant, but he quit the job before he even got paid. He said he felt uncomfortable with some of the people who worked with him. Mike wanted to go up to Kenosha to get an apartment closer to his newest girlfriend, who was about to start college there. He agreed to work with his dad on finding an apartment and a job or maybe some classes he could take. Mike had applied to the local community college in Kenosha, but they did not accept him due to the low grades on his transcript. He did *not* want to start over and retake classes he had already taken. With his father's help, he was accepted into an adult evening program at Carthage College and found a small room to rent that wasn't too expensive. He could be close to his girlfriend, and the agreement was that he would work and live independently.

I don't recall any other incidents that stood out as problematic that summer, and I was unaware of any visible drug use. I put my brain on pause to get through it. I immersed myself in setting up my classroom and preparing for the new school year. That September, Mike moved up to Kenosha with his car, enrolled in night school, and our home became a much-appreciated empty nest. I was thankful that he was trying school again and allowed myself to stay in denial of any hidden problems.

Later that year, Mike and his girlfriend parted ways. He had completed some of his coursework by that time, but not everything he needed to pass. It was his last attempt at college.

"Mom, when I grow up
I'll still be me
I'll still find love
I'll still find my way to the stars."

"Mom, when I grow up
I'm gonna be an astronaut."

Jolly Jackson
Excerpt from *Astronaut*

Gail

CHAPTER 41—MIRACLES OF LIFE AND LOVE

2010-2015

In January 2010, Mike started dating a new romantic interest and moved into an apartment with his girlfriend. They seemed happy. We helped the two of them when we could to buy groceries and pay for car repairs when necessary but never handed over any cash.

He and some of his new friends formed a rock band called *Fur Coats for Sportsmen*. They played at local bars and, over the next few years, recorded several CDs. They became quite popular in the area and even played several concerts at a well-known event in Milwaukee called September Fest.

Mike and his girlfriend visited us for the holidays and joined us for a few vacations. We welcomed her at Matt's wedding as part of the family. Things seemed to have settled down for them, and Mike seemed healthy. They moved several times in and out of different apartments and in and out of rooms in friends' houses, but they always seemed to make things work. Mike got his bartender's license and became one of the bartenders at the restaurant where he worked. The promotion was an excellent financial move because he started getting consistent tips. At about the same time, the band was getting more paying gigs in Kenosha. Everything was moving forward from *my* perspective. Not having him live under our roof was a relief.

We can never know what is going on in someone else's life, can we? I was surprised when Mike told me he and his girlfriend of three years had split. He struggled to pay the rent by himself for their apartment, and so when the lease ended, he moved into a room in a house owned by a band member's grandmother. Another girl soon caught his eye. I was used to this and worried that he was trying to rescue someone again. But he was very cavalier about this new girl and didn't want to rush into a shared living space. He stayed in the room he rented for almost a year. Eventually, they did move in together in a little house her parents owned in town.

Sylvia was a student at the local state university and was on target to graduate later that year. She was also employed and had several jobs in addition to going to school part-time. She was a figure skater, which she had in common with our daughter, Michelle. It was fun to discover that we knew some of the same skating coaches and had traveled in the same circles. Our son worked hard at the restaurant and enjoyed playing with his band. I witnessed a new level of stability for Michael.

In 2013, I retired from my teaching position. Doug also retired from his physical therapy practice soon after that. We found a beautiful home on a lake and moved from Illinois to Indiana to be closer to Michelle and her growing family in 2014. At that time, Michelle and Brian had two grandbabies, and Matt had a daughter. Matt came back from New York to the Chicago area to study at the Art Institute of Chicago. He and his wife returned to live in our Schaumburg home when we moved out in October of 2014. I loved having them all close enough for visits. Doug's elderly parents passed away within a few months of each other, and during that same period, we welcomed a new baby boy into Michelle's family. Grief *and* joy faced us each day that summer.

We had moved on from the pain of having an addicted child living with us. We *all* had moved on. Life seemed to be stable. Mike was happy and in love. He and Sylvia were both working and making ends meet. They bought a new car and a washer and dryer for the house. They came to see us for Thanksgiving, and we had a wonderful family reunion at our new home. We had plenty of room for Matt and his family, my mom, Mike and Sylvia, and Michelle's brood. We were thankful for all of the blessings.

In November of the following year, we learned that Sylvia was pregnant and due in July of 2016. We always welcomed little ones into our family with open arms. Life is full of surprises. This one felt like the gift of life wrapped in love, a commitment, and a period of relative sobriety for Mike. Sylvia told me that Mike was saving money to get another tattoo. He wanted a ring around his wrist to signify every year that he had been clean. I knew then that they had talked about his addiction issues and that she saw the possibility of a better life for them in the future. I felt hopeful for them *and* us. Maybe this *baby* would grow up to be an astronaut.

IT'S LIFE

Beautiful, new precious
Growing, changing, developing
A miracle of life and love
Awe and amazement
At how You work
Expectant grandmother
Waits for a new life!
You have blessed us!
Praise to You!

Gail Mehlan

SYMPATHY FOR A LOVE SONG

I sing a sad song every time I wake up.
I sing a love song, not for me, but for your sake.
I don't know if I can stand on my two feet all alone.
I'm locked inside this tomb without a telephone.
So, I can't call my friends to help me roll away my stone.
Sit back and relax. We can still get out of this place.
You look at my lips, you hoped for a kiss,
and to my surprise, we miss.
Some would say that's not up to us but up to fate.
We came into this world too late.
But we are the ones who feel the reactions,
the guilt, and pain, pleasure, and satisfaction.
The world is a stage, and we are the actors.
We choose our own player, and we play from a reaction.
Which one are you, and who am I?
Which am I to be, and how am I willing to try?

Jolly Jackson

"Mom, when I grow up
I'm gonna be a rock and roll star
I'm gonna be louder than anyone else
I'm definitely gonna be a star
Everyone will love me. I'll be living large."

Excerpt from *Astronaut*
Jolly Jackson

Gail

CHAPTER 42—HOLY GHOST

2016

The evening was stormy and unpleasant for sure. We walked out of the rain into the bar, not knowing what to expect there. We entered the darkness and shook the water off of our shared umbrella. Mike told us that the show would start at 9:30, but nothing but loud recorded music blasted throughout the bar. The show wasn't happening yet.

A bartender shouted at me: "Bud Light or PBR?"

"PBR, thanks!" I yelled back. The noise level was up tonight.

I grabbed a beer and headed toward the stage. Half curious eyes glared at us as we walked through what appeared to be the replica of a cavern.

I was wearing a bright orange dress and a cute jean jacket with beige sandals. I was a bright spotlight in a sea of black, black stockings, black leather jackets, black hair with streaks of purple, well-worn Doc Martens boots, a few tattoos and piercings, and something with a chain. My husband stayed close by as he walked cautiously beside me, guiding me. His silver hair shone brightly under the decorative lights as we walked through the bar.

The air was fragrant with stale beer and the fog from the vaping patrons. Each whiff reminded me of smoked cherry, actually pleasant. Dark corners erupted with laughter as we passed by. I'm sure we looked like lost souls, but we were there to support someone special that night.

Suddenly, above the chatter of the crowd, I heard: "Hey, Mom!"

My son, Mike, called out to me above the noise, and as I turned, I was immediately enclosed in strong arms. The. Best. Hug. Ever. We lingered there for a moment, both of us comforted, welcomed.

"I'm so glad you came tonight."

"I'm excited to hear you play!"

"Yeah, we should be starting here in a few minutes. We're waiting for more people to show up."

"Did you get your CD?"

"No. They didn't get me one."

"I'll go get one for you."

Today was the CD release party for my youngest son's band, *Fur Coats for Sportsmen*, at a bar called *Hattrix* in Kenosha, Wisconsin. It was a big deal for them as this was their first *real* album, *Loud Noises*, and this was the first day it would be available in stores or on iTunes. They'd gotten some very positive press before the show. Even though we'd had some ups and downs in the past, we wanted to show Mike that we cared deeply about what was happening in his life and had come up to Wisconsin to put in an appearance to support him.

We hadn't been to one of his shows for a long time. His father and I didn't usually hang out in dark bars, and it was a long drive for us. We were thrilled to have the opportunity to spend a little time with our son's fiancé and grabbed a bite to eat with her before the show. In a few short weeks, we would welcome grandchild number five to the family. Sylvia wasn't sure how long she would last at a rock show. We understood and enjoyed our brief visit with her.

So, we waited, trying to relax, for the music to start. Sylvia was rocking side to side and tenderly rubbing her swollen belly, trying to get comfortable. Doug looked around, and there weren't any chairs for her to sit in. I was concerned for her comfort but knew she wouldn't stay long. Before the music even started, Sylvia leaned in close and said, "I'm going to head home now. Thanks for dinner." She snuck out without notice, and we were left standing in the corner by ourselves, waiting for the show to start, trying to relax. An older man came up and introduced himself.

"Hey—are you Mike's parents?"

"Yes—we are."

"I'm Roland, one of Mike's customers at the bar at Ron's Place. He's such a great guy."

"Always kind, always friendly."

"So smart—and so talented—I'm waiting for him to give me private guitar lessons!"

"Ok, great—so nice to meet you." And then someone else overheard us.

"Oh, my gosh! *You're* Mike's mom? I love Mike—I work with him at the bar. He's a great guy!" She laughed as she told us, "He always talks about his awesome parents. So glad you could come tonight! I'm Julia."

"Nice to meet you, Julia!"

Suddenly I felt as if I were floating up in the vapor surrounding me to a place of pride and happiness for Mike, a place I hadn't often been.

I repeated to myself—a *great guy*!

You see, it wasn't that long ago that I felt like I was a *failure* at the whole parenting thing. Mike and I had battled over so many things in the past. I always felt he was a rebel wanting to go against the status quo. We'd made hard decisions. But now we were letting him work out life on his own. We were loving him and letting him be his own person, in his own way. As I sipped my beer and waited, I was lost in my thoughts about how he'll soon be a dad. I almost couldn't believe it.

When the music started, I was awash in the sounds and the lights. Dancing, moving bodies were waves undulating as the music crashed against my eardrums. The energy of the crowd was contagious. They moved in close and swayed and sang along as the band played their music, familiar to the crowd but loud and harsh to my unaccustomed ears. It seemed as if an electrical charge ignited the audience as the band played all of their Fur Coats favorites.

Between songs, I heard Mike's voice over the loudspeaker.

"Hey—I'd like to give a shout-out to my parents, who came all the way from Indiana tonight to hear us play! Thanks so much for coming to support us!"

Loud cheers, screams, and whistles erupted as curious faces turned and grinned at us with a warm welcome. Who would have thought? Again, I was elevated to a level of pride and appreciation that had been a long time coming, long past the expectation of it. Suddenly I heard in the midst of a very heavy-metal rock and roll song the words,

"Holy Ghost—Holy Ghost—"

And I thought my ears were wrong, but no.

"Holy Ghost, Holy Ghost

Tell me what you know

Holy Ghost, Holy Ghost

What do you know?

What you know

What you know 'bout me?

Holy Ghost, Holy Ghost
When's that push gonna come to shove?
Holy Ghost, Holy Ghost
Who do you love?
Who do you love?
Who you love the most?

Holy Ghost, Holy Ghost
Please stand now, and let's make a toast
Holy Ghost, Holy Ghost
We're still alive on the mid-coast
And if you didn't know
You're 'bout to know 'bout me
Yeah, if you didn't know,
You're 'bout to know, 'bout me."

Justin M. Misch

I was not sure at the moment what this meant. I experienced a personal sort of Pentecost there. The spirit itself descended into that bar and touched me. This place would have been more like *hell* to the *judgmental* me than a place to receive the spirit, but it was there that I did. I experienced it. It was a blanket of reassurance covering my doubts with comfort and warmth. The *Holy Ghost* was there just as, if not more than it would have been in a sterile church. This bar was where the spirit found those it needed to touch, including me. And indeed, the spirit touched me. I was "*'bout to learn 'bout*" my son!

In the quiet after the music stopped, my ears were ringing, and my heart was full of love and respect, my doubts diminished.

With a splash of pink hair and skeletons on her stockings, another young woman came forward and introduced herself to me. "Hello, my name's Katie—and I just want you to know that your son has been such a good friend to me. I love his music—he's a good man."

My heart soared. It almost burst.

"I'm Gail. Thank you, it's so nice to meet you!"

And I thought but didn't say it. *Yes, we have raised a good man, a kind, gentle, generous, and talented man.*

GUITAR

Following the lines to
the curve of her spine
Her hips telling me
lies in forgotten crevasses
"She is mine."
Oh, "Now kisses must be earned.", she says
Time has worn her
Time is tired
Time loses its soft meticulous touch
"Kisses, my boy, must be earned."
Lateral space opens between my ears,
Melodies in dark temples fill the empty halls
Each scar worn a little deeper than the next
Soft tissue between her ribs and thighs
My fingers can only now softly touch
Flowers blooming in her harmonious eyes
Screaming in pleasure, shivering nights
Only now, while gently playing

Jolly Jackson

LIVING IN THE FUTURE

It's four AM, and I can't sleep,
Why do I keep having all bad dreams?
My wristwatch a day behind
But the right time?
Working up to every moment
I'll take the abuse, hear all the white lies
I'm living in the future
I'll tell you the truth no one really knows their use
until we're forced to choose
And I'm almost out of all good excuses
I'll tell you the truth
I'm going to share and compromise
to your surprise! I'm living in the future
One future at a time
I'm living in the future.
You'll show me yours;
I'll show you mine,
I'll trade you my memories for your time
I don't want them anymore
What good are they?
You'll show me yours; I'll show you mine
My wristwatch is a day behind
but the right time
I'm living in the future!!
I'll tell you the truth; no one really
knows what happens when you die
But if you're a lucky man,
they'll dress you in a suit and tie
Say a few good words,
all your family will cry
Is that living in the future?

I'm living in the future
Living in the future
One yesterday at a time.

Jolly Jackson

"Watching the sunrise—
Manic trying to relax—
Waiting for my lovely to come."

Gail

CHAPTER 43—MEETING DOUGGIE

July 2016

July 19, 2016
Darn Facebook! This post gives me just glimpses of thoughts from my son, so far away. A baby is due any day now, our fifth grandchild. Now I feel it too. Anxious.

I don't like the word 'manic'. It frightens me because what follows a manic moment is never good, helpful, or healthy for my son. So, I stop and say a prayer that he will be okay and take care of himself and his new young family.

He's going to be a father very soon. His fiancé spent the night with her mother; he is alone and doesn't know what's going on. Her love and her sweet disposition have grounded him. But this morning, he's feeling restless and anxious again. I can sense it. Much is going to change for them so soon. It is a scary thought. A second post appears on the page a few moments later.

"Beautiful, I don't know why I can't get tired, but that makes living worth it, sunrise over Lake Michigan."

He will be a good father. He doesn't know what the day will bring, but facing it somehow seems worth it and beautiful. My prayer did not go unanswered this time.

My son was going back and forth between the labor room and the waiting room, and each time we saw him, we sensed the fear and anxiousness in his face. He was pacing. His sighs were deep and stressed. He needed a cigarette but didn't want to be gone too long. He didn't want to miss anything.

We had been sitting there for over two hours, waiting to hear that the baby had arrived. We'd heard nothing. The last text from two hours ago was,

"She's dilated 10 and 0. It's gonna be soon."

I sent Mike a quick text, praying that everything was okay.

"She's resting now, giving it a little bit to finish moving down, fingers crossed. I'm calmer now."

Phew! I breathed a little easier. At least he'd calmed down.

"Good—hang in there!" I texted back.

After another agonizing hour, I couldn't help myself, so I picked up my phone and sent another text. "Any new news? Just wondering—"

Please, God, let everything be okay, I thought to myself.

"They slowed the contractions. We're just waiting on the doctor and for him to get down more—He's +1, +2. I don't know. The doc needs to check. The nurse isn't sure."

"At least there's progress! We're not leaving!"

After a few more minutes of anxious waiting, another text comes through.

"Okay, I guess we're just doing this full-on labor pushing and everything. Doctor's words, "Okay, babe, let's see what you can do!" to Sylvia."

We were going to have a baby soon!

I was a mess. I was so tired and groggy as it was almost three o'clock in the morning. I dozed off and on in the chair, watching the history channel. My cell phone was almost dead, so I couldn't entertain myself on Facebook any longer. We were just waiting.

I thought: *You should pray,* but my mind seemed empty. I did it anyway.

Please, Lord, bless this new little family. Be with them at his birth. Make his entry into the world safe and healthy. Give my son patience and endurance to be the father I know he can be.

All of a sudden, my husband jumped off the chair, startling me, and headed for the door. Mike was walking towards us, pushing the hair out of his face. He came up to me and reached out with open arms. I embraced him with a strong, loving hug, and he whispered in my ear,

"I'm a dad. I'm a dad! He's here!"

"Is everything okay?"

"Yes, he's perfect."

"And momma?"

"She's fine."

I glanced up into my son's eyes, and he looked so relieved and happy. I felt it too. Relieved. Happy. Blessed.

We still needed to wait a few more minutes to go back and see the baby. So, we waited and waited—it seemed like forever! Didn't they know how anxious this grandma and grandpa were?

Finally, Mike texted me to say we could come to the room. We walked down the hall and knocked on the door. Mike met us there, and as the door opened, we peeked around the curtain. There he was, baby Douggie. He was lying on the warming bed next to his mother.

I gave her a quick hug and congratulated her. She looked exhausted and dazed after doing all the work. Poor thing! I wished I knew what to say to her.

"Thank you!" I said, but I turned away quickly. I just wanted to see the baby.

I got my chance. He was there, looking around this big bright room with eyes so alert and focused that it was hard to believe he'd just arrived.

I studied him closely. He looked so much like his father did as a baby, perfect in every way. He had ten tiny fingers, ten tiny little toes. (Trust me, I counted!) He had a cone head that I knew would disappear soon. He looked deep into my eyes as I greeted him,

"Hello, there, precious little one. I am your grandma. Welcome to the world, sweet thing. Grandma loves you."

He looked at me intently and began moving his little arms and legs, stretching. It felt like he heard me and understood each word that I said. I touched his tiny fingers. He turned to follow my face. Such a precious gift we had received! I was overwhelmed with a sense of gratitude and love. It started right there. The love for this new grandchild grew with each breath he took as he looked up at me with such trust.

My son came over next to me, and I put my arm around him and gave him a slight hug. He said,

"Hello there, little guy!"

Douggie turned his head to follow that familiar voice.

"He recognizes your voice! Look at that!" I said to my son.

"Hey, what about me? I didn't get to hold him yet!" Sylvia said.

So, we asked the nurse if she could hold the baby, and the nurse wrapped up Douggie and gently handed him to his mother.

She looked at him and began to cry.

"He's so beautiful—I can't believe it!"

Welcome to our world, Baby Douggie. You are a special blessing.

We are so glad you are here!

LOVE AND BARYONS FOR BREAKFAST

What is this adulthood that has sacked me?
Oh, how these computers have hacked me.
But "I'm alive," I hear as my tongue speaks
Aging less than a sack of human meat.
Liver's quite pickled in spice, a treat.
The pleasures of virtue sold out by the pound, the happiness,
I've scraped off the last of it.
I've choked it down, hacked it up, the wholly unrepentant
wrenching sound.
Bury it in the dirt, and cover it up
in fresh ice with sugar so sweet.
I've dug into the ground to plant the seeds to grow a house
but repaired it out of paste,
to break it up for who is to burn it down.

Softly—
Softly, I asked of you, "Are you feeling okay?"
The nausea has taken you down, so we sleep the hours away.
Watching TV—*Touching softly*
We spend our time saving, spending little.
"Since when did things get so costly?"
I love you. You love me. We are having a baby.
I've tucked you in every night
and cooked supper in the evenings.
I've cleaned our rooms in the mornings,
prepared but baryons for breakfast.
I washed our things in hot water.
So how clean should we be if the stain of sin were no more?
I cooked my livers in fresh oil,
for this is all that's left of our spoils.
I love you. You love me. We are having a baby.

The rain is now making me rhythms,
Feeling worse, I've seen the symptoms.
Oh! How I just want to be happy and
find the little place to call my home.
I just want to love them,
make them feel the world is in their hands.
I love you. You love me. We are having a baby.
I thought I could end the truth, assassinate it,
a two-faced halcyon of evil thoughts, the truest corruption.
The despot, the tyrannous, maligned the history
we've seen for ourselves the folly of the wise man,
How stupid the comforts we toil in this life for?
For the better part of hundred years,
the rest is but jesting and mud in our eyes,
Oh, the better part of a hundred years,
the sun will shine, and we shall see.
Greetings, Oh, posterity!
I love you. You love me. We are having a baby.
I lack time as it goes by. Who said I'm not afraid to die?
Who said I should be afraid to cry
I wish to fly, the same as the bluebird flies
But gravity brings us down, makes us feel ashamed.
I don't want to feel this way anymore
I want to be free, free as the winds go by
Free as the summertime,
Enjoying the daylight.
I want to be free, free to dream the way babies dream,
sleeping all day long,
As free as the lullaby from momma's lips,
as we grew up way too quick,
And Time, he plays his tricks.
Free to be kind,

This love makes everything alright,
"Tell, me. Is it lonely and cold down deep in the hole?
Is the moonlight a guiding sight?
I can't wait to help you out."
I love you. You love me. We are having a baby.

Awaken early to laughs, loved into a battlefield.
A plastic prophecy strewn about the kitchen
Suspicion itching at the back of my eyes
I'll trade you back the "Noes" for sighs
I love you. You loved me.
AREN'T WE having a baby?
I've left this house bones broken, heavily worn
I've cooked my dreams till burnt to hot sludge
'Til worry and sorrow came home
Did you miss me?
Pregnant stomachs like swollen feet—defeat
Is this the food that we eat?
I loved you. You loved me. I love this baby.
But it's all gone now.
Daddy's gone crazy!

Jolly Jackson

"Glittering flakes peeled off a colorless world
A faint sparkle shining bright in the iris of confident stares
None have had your lovers embrace,
But I've felt your soft, harmless hands
A long reach of hopes amending "Grace.""

Jolly Jackson
Excerpt from *Grace*

Gail

CHAPTER 44—PRESENT STILL

2016

Yesterday, we went up to see little Douggie at the hospital, and there was a moment when Mike left the room, and I was talking with his fiancé alone. I was leaning over the baby bed, marveling at how precious this new life was, looking at his perfectly formed little hands and feet, when Sylvia shared with me, "I've been worried about Mike's drinking lately. A few weeks ago, he had a couple of nights of excessive drinking. He was so drunk he was doing crazy things."

She wasn't sure she trusted Mike to care for the baby if he had been drinking. She told me about some of what had happened, and the stories were all too familiar to me. They'd had a serious talk, and he promised he would do better.

Red flags and warning lights went off in my mind. I told Sylvia that she *had* to protect this precious new life. I told her she had our promise that we would not walk away from her or this child if she ever had to make those decisions necessary to take care of the baby. I said,

"I cannot change anyone else. I've learned that lesson over the years. But I *will* support you through this."

"He's been much better the last few weeks since we talked." She admitted.

And he *had* done better. A fragile peace had settled between them.

Somehow, I didn't feel reassured. The wheels of my mind had started spinning.

Of course, I had trouble sleeping that night. I wanted to *fix* the problem once and for all, *again*.

I woke up early on Douggie's second day of life and decided to go for a walk. Home. At least it felt a little bit like home. We were staying in the house we had lived in for 20 years. Matt and his family rented it from us. It was still our house, but it hadn't been *home* for two years.

I decided to walk up to the small park nearby with a path around a beautiful lake. I had walked around this lake so often when I needed to decompress from any stressful situation over the years. I had walked around this same lake on that rainy day in 2004 when a presence took my hand and pulled me out of the depths of despair to step forward into the future. I felt back then that God was walking with me.

As I walked along the path again, I had the feeling that the Spirit was walking with me still. Today, my thoughts were almost as confused and crazy as they were many years ago. *He's drinking too much. My son's not taking care of himself. What's going to happen to this baby?*

The vision of a father who couldn't be present for his child's life flashed across my mind as I projected into the future all the *what-ifs*. I let my mind go there for a few minutes, having a little pity party in my head. Tears dropped from my eyes, and a lump formed in my throat as the thoughts filled me with sadness. The icy fingers of fear crept into my heart as I worried about the whole situation. In an instant, it dawned on me, and I *knew*.

I simply *knew*. It was almost as if it was knowledge I carried in my body, not just my mind.

I am powerless over any of this.

I kept walking, and as I did, I noticed that the sun was shining, and there was a cool breeze. It was a beautiful day, not raining and dreary.

I noticed that the path around the lake was smooth and recently repaved. I held my head up high and looked up towards the sun. The leaves were flickering in the breeze, glistening, and the trees seemed taller to me. The lake was blue and sparkling as I appreciated the beauty of the scene around me. A white crane almost seemed to nod its head at me as I walked by. A thought calmed me.

Things CAN change. Renew. Repave. Repair. Redo.

There was still a loving God who walked with me, with all of us.

I said a quick prayer.

Lord, thank you for showing me all the changes that have taken place in the physical world around me. These changes remind me that life is continuously moving forward. Change is possible and positive things can happen. Gray, dreary days can turn into beautiful sunny ones. Paths that are worn and cracked can be repaved and smoothed out. The old can be made new, and the dead can receive new life. New life is here. You've shown me that. Perhaps you have a plan. Help me be strong and involved in this new precious life with love. Give me the strength to support them through the good times and the tough ones. Amen

Step One
We admitted we were powerless over alcohol—
that our lives had become unmanageable.
Step One of the 12-Steps

Gail

CHAPTER 45—POWERLESS

2016

Doug and I took a vacation to Spain and Portugal about a month after Mike's son, Douggie, was born. As usual, time away was good for us.

September 19, 2016
I feel like I am a lifetime away from all that happened in the Vale de Mendiz. We are in a beautiful hotel, and I am safe and sitting on the balcony, looking out in the distance at the hills and mountains surrounding me. Portugal is a patchwork quilt of green, brown, and tan. I look out at the beautiful views and am amazed at all that was created by God and nature combined with man's handiwork. I see the white buildings, the red tile roofs, and the roadways that wind through the mountains, and it is just beautiful. It is a woven piece of art. We don't notice it on our day-to-day journey up close, but we can see the beautiful tapestry of the scenery when we stand back and look from a distance. Being away on vacation gives us a chance to see from a distance what our life has become. It's a time of reflection.

A few days ago, we headed out from our hotel room in the mountains of Portugal for a short road trip. Our drive back to our hotel was uneventful, or so it seemed at first. When we were getting closer to the area we recognized, I turned on the GPS to help us navigate back to our beautiful hotel.

The cheerful voice said, "You will arrive at 8:15 PM. You are on the shortest route."

Okay, I thought, *let's go!*

We proceeded to follow the route. The road began to become narrower and narrower. We came upon a town that was a mere two houses and a bar. There were tables and chairs set up on the road. It was a beautiful evening, and the locals were outside enjoying a drink. The servers moved the chairs and tables out of the way so we could pass.

My husband turned and said to me, "Are you sure we're going the right way?"

"I think so—that's what the phone says."

So, we proceeded. The road we were on was disappearing even as we drove along it. However, the GPS voice maintained her positive attitude as she directed us, "Turn left—turn left! Sharp turn to the left!"

We were going down the mountain on what appeared to be farm roads used only by tractors tending to the vineyard. Doug kept his foot on the brake as we traveled downward on one particularly rough cobblestone road that seemed to be heading straight *DOWN*.

As we approached what appeared to be the end of the road, the friendly GPS blurted, "Make a sharp left! Sharp turn to the left!"

We were literally in the middle of nowhere. Dusk had settled in, and it was hard to see. The road ahead of us seemed to drop off the mountain, and the road to the left (sharp left) was a severely steep *trail* leading nowhere.

My husband stopped the car suddenly and announced, "I'm done."

"What do you mean, you're *done*?"

"I can't do this!" he said, defeated.

Creeping threads of anxiety came up inside of me.

"What do you mean, exactly?"

"I can't DO it! We're stuck!"

My strong, reasonable, and constantly reliable husband was frozen with fear.

"What do you think we should do? Can't we just keep going? The GPS says we should be at our destination in only eight minutes."

"I'm DONE! You need to call the hotel and have them come and get us! Call the police! I AM DONE!"

In a bit of panic myself, I complied, not knowing what to say to the hotel receptionist because I had no idea exactly where we were. Not to mention, I didn't speak any Portuguese.

NO ANSWER at the hotel. No idea how to call the police either. PANIC.

But I *KNEW*—I felt that strong deep sense of honesty in my soul—the only way we could get out of this valley was to *push* forward, little by little. I knew this in my heart, even as I felt the complete terror my husband was experiencing.

So, I said I was getting out of the car to see exactly how steep it was and how the road looked. It didn't look good. But I told him calmly, "We have to keep going."

By now, it was completely dark, and I mean DARK. There were no streetlights in the valley. We were between two mountains on a tiny cobblestone road, dare I say, *path*? Both of us were riddled with fear of the unknown. I said, hoping Doug would take this well,

"We can't stay here all night. Don't you think it would be better just to continue slowly, carefully, and see where we end up? I'll drive if you can't do this. I think it's our only solution;

move forward slowly."

I'm sure it was my offer to drive that did the trick. My husband wasn't about to let me practice driving a stick shift down a 45-degree incline in the dark on a mountain. So, we got back into the car and headed down—inch by inch—into the sea of darkness all around us.

We moved forward so slowly it was almost painful. We took each turn with great caution, following the cheery voice of the GPS, "Turn right, turn left." Bumpy cobblestone roads and the gravel under our tires were the only sounds we heard as we proceeded forward.

When we finally hit a stretch of smooth pavement, a REAL road,

"Sigh—"

Both of us let a large amount of air out of our lungs. We didn't realize we'd been holding our breaths. Even though the pavement was smooth, we still had a long way to go. Slowly and cautiously, we inched our way through a town called Vale de Mendiz. Then the road began heading uphill out of the valley. We began to feel a bit better, hopeful at last that we were making some headway.

I said a quick prayer of thankfulness. The GPS *was* correct, after all.

Doug wasn't so kind to the GPS. He blamed the whole fiasco on that poor female voice on my phone. After the ordeal was over and we were back in our hotel, with no visible signs of injury, he typed out a text to our children saying that the "GPS nearly killed us on a mountain in Portugal." They were all concerned and responded with many questions. I grabbed his phone and typed a message back to reassure them.

"Everything is fine. GPS knew exactly where we were every single minute!"

The weird thing was, the phone autocorrected "GPS" to

"GOD." So, the message they received was,

"Everything is fine. GOD knew exactly where we were every single minute!"

And I believe that he did! I don't think we were ever in any incredible danger, but *fear* can paralyze you and prevent you from moving ahead. We needed to move on anyway. I believe God *was* there, pushing us forward. Doug said to remind him that if he ever gets *stuck* again, all I will have to say is, "Vale de Mendiz!"

The very next day, as we drove past the mountains in which we felt we were lost, we could see how each road carefully turned on had brought us down to the lowest point of the valley and then gently lifted us back out. The roads formed a kind of zigzag through it all, crisscrossing across the mountains. It was breathtaking to see how it looked during the day with full sun. It was beautiful. We could see each turn and slope for what it was.

In the dark, it all felt so different. We could *not* see where we were, where we'd been, or where we were headed. It was dark, scary, and uncertain. In the dark, we had to trust the path before us, knowing it was laid out for us in some sort of master plan. Trust.

In the light, we could choose which way to go because we could *see*. A fundamental and mind-blowing idea is that the path *was there* in the light *and* the darkness. The road didn't change. It was our perception that changed. Sometimes, most times, whether we can see the light or not, we just need to keep pushing forward in trust even when we know we are powerless.

THE CRACKS

I built it up strong once
A fanciful presence, glistening concrete
Every tiny crack begins to show

How do people forget?

"Sticks and stones," they said
"Never broke my bones!"
But the cause of tiny cracks begins to rupture
A serving full of suffering means,

Slop!

I had wiped the slate clean once
Cleared the air of the stinking shit
If people knew the strength I'd had
Maybe they could take a share, one or two
If you feel like I do, maybe you'd care

How do people forget?

Shades of a sober temperament
How long have I suffered in pain in darkness?
Through angry "spirits" and drunken teardrops
It came in calm winds through red-headed beauties
Laughing through the broken hearts
Fair-skinned brilliance through hard work and earned duties

How do people forget?

Tell me I was good once, vying for truth, muscles burned hard
Searching for waters in fountains, turned off
Home was where the heart died, beating its last,
On the bloodied cutting board
Every twitching wince a lie of new life
Tribulation masked in your deep suffering breaths

Jolly Jackson

"In public, I tried, putting on the charm,
But my lack of enthusiasm should have rung alarms
Music rang out to silence as I searched to find the veins in my arms
Blinded by exquisite suffering, ended
Oblivion felt as sweet dripping nirvana
I remember it all, the roaring serf,
Before it falls, relief."

Jolly Jackson
Excerpt from *The Cracks*

Gail

CHAPTER 46—I DON'T WANT THIS TO BE OUR STORY ANYMORE

January 2018

I'm going to say this upfront: "I don't want to be a part of this story anymore."

I am opting out of my involvement and participation in this drama, which seems to have no happy ending. Even as I write this, I sigh because I cannot opt-out of my own life or my son's life.

When I began writing down the story of our son's involvement with drugs and alcohol, I found myself reliving some challenging and unhappy days. Writing about them brought them to the surface in their raw, frustrating messiness. These moments from the past were mixed with bittersweet snapshots of happy memories that kept me going, kept me writing. I wanted to write a happy ending to our story. I was *planning* on a happy ending.

The reality is that drug and alcohol addictions are not just bad dreams we can wake up from, shake off, and move on. They are not nightmares where we can go back to sleep and dream a different ending. Those of us who are affected by these addicted relationships keep on living as the saying goes, 'one day at a time'.

A few weeks ago, my husband called our son and, in a moment of nostalgia, told him that he was proud of him. He said he was glad he was our son, loved him, and wanted good things to happen for him.

"I love you too, Dad, but don't be proud of me—things aren't going great. I need to tell you something—I'm using again, and I can't stop. I need help."

I'm so thankful that my husband took the time to listen and offer his support. He was compassionate and concerned but held to the boundaries we had established. Doug wanted to help our son, but the *help* he wanted was the same old thing, money. Meanwhile, I was busy getting organized as we packed up to leave for a two-week vacation the following day. There always seemed to be a crisis when we were planning a peaceful time away.

"I want to come to stay with you guys so I can detox and get this shit out of me," Mike said.

"Oh no, Mike, that won't work. We're leaving tomorrow. We're not going to be here. What other options do you have? Don't you think you need to get into a drug treatment program?"

Mike told him that if he couldn't come to stay with us, he wanted to go to a hotel for three or four nights away from his family so that he could detox on his own. Unassisted detox is precisely what he decided to do. We both knew this was dangerous, but my husband agreed to pay for a hotel room in another town. Doug told Mike to stay in touch by phone.

The entire situation made our first few days of vacation challenging. Despite my years of meetings, and everything I knew, my brain would *not* shut down. I could not *let go and let God.* I was so worried about my son's well-being. I tried to work *my* program. I thought I knew what to do, but Mike's relapse became *my* relapse. I kept thinking to myself, *Gail, you are not in charge.* This drug relapse was not *my* problem. It was my *son's* problem, but detoxing from heroin on his own could cause death without professional help.

On vacation, my mind continued to work overtime, perseverating about his situation and what was happening to him. I'd grabbed my support group's literature right before we left and stuck the books in my backpack. I *needed* them and spent time studying and praying while we were gone. I tried to stay detached, but I anxiously waited for a phone call or a text with a word on how Mike was doing each day. I still wanted to *fix* everything. I thought I was beyond this, that *I* was healthy and could handle it, but there I was, powerless once again.

One night after we returned home, I was getting ready for bed. I lowered the thermostat and shut the lights off. As I turned around in the bedroom doorway, I faced a wall of blackness. It was so dark that I could not see a thing in front of me. It felt like the darkness was coming back at me as an unexpected slap, and I actually flinched. I was in a black hole, and it was sucking me in. I took a deep breath, slowly reached my arms out in front of me, and started moving through the dark, feeling for the bed, wall, or something to grab onto. Gradually my eyes adjusted, and the light from a sliver of a moon outside the window illuminated the way to my bed. I climbed under the covers and felt the warmth of my husband sleeping beside me. I was safe.

Michael's attempt at detox on his own was *not* successful. In reality, it was a nightmare. He was so sick that he almost ended up in the hospital, but after four days, instead of trying to enter a rehab program, he returned home to his one-year-old baby and attempted to face life on his own terms. He hadn't fully disclosed the extent of his problems to his fiancé. He was continuing to live in denial. It was the baby, our innocent grandson, living in the mix of addiction and the lies that permeated the situation, that bothered me the most.

I didn't know what the outcome would be for my son or his precious family. His relationship with Sylvia was fragile, but I never doubted how much he loved his son. I knew he felt ashamed of his problem. Still, he was not ready to get the help he needed.

The first time I saw my son, he was lying in a clear plastic box—wires extending from his head, heart, and tubes coming out of his nose. I couldn't give birth to him—he was cut from me as I lay bleeding on the table, losing too much blood from a placental abruption. He was very tiny, born a month too early, seeming to embrace the life he'd been given.

He was whisked away from me and sent to the Neonatal Intensive Care Unit before I could even open my eyes after an emergency c-section. The first look I had of him was bittersweet. He looked at me with wide-open eyes, blinked when I spoke to him, and touched his tiny hand, perfectly formed. I loved him so much, and my arms ached to hold him and my breasts filled with sweet milk, ready to feed him. The waiting seemed endless as he needed to stabilize and grow first. I prayed even then for swift healing. The incubator was adorned with his name, 'Michael', in rainbow colors made by big sister and brother. The Hebrew meaning of his name is *Who is like God?* The whole family was impatient to meet him. He *did* grow and become healthy and had a robust sense of *life*. I still think of him as the bright, toe-headed little boy who made me laugh yet constantly challenged me.

The precious baby I fell in love with was in *danger* of losing his life to addiction. I wasn't ready. I felt the need to guard my own fragile heart. I didn't want to get sucked in again to the spiral of obsessive thinking that could overtake me and make *me* sick. So, every day, I reminded myself that I must also remember *self*-care. I had to keep my boundaries firm and lean on God to carry me forward. "There is no sin in avoidance." is something a friend said at a meeting. I avoided *involvement* in Mike's life to care for myself, but it was extremely difficult. All I wanted to do was jump in the car, drive up to Wisconsin, rescue Mike, and *fix* the situation. Did I miss the clues that foreshadowed this horrible situation? I kept thinking about the last time we had been up to visit.

After the New Year, we visited Mike and Sylvia to bring Christmas gifts for them and Douggie. We went to eat at the local German restaurant, one of our favorites. As we sat there talking, I noticed how jittery my son seemed. I remember commenting, "Gee, Mike, it looks like you've lost a lot of weight."

"Yeah, me and Sylvia are trying to eat healthier this year. It's one of our New Year's resolutions. I'm trying to take better care of myself." I noted that he had ordered a Coke instead of a beer. I didn't mention that. Then I asked Mike to tell me more about his health. He had informed me recently that he had been diagnosed with an autoimmune disease called lupus. He spoke about a new therapy he was receiving at the clinic that involved injections. He showed me his arm, full of tiny scars and bruises.

"They're giving me these shots, and it's bruising my arm, but I think it's helping with the pain and the rashes."

"Wow—that looks uncomfortable!" I responded, not suspecting anything.

We ate our dinner, and Mike spent most of the time running after Douggie, who was about 18 months old and a busy little toddler. After dinner, we stopped at the local grocery store because I needed some batteries for a small race track we had gotten Douggie for Christmas. Mike came into the store with me, grabbed the batteries, and said he'd pay for them. When I looked up at him to thank him, I noticed that his pupils were just a tiny pinpoint in size. I had a vague recollection of that look. I'd seen it before when Mike was high on cocaine.

"We aren't doing this for now. We're doing it for ten years from now," Tami's husband used to say after parent meetings when our boys were in the Dominican Republic. Well, ten years plus have gone by since my son's joyous return from his time in the program. He was, on that day, our flesh and blood prodigal son. He seemed to be doing better. He had a fiancé, a job, and an adorable toddler. He and Sylvia had been planning for the future. We thought that in ten years, he would be past the struggles. I'd become complacent in my recovery, ignoring the warning signs. I didn't see this complete relapse coming.

The wall of darkness I faced that night represented shadows that consumed me. I couldn't see the end of the darkness. After all my praying, I expected the miracle ending. *This relapse was not the end of the story. There would be hope for recovery until the end of his life.*

A LOSS I HAVE NOT GRIEVED

—is the one I haven't yet experienced. It's the one that sits on the edge of my security—the loss that is simply as close as the next shoe to drop, the next close call, the next turn around the corner. It's the grief I prepare myself for by imagining it in my worst-case scenario thinking.

I fear that one day I'll lose my son to his addiction.

When he was younger, I used to dread the sound of the sirens in the distance, and my heart would do little flip-flops inside my chest. Is this the day?

There have been many close calls that I've known about and those of which I am not aware. The end is not the end until the end. My instinct is to pray for my son—knowing how insidious, cunning, and baffling addiction is. My prayer is always that if—the moment arises for him—when the day comes—God will welcome him home into the loving arms of the Divine as I would welcome my son home as his mother.

Gail Mehlan
March 2021

DREAD

It's pretty much all I feel these days
Why? Don't know
But it's there
Looming.

Jolly Jackson

Gail

CHAPTER 47—SOMETIMES PRAYERS AREN'T ENOUGH

2018

I feel as I write this that I am vomiting. I'm hurling words out onto the screen as fast as I can, spattering the pages of our story with the garbage-smelling contents of my head as it continues to unfold. Maybe I can't get it out fast enough, searching for what will provide momentary relief from the pain of the situation once it's all out there. There seems to be no end to the saga. I didn't want this to be the end of the story, and it's not. I continue and keep regurgitating again and again. The words that come forth don't seem to touch my despair.

After we arrived home from our vacation, we continued to be in contact with Mike. His father was diligent about talking with him and advising him daily. Many phone calls came frequently, and each time I heard the little jingle that signaled my husband's cell phone going off, my heart skipped a beat. Each time I heard it, I asked myself, *could this be it? Could this be the end?*

My steadfast husband was always so upbeat, and despite the pit in my stomach, each time he answered, he always said, "Hi, Mike! How're you doing?" No matter what Mike said was happening, he responded with what seemed to be the same advice, repeating it almost like a mantra.

"If you want help, you need to get into a treatment program."

I maintained my distance. I allowed myself this luxury with the excuse that I was working on my own self-care, struggling with my fragile heart, and I was. The 'Let Go and Let God' slogan was my go-to phrase, and *sometimes* it soothed me.

Several weeks passed, and Mike still asked for financial help regularly. He worked as a bartender and watched his son during the day. The knowledge that he was responsible for our beloved little grandson while he was *using* left me heartbroken and furious.

January 10, 2018
I'm writing Mike a letter.
   Oh! Mike!
   Is this who you want to be, son? Now, you want to lose your family? Your son?
   I don't want to lose MY SON or my GRANDSON in my life! But I'm tired. I'm DONE! I'm done picking up the pieces of YOUR life and holding them together for YOU! You KNOW what this will do! You could DIE! What are we going to tell your son about you? What will your legacy be? Who cares about money? What matters is relationships! That CHILD! Oh! What a tangled web you've created.
   The story of Abraham came up again in my Bible study this week. Just as Abraham did with his son, I have ALREADY struggled to carry you up and over the mountain, and I've offered you up as a sacrifice to God—and He saved you once—twice—maybe even three

times. God provided the lamb. Now I feel like I'm right back there again this very moment trying to carry you up to the mountain and let you go. This time you are too heavy for me, Mike, too heavy!
ARE YOU THERE, Lord? Can you help? I cannot bear this burden again!

I could not even end the letter with a closing, knowing I would never send it.

Day by day, one day at a time, I tried to keep myself detached from the situation and prayed fervently every day that nothing terrible would happen while Michael was in charge of his young son. We watched from a distance and waited for a few miserable weeks, holding our breaths for fear of some disaster. Then things began to deteriorate quickly. The subsequent few events are like one long run-on sentence that never reaches a point that ends in a final period.

First, Mike took some cash from the register at the bar where he worked and got caught by his boss. His boss fired him on the spot but did *not* press charges. Lucky for Mike, I guess. I was disappointed, praying for a situation that would *force* him to get some help. I'd heard that sometimes that's what it takes for an addict to seek help. How low can a mother's prayers go?

He was out of work and trying to keep himself from going into withdrawal and experiencing terrible symptoms. I learned later that he was "only using enough to stay functioning" and never cared for his son when he was *high*. This excuse sounds pretty sick to me, but I am not an expert on opioid addictions. He told me that the symptoms of withdrawal would've left him unable to function at all.

One evening, Mike arrived home to find Sylvia waiting at the door for him with the news that the police had been looking for him and asking for information about his involvement with certain crimes in the area. Mike had also taken money from their joint account that she needed for expenses. She was livid. Sylvia's concern and frustration came to a head. She did not want him near her or their son. She told Mike that it was time for him to leave.

When I heard this, I was glad she'd finally stood up for herself and Douggie. I felt guilty for holding back information about what was going on. I was selfish in my silence because I also knew what that meant for Mike. I was concerned about my son, who would be out on the streets, unemployed and homeless, in January.

Mike was not in good shape that night. I stood back, waited, and silently prayed for *something* to change. How could a mother pray that her son hits rock bottom? That's where I was. My husband spent several hours talking to him on the phone. Again, he begged to come and stay with us.

"No" was the answer, along with my husband's mantra, "If you want help, get into a treatment program."

Mike was driving around in his car with most of his belongings, not knowing what to do. I believe he was high on heroin and drinking alcohol. Doug coached him to drive to the nearest emergency room. He refused to go anywhere local because he was afraid of an arrest. My husband, always trying to be protective, didn't tell me his deepest fear that night. Doug feared that Mike was suicidal.

Doug convinced him to drive to the nearest hospital in Illinois. He stayed on the phone with him and gave him directions. Several times Mike needed to pull off the road to take a nap. My husband told him to answer his calls *immediately* and threatened to call the police if he didn't answer the phone or call him right back. We were both on pins and needles. If we had been closer, we might have gone out searching for him. The need to *do* something was so strong in both of us. Thoughts of being able to rescue my son entered my mind in rapid-fire succession. If we left right away, we could be there in four hours. But then, what would we have done?

Finally, after what seemed like many more than four hours, we heard the jingle of Doug's cell phone. Holding our breath for a moment, we learned Mike was in the parking lot of a community hospital in Illinois. By the grace of God, he had arrived there safely. He said he was going to take another rest before he went into the emergency room. Doug warned, "Go into the hospital, or—the police will be notified."

When the phone jingled again, Mike was calling us from *inside* the emergency room and was waiting to be seen by a doctor. Doug and I both let out a long sigh, not knowing what the next steps would be. Mike told his dad that someone had come up to the car, knocked on the window, helped him get out, and walked him into the emergency room. I am convinced it was one of God's angels. He was transferred by ambulance to another hospital and entered into a detox program at a treatment center.

I was stress-free the whole week Mike was in the hospital detoxing. I know that sounds weird, but it was the feeling of peace I would get each time Mike was in treatment. *Someone else* was caring for him. *They* were feeding him. *They* were helping him. My prayers were still flowing, but I felt a slight lifting of the emotional burden. The detox lasted but a short week.

When he was released, his brother, Matt, went and picked him up, thinking he could convince him to enter treatment, but Mike was determined to go back and try to find a new job and an apartment.

"When I get that all figured out, I'll go into an outpatient program," he told Matt.

He had nowhere to go, though. We continued to say "no" to

his coming to live with us. One of my friends from my Twelve-Step program reassured me at a meeting, telling me, "Each person has to move through their recovery in their own way." This idea gave me the slightest bit of hope. Mike wanted to do recovery his way. He had detoxed in a hospital with medical assistance. By his standards, he believed he was now *clean* and that life would return to *normal.*

For the first week, Mike stayed in various homeless shelters in the area. The following week, and week after week, Doug and Mike would talk. Mike applied for and got a job delivering pizzas and somehow managed to find several friends to put him up so he didn't have to sleep in his car. Sylvia was not allowing Mike to see his son, but one day, she couldn't find a babysitter and was desperate. She called Mike and asked if his brother would allow them to stay in Schaumburg. Sylvia offered to bring them both down to Illinois. Matt graciously agreed, so they spent a couple of nights at his brother's house.

Mike's ability to stay clean was fragile, and although he stayed with several of his friends for a few nights here and there, it didn't last. He was spending more and more nights in the car, fearful that the police might pick him up. Sylvia finally agreed to let him park in her driveway and use her bathroom and Wi-Fi so he could look for a job online.

Doug tried searching for community resources for Mike, homeless shelters, rehabilitation programs, and other opportunities. He could not do much from a distance, and he found that most places didn't give out information to *parents* of adults. However, one community resource counselor called Mike personally to see if she could convince him to come in for some counseling and support. They had beds there that were available the day she called. Several days went by before Mike made his way there, and there were no beds available when he arrived.

Finally, one afternoon, Mike did walk into the center again, and miraculously they *did* have a bed for him. We were hopeful he was going to get some help. The center set him up to get some counseling and enter into an outpatient day program for rehab the following day.

Just after Mike had taken a shower, eaten breakfast, and was getting ready to start meeting with a counselor, the police arrived at the center to arrest him. They took him to the county jail.

The following day he was charged with twelve counts of breaking and entering, credit card theft, and unlawful use of a stolen credit card. His bond was set at 100,000 dollars. We got a call from the correction facility after figuring out how the system worked and spoke to Mike. He asked what he should do.

"I can't put up that kind of money for you, Mike. You'll have to stay there and ask for a state's attorney," My husband said. We put a small amount of money into his account at the commissary to make phone calls and get a few essentials. Jail is not *free*.

I felt betrayed by my son. His choices and addiction had put a wrench in *our* plans *again*. Even though my concerns seemed trivial and self-centered, they were very *real*. We were getting ready for another big trip to Spain. We planned to be gone for three weeks with Doug's sister and could not change our itinerary because our son was in jail. Contempt for Mike and his circumstances helped me look forward to having time and space between us. The distance couldn't stop my *own* addiction to worry about this adult child of mine, though. That was my biggest obstacle. How could a mother stop thinking about a situation like this when away on vacation? An ocean wasn't nearly far enough. I felt like that hamster on the wheel again, consumed by my runaway thoughts. Round and round they went, never ceasing, never coming to an end.

We heard from our son, Matthew, on the second evening of

our trip that Mike went before a judge at a bond hearing, and his attempt to get a reduced bond was refused. He would be in jail for at least a month. Another hearing was scheduled.

I breathed a sigh of relief at this news. I was unhappy that my son was in jail, but he was not out on the streets and couldn't *use* drugs. I began to relax and enjoy our trip, free from the daily reminders of where my child was. No mother ever brings a child into the world, hoping they will grow up to be a drug addict. I know I've said this before. No mother loves a bright-eyed toddler, thinking, *I can't wait until my child goes to jail.*

My hopes and dreams for Mike were destroyed, yet he was still *alive*. I felt like God had not answered my overarching prayers to beat this addiction, even though I'd had little glimmers of hope over the years. I kept telling myself; *God's will, not mine.* Somehow this must be a part of a larger plan.

One day, while we were in Spain, I got up early and dressed in silence so I could go for a walk along the beach alone. The morning was chilly, but I kicked off my sandals anyway and walked barefoot along the shores of the beach in Mundaka, a town along the northern coast famous to surfers for its excellent waves. I arrived at the beach just as the sun illuminated the sky over the water. The bright reflection of sunlight on the water was so beautiful. The only footprints in the sand were mine, but somehow, I did not feel alone.

I thought about my son in jail, and through my head, I kept thinking: *When prayers aren't enough—when prayers aren't enough—when prayers aren't enough.* That was precisely how I felt. My prayers hadn't been *enough* to end the awful disease called addiction. Maybe I hadn't prayed the right way, but oh! I had been praying! The prayers just didn't seem to be enough.

I thought of the story of the prodigal son. I suffered as he *left* our family and *welcomed* him home, but do I do that again? *Can*

I do that again? How many times would the father in the story have kept welcoming his son back? What about the mother? I asked myself those questions.

It was quiet for a long moment, and then slowly, I began to listen. I could hear the waves crash upon the shore over and over again—and over and over again. Continuously. It dawned on me then; the father *would* keep welcoming his son back, over and over again. So would the mother. The answer was in the roar of the ocean waves as I watched and listened. As each wave hit the shore, it receded, swelled up again, and crashed upon the beach. They came one after another. Continuously. A thought entered my mind, *as many times as that!* I knew *God* would forgive, love, and welcome him back time and time again—always.

Siempre.

I JUST MIGHT BE THE DEVIL—PART 1

Perhaps I was created to fall forever—
Just like my dearest friend the devil
Fall and fall and fall over and over again
In and out of your presence
I just might be the devil
I just might need to be in your glory of gods
but perhaps your life suffices
"Perhaps I can never have you."
And I've offered up this damned thing as a sacrifice
And damned forever in your pit
A flaming river of despair
I just might be the devil
Perhaps what is broken can never ever be repaired
I believed you when you said you loved me
And now that was only the present then,
but it is not the present now
But I believe it still might be true, a million different ways
In a million different worlds, while a million different times
We've shared some words of truth
Or perhaps I'm the father of lies
Perhaps I've exhausted my resources
At least I've tried.

Jolly Jackson
Excerpt from *I Just Might Be the Devil Part 1*

"Silence is the loudest of sounds
when you're used to hearing everything."

Jolly Jackson

Michael

CHAPTER 48—WHO *IS* JOLLY JACKSON?

2019

Life has always been full of jokes and subtle little ironies. To find joy in the suffering, you simply have to laugh at it, like dogs looking like their owners, skinny folks complaining that they're fat, how we sleep in the dark, yet we're afraid of what lurks there.

When I got outta jail, I had no place to go, no job, no money, and at every turn, there was a trap. I was ready to make a change but was still so broken on the inside; my family was gone, their trust gone. Sylvia was more than disappointed, Douggie didn't have his father, and I had no idea how to get that person back. My friends, my band, and everyone hated me. My face had been plastered all over the five o'clock news, "Searching for this individual wanted concerning a burglary." I was a marked man, a criminal, a degenerate, and I couldn't be Michael anymore. That guy was gone, dead in the water. I didn't feel like him. I didn't want to be him, but I couldn't shed the shame of being him. Time and time again, people will form opinions of you without knowing the truth, without caring about the details. In the last six months, I had been a criminal, and nobody wanted to give me a chance, and now I had been marked a monster.

Several months before all this had transpired, there had been a moment when I destroyed my band. I fought my bandmates on stage at a show in a moment of drug-induced anger. I smashed my bass clean into the guitarist's amp, then proceeded to punch and wrestle my friend to the ground. My music was falling apart. I stormed outta that bar, a broken time bomb of disappointment. People saw me being violent. I had never been violent before, except for a few schoolyard scraps as a kid. Still, I had taken out all my anger with myself on my best friend and bandmate. I was easing all my struggles, juggling work, baby and girlfriend, and stress by using drugs again and drinking heavily. I considered him my brother, but I made it all his fault. He was holding me back. But that was just a lie I told myself. The band was over. I had lost my best friend and collaborator, someone who believed in me, one of the people who kept me grounded and working. But I was the one who was broken again, and now I was marked as violent.

Next, I destroyed my relationship with Sylvia and broke her trust in every way.

I lied, I stole money, I ruined holidays because I was dope-sick on heroin. I cared for my son when I was using. At times, he was in the backseat, happy as could be, when "Daddy" had to cop drugs and shoot up in the front seat so I could function as a person. I'll never forgive myself for that. Hopefully, he doesn't remember Daddy like that. I pray he never does. I left Sylvia alone. I wasn't there even when I was there. I didn't make her feel loved. I abandoned her because I felt like she wouldn't understand or love me anymore. I couldn't tell her what was really going on; I didn't know how to get help, so I left her alone with our son. I left him alone too. I was still there physically, but they didn't have me. I wasn't Mike anymore. I was a dead man walking.

Then the money started to run out. I wasn't making enough to support my habit and take care of bills, food, and everything Sylvia

AMONG THE SUNFLOWERS

wanted for Douggie, toys or clothes for me or anyone. I began stealing things to help get by. I broke into cars late at night, high on cocaine, and was hanging around gang members who would pay me with drugs to do favors for them. I had a junky friend who was also doing the same things, and we would often work together to steal and swindle to get the drugs we needed.

"Hey, I got these credit cards from my aunt!" he said to me, and we used them. He told me his aunt gave them to him to get new stuff for himself, but instead, we used them to buy items to trade for drugs. In the end, I had willingly become an accessory to the burglary of my neighbor's house, my own neighbors! My friend had broken in through the screen door and stolen a purse. That was where he got the credit cards, not from his aunt. The police saw me on a security camera using one of the cards illegally and came looking for me. Now I was the one marked as a criminal. I lost my home, was on the run, and my family was gone.

"Mike" was now violent, a criminal, a family deserter, a bad father, a wanted man.

I had to get clean.

After I got out of jail, my friend gave me a place to stay, an air mattress on the floor, and a job working for him fixing refrigeration units. We'd get up, do breakfast, and work ten-hour days. I was sober, in the district attorney's diversion program, on Vivitrol (a medication to reduce cravings), and trying the best I could. But I wasn't "Mike" anymore. I was different and wanted so badly to shed the image people had of me. I wasn't what people thought I was anymore.

While I was in jail, some of the other inmates mocked me as sad and morose, and because of post-withdrawal, all I craved were Jolly Rancher's candy. The inmates started to call me "Jolly" as a tease, and I refused to correct them. They'd say, "You Jolly?" and I'd return with "For now?" then laugh. It was all a joke to me, really, but when you're in jail, things are tough, and it's better not to get to know people too closely.

One night, I sat and pondered that nickname while listening to Michael Jackson. I'd always had a fondness for the King of Pop's music ever since I was a kid, and the "Jackson" just stuck. I had a new name, a new identity. I didn't have to be "Mike" anymore. I changed my Facebook name to JOLLY JACKSON and said to myself, well, I guess you're "Jolly for Now," kid. I laughed at how ridiculous I was, sitting on an air mattress with nothing to my name, nothing at all. I was a clown, a joker, an absurdist. It was all a joke, I was a joke, and I laughed till I cried and felt the cold emptiness of having to start all over again wash over me. I had nothing, no family, no home, no money, nothing at all, but I was sober. I was clean. I didn't have to be "Mike" anymore. The world that scared me so long ago was now a sad joke. I had to be strong. Was this going to be my life? Was I gonna just keep having it all, then throw it all away again? Or was I gonna be different? Could I really change who I was, or would I keep doing this to myself? It wasn't over yet. I still had to do the work.

The following two years would be hard. I'd have to learn many more lessons. I'd have to dig my way out of the trap and hole again and again and again. I'd tangle myself up with demons just to have to exorcise them from my life. I was beginning to see what I could be if only I tried. I just wanted to be loved and whole, but first, I had to wipe the slate clean, so I did. Becoming that new person is unheard of. Can you become a brand-new person? Well, you'll never know 'til you try. The first step is always forgiving yourself. I had to forgive myself.

"I'm sorry, Michael, I'm sorry you lost it all. I'm sorry you're hurt and suffering. I'm sorry your life has been hard. I'm sorry you don't fit in. I'm sorry that this happened to you, but I'm trying to make you whole. In order to do that, we have to heat you up and pound out the slag over and over and over, then grind away the rest till you're a new bright and shining blade. It's not gonna be easy, but I do it because I love you. I do it because you are good. I forgive you for who you've

been and for who you may be again. I forgive your doubt. I love who
you will become."
   Love, Jolly Jackson

"I was there before you were born. I'll be there when they
   weigh your heart
I may not make my presence known but you and me; we've
   never been far apart
I was beside you moving your hand way before you were
   in dragon-infested lands
I was there when joy would move your parts and make
   you dance
I was the one who gave you, yes you, another chance
I moved the tides from high to low
I made you special, and this you should know
I know I made you feel much stronger than most
But I was your mover, your holy ghost
I was there watching when you pulled Sylvia close
And told her you'd love her better than those
I was the one who gave you your child
I will be there for him, too, if he's wild like you
I was the purpose; I was your point
I was your maker
I can tell you it's true
You called me Lord, and I called you son

But you're Jolly for now, and your games are no fun
Your burden is heavy; now pull off that yoke.
You say you're Jolly for now, but no one laughs at
your jokes
You forgot me before
You'll forget me again

In the darkness, you'll ask me and say it in prose
When you want to be free, no longer tied like a dog
    to a post
You'll remember me, Jolly, when you pull your loved ones
    in close
Because I am the one who loves you the MOST."

Jolly Jackson
Excerpt from *The Ballad of Jolly and Sylvia*

THE MAGICIANS

This insidious death that crept into the spire
of my blood that has led me here
to this realm of shadows
Peeking through the veil to see my beloved one
Seeing the grief on your flesh worn
as if like a badge to signal your chance at change
I'll send you magicians to make but wonderful workings,
turn your water into wine, pour your sadness out into joy—
Send you the witches and shamans to prophecy your future
Send you the healers and teachers to build up all your knowledge
Send you an angelic host who can defeat the devils
that reside in your homes and hearts
So, you may take off this badge of grief
and sire new clothes for yourself
Grow my sweet child, my love, grow and grow and grow and grow
and heed the signs I've posted on the walls,
in paper leaflets balled up in a drawer,
these artifacts I've left behind
For I am gone, a ghost just hiding now
Here between the shadows
Here just here—watching your light burn, so incredibly bright
So, grow my sweet child, my love, for I will send you magicians—
To water the seeds of your life

Jolly Jackson

"We've opened Pandora's Box
A wrath of rebukes, a parasitic sentimental pride
Shame on you for your fruitless ways,
your children buried in a pit of your own destruction,
shame on you for cauldrons of love spilled out for fanciful whims,
desires never fulfilled searching for the dead in empty tombs."

Jolly Jackson
Excerpt from *My Sweet Queen Marie*

Gail

CHAPTER 49—WHY DID WE HAVE CHILDREN?

2019

One night after a frustrating phone call with Mike, my husband asked me a question that reminded me of a similar question Mike asked me years ago.

"Why did we even have kids? Was it for us? Or for them?"

We got to talking about life and the endless struggles that our children, not just the addict, had been having. Each of our children faced differing situations. Severe health problems confronted our daughter, and we were helping her search for answers. We also helped take care of her young children every day. There never seemed to be enough money available to fulfill the dreams they each had for their lives, and misunderstandings arose between spouses. I forgot to tell them that marriage wasn't a fairy tale. When job searches had not produced the desired results, there was much disappointment and uncertainty for the future. The list of difficulties they each faced just seemed to grow and grow. As parents, it's hard to watch your adult children struggle with real life.

Michael's recent relapse had sent me into a tizzy again with my obsessive thoughts and desire to control. This journey through addiction had placed an enormous burden on our family. Our children each had serious problems, but this one *thing* still held *my mind* hostage.

"I don't know. I had a *good* life growing up in mine. It's a natural progression. I always wanted to have children. I always enjoyed being a part of a family, and I wanted to have one of my own. I love children. I love my grandchildren."

"But, did we have them for *them* or *us?*"

This question burned in my heart. I couldn't even imagine life without our children in it! I experienced great joy in growing new life inside my body, giving birth, and holding my babies in my arms, nurturing them from the milk my own body produced. Yet, I admit, I never asked myself, was I being *selfish,* wanting them in my life and my family? Did I want them for *myself?* Did I have a choice? Maybe I did. There *was* some sacrifice of my own life's ambitions that I gave up to be their mom, but I never resented it. I always viewed mothering as my mission field. I was always willing to do the work for *them,* for *their* lives. Mothering *was* a life ambition for me. "Holy work is hard work," my pastor said to me once. That's what being a mother was for me, hard *holy* work.

I always thought I would be content if my children all grew up to be contributing members of society. I tried to guide them in that direction, but I never asked them if that was what *they* wanted. *What about life and living has any value?*

I failed at adequately adding anything profound to this discussion until I read a quote on Facebook a few days later from the author, Donald Miller, saying, "I hope the word *successful* will not be used in heaven. I hope it is replaced by the word *beloved*." This quote resonated with me. Being *beloved* is what we all crave from this world, especially from our families.

In my attempts to figure out what the longing to have children was for me, the only word I came up with to share how I felt about my children's lives, or any life, is LOVE. They are here and living their lives because my husband and I loved each other. They learned to love growing up in our family. We showed them love and love them still, despite the difficulties. We demonstrate to them daily that they are *beloved* by walking with them through their problems and valuing them and their families to the best of our ability. Yes, we were selfish, wanting our love to grow into something special, something *successful*, the *perfect* family. But now we take the word successful out of the equation because we know how variable that can be. Focusing only on the goal of *success* is based on prejudice and misunderstanding. We certainly know we are not perfect. We simply chose to love them. That is how *I* want to be loved. I believe it's just like God loves us unconditionally. They are *beloved*.

Not too long ago, we had the opportunity to spend a few days with Douggie. He is a sweet and spunky little guy, yet not so little anymore. He's a toddler. He ran circles around me as he played with his Hot Wheels cars and trucks and asked to go down into the basement to play "toys"! He was full of smiles and hugs and brought a light to my days as we spent time with his cousins here in Indiana.

"I a hungry, hungry boy!" he told me as he chowed down his lunch or dinner. He never turned down food and never forgot to say "thank you" and "you're welcome ." He would give me a great big hug, snuggle into Grandma's big bed and go right to sleep.

Spending time with him made me feel so full of love that I

had a sense that life and love were coming full circle for Mike and me. If Mike weren't here, we wouldn't have Douggie. If Mike weren't here, he would also be free from addiction *and* non-existent. He would not even have had a chance. But this immense *LOVE* for his child would be missing, and we wouldn't even know it was possible.

No, we cannot go back and question our motives for having these children in our lives. Their lives were not up to us to choose. We did it for ourselves *and* them. They are here, and there is love. Sometimes it has to be *tough love*, but all of my children and grandchildren are *beloved*, hard as that can sometimes be. All of them are human, *my* favorite humans!

As I reflect on the past few years, Mike's relapse and arrest, his incarceration, and his treatment following all of this, I realize that life moves forward whether we are ready or not. There are always consequences for actions, but if there is still *life*, there is *hope*.

After Mike was in jail for about six weeks, he was offered an experimental medically assisted treatment program by the district attorney. He could enter into the two-year rehabilitation program, and upon completion, all charges against him would be dropped. Michael agreed to do this and continued to work on his recovery. He has done well with just a few minor slip-ups. When supervised and away from the house, he can see Douggie, but not enough, in Mike's opinion. These restrictions upset Mike, but graciously, Sylvia's family has allowed us, as grandparents, to spend time with our grandson often. That has been a blessing for all of us. He is still involved in our lives, loves us, and wants to spend time here in Indiana with us. I give much credit to his mother and her parents, who have cared for Douggie and loved him thoroughly.

There is still a long way to go, but Mike has a job, is living in a sober house, and doing his best to keep up with the program's requirements. He is responsible for his own life and his own decisions.

Sometimes I withdraw from interaction with him because I still feel fragile around him. He's an addict, and *I* can become addicted to *his* addiction. I need to protect myself from being sucked in. My husband is a little stronger than I am and calls Mike almost every day. We are still worried about his circumstances, and even though he's been sober for many months, his sobriety feels new and fragile.

Last night he called his dad because he was frustrated that he doesn't get to spend much time with his son. My husband patiently listened and tried to come up with some reasonable suggestions that might help him be in better graces with his ex and smooth things out without going to court, but my son continues to be stubborn and impatient.

The following day, I asked my husband about his call with Mike the night before.

He let out a huge sigh and said, "I don't know—It's hard."

I smiled at him and couldn't help letting these words come out of my mouth,

"Why did we even have kids anyway?"

He smiled back at me and sighed,

"Good question."

"Beloved, let us love one another because love is from God; everyone who loves is born of God and knows God. Whoever does not love does not know God, for God is love."

1 John 4:7-8 (NIV)

"I'd be remiss
If I said there are no monsters
There are
And they're us
We all have it in us
I'm not here to say we are
But we could be"

Jolly Jackson
Excerpt from *Monsters*

Michael

CHAPTER 50—IS THAT A MONSTER UNDER THE BED?

2020

Things hadn't been going that well for a long time in my mind. I had been dating and living with a girl, someone who was kind to me and wasn't using drugs or drinking. She wanted me but didn't understand me or what I was going through to keep my sobriety. I was lonely and thought that I loved her. I loved being in love with her. She wanted me to empty my soul to her daily and wanted my complete loyalty. She refused to understand that I was already loyal to the family that I had. I wanted so badly to love her and make her life happy. I felt that if Sylvia, my ex, had moved on, so could I. I deserved a little happiness. At times this girl brought me that happiness, and I did everything in my power to hold on to it. What I did do was hold back from sharing my deepest thoughts with her. I was never completely honest with her. I never told her what it was like to lose yourself in a sea of addiction. She wanted my total fidelity, my heart, my mind, and my soul. I was just unwilling to hand it over freely. She needed more support than I was able to give. I led her on, partly to get back at Sylvia for treating me like a monster and not letting me see my son. But in the end, I did end up caring deeply about this girl.

Even though I cared for her, our relationship was always tumultuous. I was too old a soul, and she was too young and broken. There were ten years between us. I know what that's like to be a broken soul. Once again, I thought I could heal, fix, and mend her. I could help her, and she could help me. We could live happily ever after. Unfortunately, that did not happen. We constantly fought because she knew deep down; I still loved my family more than I loved her. That idea hurt her deeply, and no matter how much I wanted to change my feelings, I couldn't. She felt terribly hurt by my lack of commitment. I'm not a monster, and neither is she, but no matter how much I cared for her, we could not change some fundamental things.

One day we started fighting. She had been scrolling through Facebook and had noticed that I had added a new girl's name to my friend list. She began yelling and screaming at me, accusing me of cheating on her when this girl was utterly harmless, just a casual friend. She was so jealous of me and didn't seem to trust me anytime I was away from her. Another time she found a note from an ex-girlfriend as she looked through my personal belongings. The fight escalated.

"Who wrote you this note?" she yelled at me in a screeching voice.

"What the f**k! Are you going through my stuff while I'm at work? You're nuts! I was at work! Dammit!" I angrily grabbed her phone and threw it aside. I had finally had enough of her tirades and wanted to leave, hide, and escape the madness of everything, but I couldn't. Something always held me back. I tried walking out that day, but she followed me everywhere as I was preparing to leave.

I went into the bathroom, and she snuck in behind me. In a fit of anger, I pushed her down onto the floor. I started pulling her makeup out of the medicine cabinet as she watched me destroy it all, sobbing. She tried to get out of the bathroom door, finally grabbing my phone and scratching me to get me to stop restraining her. After she finally broke out of the bathroom, she was so angry that she quickly turned and walked over to the other side of the room, picked up my beloved guitar, and threw it to the ground, demolishing it. I grabbed one of her hoodies and tore it up in retaliation. I furiously packed up my stuff, continuing my attempt to leave as she threw my cell phone to the ground crushing it completely. The next thing we knew, we were wrestling on the floor until I snapped and slapped her across the face.

I had hit a woman. I had never done this before. She began to cry. At that very moment, her mother's boyfriend came into the house and started threatening me with my life.

"Help me! It's all his fault!" She pleaded.

I had done the unthinkable. Was I a monster?

I gathered what I could of my things and left in a hurry. I picked up my cash paycheck from the restaurant where I worked. The first words out of my mouth were to my drug dealer: "I wanna get high."

I had let the monster out from under the bed, and it was too much to handle. During the course of the next two days, I injected two grams worth of cocaine and crystal methamphetamine into my veins in an attempt to lose myself.

In my drug-induced paranoia, all I kept thinking was: This is all a setup. I'm gonna go to jail. The government is after me. I have to run and hide. I was running, scared. I began walking. The whole time I walked, it was all on repeat; This is all a setup. I'm gonna go to jail. The government is after me. I have to run and hide. I had to walk. And I walked, and I walked, slipping in and out of every alley and avoiding streetlights. I walked clear across the state line from Wisconsin to Illinois into a neighboring town. I found myself running through the woods, thinking there were men in the trees watching me, chasing me down, until I finally screamed out loud: "I just want to see the lake again before you take me away!"

The shore of Lake Michigan came into view, and I slowly approached it to be close to the edge. I stood there for a long time, staring. I peered deep into the cold frigid water and contemplated jumping in. That would be better than getting caught, I thought. I wasn't afraid of death but felt extremely afraid of everything else.

When the sun broke above the waterline, and the light began to make its way into my eyes, I suddenly came to my senses and realized it had all been a hallucination. I had walked ten miles in cowboy boots through the night, and now I was there at the edge again, staring into the abyss, and nothing was real. None of it. Now, I wasn't afraid. I had walked through hell and came out the other side alive. Again, the sun broke in and took my mind back to reality, and I said to myself, No! Never again! I was done. I had hit a wall. If I kept doing this, I would be dead. There was no monster under the bed, no monster inside of me. It was all just me, my doing, my actions, my fear, leading me down this path of destruction. I no longer needed to distract myself again with other things. It was time for me to do what I needed to do. I needed to do things for me, fix me, fix all of it. I couldn't do it anymore. I had to stop, or I would go insane. I walked back. I went to the hospital and tried to convince those in charge that I needed to get myself into a sober living house again.

I felt a presence as I walked, something guiding me to do the right thing, leading me back. I had strayed again too far from the path. I had to see what true hell was like before it made sense to do the right thing. I had to break completely to see that I had been making so many mistakes. I had to listen and walk the path, knowing that if I didn't stay on it, all would be damned. I had forgiven myself, but I had to fix myself first. I needed to make a course correction.

Recovery isn't a straight line; it isn't static. It's good. It's bad. It's ugly, and it's full of tough choices: To be fulfilled in one way and leave the rest, or be lonely and follow the path you know will lead you to salvation, to the truth, to being and doing good. It is a path that isn't easy to see, and the choices aren't black and white, but if you squeeze through to the good decisions, you get colorful outcomes. If you focus on the black, all you find is darkness, deep in the cold frigid abyss of the lonely water of death. I chose to live that day and tried to be good. I thought to myself. I'm sorry I couldn't fix you, love, but everything had to be different. I am only able to help myself right now, and that's a tough vision to see.

God was pushing me back to my family.

THE BLUE BONE DISEASE

Walking—Walking until my feet begin to bleed
Shadow men chase me down with shadow dogs
Watching slyly through red-curtained windows
Video electric eyeballs documenting my every move
Wondering what it was that I had lost
I only wish to see the water again, one last time
before I go away far too far—away for good

Walking—Walking until my feet begin to bleed
Bones crunching on bones, knee to bone, bone to soft mass
You'll never catch me slipping, I whisper to myself
I won't be enticed by your traps
Why would they do this to me? I thought I was good?
Why such tricks would be had on my mind—My Memories?
It was real? This is real. THIS IS REAL!
WHY WOULD YOU DO THIS TO ME?

Keep walking—Walking until my feet begin to bleed
Snowblind soldiers armed in the woods,
hiding just there, like tigers
I can see you. I see you.
Tactical rifles aimed to capture me. Why?
Was the poison in my bones made for me? To see?
Was this a big game? Was this the one that I was to win?
Perhaps I was meant to lose—
Oh, Devil in this wilderness, tempt me no more!

Walking—Walking until my feet begin to bleed
There must be only one destination
One special home for me; I'm headed down
Deep into the cold waters, never to return

The empty cold darkness—
How could you be so cruel to me?
How could you do this to me?
My bones are filled deep with the deepest blues
Easily broken, brittle spires and stems
It's a sadness sickening disease
Being alive
A shriek, a thousand birds, swarming above my head
Beckoning lost futures; traded for fear and ignorance

But like a seam of golden thread, the first beams of light
peek over the water
Shooting me upward to peer wildly into the sky
The empty black sky broke
Blinding, shutting, wincing, and searing
the backs of the orbs
I cannot see; I'm ready with my shame
Oh! beaming God of Light, magnificent bringer of warmth,
I'm ready now
I'm ready
I'm ready

Walking—Walking until my feet begin to bleed
The journey's just begun; it never ended
It only brightened

Jolly Jackson

"I see you've
Fallen
way down
Down deep
We ride on and wonder
do you feel these surface waves?

One of ours gone over
One of ours gone over
The edge

No warning, sign no omen
No borderline nor door announce
The edge

Silently approaching
A normal day unfolding then
The edge"

Matthew D. Mehlan
Excerpt from *The Edge*

Gail

CHAPTER 51—THE EDGE

2020

"Michael walked out on me after trashing all my make-up and ruining my clothes.

He was acting crazy. I don't know what to do. His phone is destroyed, and I can't get a hold of him. Have you heard from him?"

One evening in February, I received an unexpected text from Michael's most recent girlfriend. She always referred to him as Michael, not Mike. She had never communicated with me at all. I met her one time in January when we were in Kenosha and took Mike out for lunch and exchanged a few late Christmas gifts with him and our grandson. Sylvia had allowed us a brief visit while we were there. Mike and this girl met us at a hot dog place, and we had a nice but short visit. They had recently gotten an apartment together on the second story of her mother's house. I knew nothing about her at all yet had an uneasy feeling about all of it. I knew that Mike didn't like being alone.

Should I respond to this text? I thought about it for a few minutes, worried about getting in the middle of their relationship. I texted her back anyway.

"No, I haven't. What happened?" I asked, hoping to get more information. Her reply was a long and detailed story about what transpired between them. It sounded like a horrible fight.

"Do you think he's been using?"

"I don't think so. He just got so angry."

"It seems out of character for Michael unless something's going on."

"Yeah, I know. He's the kindest man I've ever known—I want him to come home."

"Well, if his phone is broken. I have no way of getting in touch with him."

"I know. I just wish I could find him."

"I'm sorry." It was all I could manage.

It dawned on me that we hadn't heard from Mike for several days, and he had been so good about staying in touch recently. The familiar fire of fear started burning in my belly, but I reminded myself to remain detached. I knew this probably meant relapse, and the fear turned to tears of sadness when I realized he only had five months left of his two-year rehabilitation program. There my son was again, at the *edge*, and there was *nothing* I could do.

I told Doug about the text message and that Mike didn't have a working phone.

"Oh well," he said with a sigh. "Always something. We'll have to wait for him to contact us."

Sure enough, the next day, we got a Facebook message from Mike about the phone. He could communicate using his computer when he had Wi-Fi. Doug messaged him and said he would see what he could do. We didn't want to purchase a new phone for him under the circumstances, but Doug spoke with our nephew, a whiz with technology. One of his friends had given him a broken phone, and he installed a new screen and got the phone working again. Mike could have it if he wanted it. Doug's sister drove the phone up to Kenosha, met Mike at a restaurant, fed him, and gave him the phone. He was able to insert his old sim card, and it worked. I believe there *are* angels out there, and some of them are family members.

Mike told us that he was accepted back into the sober living house and was looking for another job. He told Doug that he was still in the rehabilitation program but that the district attorney had extended his time until the end of December, an additional six months.

I had no idea at the time that the next six months would involve a complete lockdown due to COVID-19, racial unrest in Kenosha, and a contested election. What was happening in the world was surreal, and I had to stay calm, stay off social media, and stay focused on what was in front of me so that I didn't go crazy too. I kept putting one foot in front of the other. The phrase, *relapse is a part of recovery*, was my mantra.

LITTLE CAGES

Trapped inside little cages, trapped up little treasures
One-part female creature, two-part midnight feature
Don't you cry, don't you cry, don't you cry, don't you cry
No, don't you cry to me

Save all your speeches; save it for the jury.
Save all your energy, 'cuz no one buys a crier
"I don't feel guilty," you once said to me.
But guilt is the pain that will set you free; can't you see that?

You're trapped inside little cages, trapped up little treasures
One-part female creature, two-part midnight feature
Don't you cry, don't you cry, don't you cry, don't you cry
No, don't you cry to me

I can't understand a thing you just said to me, can't you see that?
That your tears give me all the power?
I'm the one who controls you now; no one cares about this
anymore.
You were mine to fill; you were mine to thrill
You would have been mine to kill if only you loved me still.

But you're inside little cages, trapped up little treasures
One-part female creature, two-part midnight feature
Printed up to perfect measure, sold for a rich man's pleasure.

Michael M. Mehlan

"You're trapped inside little cages, trapped up little treasures
One-part female creature, two-part midnight feature
Don't you cry, don't you cry, don't you cry, don't you cry
No, don't you cry to me."

Michael M. Mehlan
Excerpt from *Little Cages*

Michael

CHAPTER 52—RECOVERY IS LONELY

2020

Finding support is absolutely the hardest thing to do because everyone's recovery and life experiences are different. One very hard thing that people rarely understand is how lonely recovery can be. When you are overwhelmed with the idea that nobody is gonna understand your feelings and show you the kind of love and support that you need, sadly, for the most part, you're right. Nobody is you. People say things like: "I know it's hard," and "I'm proud of you," or "It's a tough thing to go through." But like a grieving person, you go off in your head with a guttural response: "THe f**k MAN!!" "YOu Don't KNow SHit ABout it!"

What you really mean is: "YOU WILL NEVER UNDERSTAND THE PAIN I HAVE, AND YOU NEVER WILL!"

That's the truth. The lie is that although people try their best to have sympathy and empathy for your situation and do their best to encourage you, most don't understand it a bit. Those of us in recovery have to accept these words as the best others can give us. Don't complain about getting coal just because it's not diamonds. Coal can at least be fuel to keep you going. Sometimes it's all others have to offer. Cherish it, just like you would the diamonds. You will find diamonds as long as you pay attention. You cannot escape the fact that you are suffering. We all suffer. Your pain is no more real to anyone else than it is to you. Don't be selfish in thinking you're alone.

You have to be patient. It takes a long time, a terribly long time, to break out of addiction cycles. First, there's withdrawal, then treatment, and mental health counseling. After that comes regulating your diet and adjusting sleep patterns. Exhaustion is always present, and with it, irritability, frustration, sickness, diarrhea, and sexual dysfunction, and that's just the beginning. Then you will be hit with post-acute withdrawal syndrome, which is even more of the same but spread out over a more extended period. Then you find yourself trying to find stability, support, and money to pay your bills. You will become an upstanding citizen again, attending to your grooming and everything life throws at you. Taking care of yourself feels like growing up all over again. You learn to set boundaries and recognize triggers and negative behaviors. Finally, you begin the journey of self-reflection and the process of forgiveness.

The worst part is, this whole process takes YEARS! Not days. Not weeks. Not months. But years! Even then, you could fall right back into the abyss all over again. It is a fall, and it's quick, and it's far, and the ground hurts. Maybe this time, it'll kill you. All the fear of relapse is there the entire time.

I can get angry, especially at those who say, "You made a choice to do drugs!" Well, I didn't want this to be my life. None of us can say we'll never be there. Someday you could be where I am. You just never know. That's how insidious this whole thing is. Free will and willpower are tough things on which to base recovery. It's not worth arguing about it if someone is trying. That trying takes many forms.

For some, that tree of trying never grows fruit at all, and this is, of course, terribly depressing and defeating.

As much as addiction is a medical disease, it's also an affliction of the spirit. Once you fix the diseased part and the mental health aspects are regulated, you have a whole spirit in yourself you've now gotta deal with. This spirit is one filled to the brim with crap. It's like cleaning out a hoarder's house and then flipping it to be a nice place to live. The tasks seem impossible, and addicts often don't want to do such hard work. Sometimes that work includes hurting others' feelings or ignoring your own. Sometimes that work includes slowly, patiently cleaning out the crap 'til it feels better inside, and it takes what seems like lifetimes to do so. Be patient. I know it's lonely, but just think how beautiful it might be to live outside the cage.

"I don't even care if I bump into whatever's near
I'm gonna keep moving!
I'm not one to give up. You know me better than that!
I'm working!
I need that check at the end of the month.
I'm gonna keep moving!
I'm gonna get paid enough to survive
So I quit complaining for once in my life."

Matthew D. Mehlan
Excerpt from *STEPPER, a.k.a. Work*

Michael

CHAPTER 53—
THE WALK HOME

2020

"One—Two—One—Two—One—Two," I say aloud—that's how many steps per sidewalk square it takes if I'm moving at a pace that gets me home fastest without wearing myself out after work. "One—Two—One—Two," I keep saying.

Home. That word has a lot of meaning to me or once did. Right now, it's just a place to rest my head, at the sober house. Hey, it's better than sleeping in my car, but that old beast doesn't get me anywhere since the city took away my license. The job's good—I got hired on at a local sandwich shop as a "chef de partier garde" manager. I make all the cold food, in case you don't know French. I work full time plus, about 45 hours a week, and it keeps me busy. I like the work; it keeps

GAIL MEHLAN | M. M. MEHLAN

my hands and feet moving, "One—Two—One—Two." The pay's not fantastic, but I make enough. It's the most I've ever made at a job. I work hard, and the head chef likes me well enough.

I walk home on the same path every night, through some of the darker parts of town. I think, where am I going? HOME, yeah, home, the little room I rent in the sober house. It's good enough, I guess. I miss my son, though, his little smile, and as of late, he tells me he misses me too, which feels good.

"Wish I was with ya, bug!" I say aloud.

I miss him every night, deep down in my soul. The longing hurts like cutting knives, and I feel the wounds if I think about it too long. I send money for him to his mother. It feels good to do that, even though I'd rather just have the TIME, ya know, quality time, "Miss ya bug!"

I lose these thoughts, and I'm back to it. "One—Two—One—Two." Gotta keep moving, or I'm done dead in the water. Things are getting better. I gotta keep telling myself that. Twelve more weeks is what I've got left of this stupid program, recovery and all. They keep trying to harass me about "dropping" (peeing in a little cup to make sure I'm not using again). I know, I know, comply and all that. But, I'm your program's golden boy. I'm clean, president of the sober house, working a full-time job, and paying my bills! I'm doing everything right. I'm sorry my job interferes with your little flaming dog hoops I have to jump through. I'm fine, though, great, in fact. I've got my little room, guitar, and bed to sleep in. It's great, yeah, it's great. The district attorney just needs to let me graduate from their little program. I took the meds, did the counseling, and went to group therapy. I did it all for two and a half years. Just let it rest now, please!

I admit I used those credit cards, I did, but I didn't take 'em in the first place! Twelve more weeks, and maybe it'll be done for good. "Dead to rights," as they say. I got caught, and I've gotta pay the price. I paid the price. I did the work and kept doing the work every day.

I take those steps, "One—Two—One—Two," and I keep moving, moving forward, clean and sober, for my son, my family, and everyone. I want to live, not become some "sobituary."

My life has been too long, with too many strange rides. It's been hard. It's always been hard, but I'm alive! Sometimes I feel like I've been alive for too long. Even Jesus made it to my age, 33, but then he was crucified. It must have been so hard for him to live that long in a mortal body. Let's hope they don't do that to me! I'm not a martyr, and I'm no savior. I'm simply a survivor, and tonight, I'm gonna keep walking. "One—Two—One—Two." 'Til I make it home.

A GOOD DAY

When early morning drunks get their fix,
they don't want to know what makes the world tick.
I'd hate to say goodbye again; I'd rather say hello to a friend.
How many dreams must I shatter today to make it a good day?

And how many lies, like tears, that I've cried
to make it a good day?

My hands are getting old; I can feel it in my bones
as I fix myself a breakfast.
The phone doesn't ring anymore as it did before,
and friends get old and move away.
How many dreams must I shatter today to make it a good day?

And how many lies, like tears, that I've cried
to make it a good day?

I know it's an old sentiment that takes my breath away
Now go away singing words while songs lament
You know I loved you only yesterday,
but never found the words to say, so I sang them.
How many dreams must I shatter today to make it a good day?

And how many lies, like tears, that I've cried
to make it a good day?

Only once, never twice, did I make a sacrifice
For a good day. For a good day, for a good day,
Let's make it a good day.
Let's make it a good day.

Jolly Jackson

"Only once, never twice, did I make a sacrifice
For a good day. For a good day, for a good day,
Let's make it a good day.
Let's make it a good day."

Jolly Jackson
Excerpt from *A Good Day*

Gail

CHAPTER 54—A GOOD DAY

2020

One day in June, the phone rang, surprising me.

"Hi, Grandma! I coming to your house!" I heard a little voice, sounding full of anticipation.

"You are? I am so excited to see you!" I responded.

"I 'cited too! I miss you so much. I love you!"

"Aw—I miss you too, buddy! What do you want to do when you come to visit Grandma?"

"I want to see Papa and Ne-e-e-na!" (His cousin)

"I hope we can get to see her. Maybe. Do you want to go out on the boat?"

"YES! Can I see Daddy? I want to see Daddy, too!"

"I'm not sure, buddy. I'll have to talk to your mommy about that."

We'd made arrangements for Sylvia to bring Douggie down to visit us. She would stay the night, leave the following morning, and then we would bring him home the next week. She agreed that it would be okay for Mike to see Douggie on our way back if we stayed with him. Whew! *Our* son would get a chance to see *his* son!

2020 will forever be known as the year of the coronavirus pandemic. States were shut down for months, and each one opened at different times and in different ways. We wanted to visit our son, who lived in the Chicago area with cousin "Ne-e-e-na," *and* Mike up in Kenosha, Wisconsin, which made things complicated. We planned to see *everyone* on our way to take Douggie home.

It had been almost two years since Mike's relapse in 2018 and subsequent stint in jail. He continued to do well. But because of Mike's slip-up in February, Douggie hadn't seen his father since we celebrated Christmas with him. The quarantine time was challenging because it also meant Mike was without work.

He moved back into the sober living house, and we agreed to help him pay his rent until things opened up. The district attorney allowed Mike to stay in the medically assisted recovery program, requiring him to wait another six months to complete it. He was on schedule to finish sometime in December. Mike was discouraged with the additional time but continued to maintain his sobriety and focus on the future. He assured us the recent slip was a minor *hiccup* and that he got back on track right away. I prayed every day that Mike would continue on the current path. When Michael spoke of his frustration with the court system and their rehabilitation program, I always responded that I was *grateful* they had given him this opportunity even when he didn't see it the same way. I appreciated the district attorney's willingness to keep Mike in the program.

About a week before Douggie came to visit, a miracle happened in Mike's life, and he was offered an excellent job cooking at a sandwich shop in Kenosha.

Our week with Douggie in Indiana was terrific. He sped around the neighborhood on his scooter, and we enjoyed time out on the pontoon boat with all of his cousins. The family came over for pizza and made a mess of the toys in Grandma's playroom. We even hit up a garage sale, social distancing, and found a Hot Wheels track that propelled cars around a loop for only a dollar. The littlest grandsons played with it for hours after I disinfected it!

During one of my car rides with the youngest boys, Douggie and his cousin, Kell, had a conversation in the back seat. They both reminded me of Mike when he was little. Douggie asked Kell what he wanted to be when he grew up. "I want to be an astronaut! What do you want to be, Douggie?" Kell asked.

When I heard that question and answer, my heart began to flutter. I listened with complete attention.

"*I* want to *build* rocket ships!" Douggie responded.

Our visit with Douggie went by quickly, and it was soon time to take him home.

The sun was shining, and the air was warm but not too hot when we headed up to Kenosha, a beautiful city on the shores of Lake Michigan. When we arrived at the sober living house, and Douggie saw Mike sitting on the front porch, he started screaming, "Daddy! I see my daddy! Hi, Daddy!" When he got out of the car, he added, "I missed you, Daddy!"

Mike gave him a big hug and said, "I've missed you so much too, kiddo! Do you want to come on in and see Daddy's house?"

"Sure!"

Mike took us inside and showed us all the common areas of the sober living house. It was surprisingly clean and organized. Mike had been chosen to be the house president, so he held a leadership role in managing the house and keeping it running smoothly. He seemed proud of his position and how he was handling things. He felt good about himself. He was also pleased that his new job was going well. He had completed two weeks of almost full-time work. I felt so proud of him and reassured, as well, that he was trying hard to walk through these tough times of the pandemic, keeping his head up and moving forward.

We picked up a hot dog picnic at a local shop and drove to a big park overlooking the lakefront. We were able to stay a safe distance from other people and still enjoy the fantastic view. After lunch, we played on a public playground that was not terribly crowded and lathered our hands with hand sanitizer afterward. We walked around the docks and looked at all the big boats, saw some huge lake salmon caught by some local fishermen, and Douggie scooted on his scooter along the path toward the rocky beach. We found so many beautiful rocks along the shore, took some pictures, and enjoyed the time together.

I told Mike about the conversation I'd had with the boys, so he looked for and found a video online about building a rocket ship out of a Coke bottle. He wanted to shoot it off using vinegar and baking soda in the emptied-out bottle. We ended up driving around town looking for an open hardware store so we could buy a cork for his experiment. Mike and his dad finally found one. We drove out of town to a local forest preserve with wide-open spaces.

Mike and Douggie assembled the rocket and attempted an official blast-off. The first flight was a bust, but the second attempt launched high into the sky! Douggie ran as fast as he could to retrieve the rocket to try again. The third launch backfired towards Mike's foot, but the force of the rocket was fun to watch even though it didn't go up. Luckily Mike wasn't hurt. We used up all of the vinegar, so we went to get some ice cream.

Wearing our masks, we entered the ice cream shop, and Douggie picked out a *pointy* cone with Super Friends flavored ice cream, bright blue with yellow, pink, and green speckles, the kind that makes your tongue and your whole mouth blue. Yum. It was lovely to sit outside and enjoy the day and listen to Mike and Douggie chat. It felt good to watch the two of them interact and laugh. After the ice cream, we walked closer to the boat docks, and Douggie played in the park for a few minutes before we took him home. He was happy to see his mom but the first words out of his mouth were, "I got to see Daddy!"

With so much uncertainty surrounding addiction, we can never predict the future. I knew in my heart that Douggie loved his dad. It gave me hope that there could be a friendly relationship between Mike and his ex-fiancé down the road. There was no room for my two cents on their future relationship, though. It was between the two of them. All I knew was that *I* was committed to trying to stay in touch with Sylvia with the hopes that *we* could be a part of Douggie's life for now and in the future.

After we dropped Douggie off at home, we decided to go out to eat. Our favorite German restaurant had some outside seating available where we could enjoy a good meal. It was the first time we'd eaten out at a restaurant since the stay-at-home orders started in mid-March; we were excited. It was such a beautiful evening, and we sat under a tree and enjoyed the delicious German food. We spent the next couple of hours talking, listening, and spending time together. We shared stories, laughter, and most of all, love. We decided that we had experienced a good day, no matter what happened in the future. It was a gift.

As we prepared to leave, Mike leaned over and hugged me, saying, "Thank you. It was a good day—one *good* day at a time."

"I've picked you. I haven't dropped you.
Don't panic. I'm with you.
There's no need for your fear, for
I'm your God.
I'll give you strength. I'll help you.
I'll hold you steady, keep a firm grip on you.
Count on it: Everyone who had it in for you will
End up in the cold—real losers.
Those who worked against you
Will end up empty-handed—
Nothing to show for their lives.
When you go out looking for
Your old adversaries—
You won't find them—
Not a trace of your old enemies,
That's right. Because I, your
God, have a firm grip on you and
I'm not letting go."

Isaiah 41:10-13 (MSG)

Mike sent me this as his new favorite verse
while he was in the Dominican Republic in 2005.

Gail

CHAPTER 55—EPILOGUE

2021

I ended this book with a good day for a reason. This story is not
over yet. As long as my son, Mike, is alive, there is a *chance* that he

will continue to live a good life. I hope he has many, many more good days that evolve into good months and good years! There are no guarantees. I've always been on a quest to find a happy ending to our story. A friend told me once, "Maybe it's not about the happy ending. Maybe it's about the story."

I've learned over the years that addiction *is* a disease and a relapsing one. We say this in our Twelve-Step groups. Science and medicine have also proven it to be true. It is a disease that needs treatment. It may need to be treated medically and psychologically for a *lifetime*. It is *not* a weakness nor a moral failing. I read, studied, listened, and learned many things about this disease of addiction as I've lived through it with Mike. I watched him struggle through the ups and downs. I always wanted him to choose *life*. I hope he knows that my understanding of this disease goes only so far. All my learning helped me see how hard it is to overcome addiction. I *know* he is doing his best to keep moving forward. No one can choose life for him but himself. No one can choose life for me but myself. Today, I give thanks that we continue loving and understanding each other through *all* of the trouble we've experienced.

I believe that very few people have *never* been shaped by or experienced life with an addict. Addiction is pervasive in today's world. David Sheff, author of *Clean: Overcoming Addiction and Ending America's Greatest Tragedy*, writes, "Almost 80% of America's children under eighteen have used alcohol, and half have smoked marijuana or tried other drugs…Approximately one in twelve Americans over the age of twelve is addicted to drugs. In addition to the deaths it causes, substance abuse leads to more illnesses than any other preventable health condition…Drugs are also the number one cause of crime…The total overall cost of drug abuse in the United States exceeds $400 billion a year…the statistics describe only the scope of the problem, not the suffering, which is immeasurable… Drug abusers and addicts can do more than get off drugs; they can achieve mental health…"

These statistics are overwhelming. For me, they are astonishing. These facts are, however, right in line with my own experiences. The hope every parent has for their children is for their lives to have meaning. For parents of addicted children, this is incredibly difficult and heart-wrenching when hope and expectations go down the drain in the face of addiction. Treatment choices are extremely limited and challenging when treatment is only available for those with financial resources, connections to services, and good insurance. Very little data is available regarding the success of new treatment options, including medically assisted treatment. Addicts who are caught in the web of the justice system, as Mike was, are asked to try new medications and enter into court-supervised treatment programs when they are vulnerable and desperate to get out of jail. They want to end up with a clean record, so they agree to participate in experimental treatment. I believe these programs help, and addicts *can* get healthy through them, but their choices are not real *choices*. As Mike said, "What choice was I given, Mom, twelve years in jail or a forced treatment program? What kind of real choice *is* that?"

I hope that addicts in the justice system will be treated with *respect* and *genuine* care as they move through this challenging process, no matter their circumstances. Treatment can't work within a broken system. With some new approaches to treatment, extra support for mental health, and care for their physical bodies with adequate health insurance, I believe there can be hope for addicts, *one good day at a time*.

These 20 years of loving an addict have shown me the many paradoxes of this particular life. Things were never what I thought they would be. That is a paradox. I hope the reader will find the common threads we all share. In her book, *Almost Everything:*

Notes on Hope, Anne Lamott writes, "All truth is paradox. Everything in life has innate contradictions. 'I know one thing that I know nothing.' Socrates said."

When I was teaching, I had a poster on the doorway that I entered every day. It said, "What did I come here to *teach*? What did I come here to *learn*?"

It reminded me that I could learn as much if not more than I could teach. Each moment was an opportunity for growth or understanding. I always paused on that threshold and accepted that I was entering into that liminal space of either teaching, learning, or *both*.

What have I learned throughout this journey of addiction and recovery? I have learned that things don't always *appear* superficially to be what God *intends for us to understand* more deeply. God's ways *are* mysterious sometimes. I believe God accepts us through our most humble attempts at understanding. I know we are beloved. The road to recovery for each of us is a journey of self-knowledge and hard work. I must continue to be open to any future lessons. Maybe I have been teaching myself along the way. I hope I never stop.

—I have to walk through the *darkness* to notice the *light*. The symbolism of the sunflower has long been a very striking image and metaphor for me of life. In the light, the darkness transforms seeds buried under the soil before receiving the gift of life, a resurrection of sorts. The light of the sun is what the sunflowers follow to provide their source of energy and warmth. The plants need to grow tall before their beautiful blooms appear. The process of this growth takes time. I've experienced some dark times, but the light has always returned with the brightness of the sun each day, with the smile on a child's face or a friend's understanding heart. I have walked through darkness, but now I notice the light when it shows up in my life, and I'm grateful for that. Situations and scenes always seem entirely different from the very moment that light enters the space. That moment of experiencing the light is when I feel genuinely *"Among the Sunflowers."* A spiritual companion *will* walk through the darkness with me and bear life's burdens *with* me.

—I must turn my *guilt* into self-care and *acceptance*. I didn't need to be *perfect,* and I didn't need to *fix* anyone. I learned to love, deeply love my *imperfect* family and myself.

—When I was in *denial* about what was happening, it prevented me from *accepting reality* and seeing *my* part in the problem. Denial just led to more frustration and indignation. Acceptance led to peace and the strength to find solutions.

—There was *power* in *powerlessness*. I received more power when I accepted my own limitations and let God handle things. I began to allow the power of the Spirit to find me and help me notice God's presence in the most unlikely places when I least expected it. Stop, take a moment, and look around you. You might be standing on *sacred* ground.

—God might look different from how I once perceived him. My upbringing shaped my faith, believing God was an unchangeable force. I understand now that *we* were created in the image of God. When I felt God had left me alone to deal with the mess and that *my* prayers didn't count, I had a revelation. The *Divine* Love of God showed up for me as a *woman*, a *mother,* inside of *me*. Even in those situations when I didn't realize it, feel it or notice the presence of God, *I* was there. *God was there.*

—*Conflict* is normal: accepting and recognizing the *differences* between people helped me become *whole*. If I take the time to open the blinds to see things differently, I do not feel so separate from others. I listen and try to understand, take a breath—and let things marinate before responding. Feelings are not facts, and I must allow feelings, good and bad, to be a part of who I am as a *whole* person.

—*Independence* is built upon *dependence*. Addiction is a disease that affects the whole family. Sometimes I just wanted to escape it, but I would not have found serenity by leaving my family behind. Instead, I found it by *uniting* with people in recovery groups and realizing that I was not alone in the recovery process.

—*Detachment* with love from an addicted loved one is a journey *together*. I used to think that addiction had robbed me of my loved one. What happened was that it robbed me of my life. When I attached to the recovery process myself, and to a spiritual path of trusting God to hold up the other end of the yoke, I was more able to detach from the things that hurt me. When I attached myself to others on the recovery path in mutual support Twelve-Step groups, I was healthier and happier walking through my *own* life.

—When the *negative* thoughts controlled the vision, it trapped me in that negativity. When given a positive image, *I* could move forward freely with hope, and my loved ones could also move forward. When I sit and dwell on the negative and hold my little *pity party*, I miss the *joy* that could be right in front of me.

—If I *judge* others, I am *convicted* and locked into a cell of my own thinking. And this cell, created by me, will not break open until I accept and offer *forgiveness* over and over again. I cannot do this alone. God helps me with this, even when I am incapable of it. The power of forgiveness was real even when I didn't believe I gave it. Mike told me one day, "You said you *missed a chance* to offer forgiveness—but in the end, *I learned* forgiveness."

—I must look *forward* with hope, and I cannot *look back*. I am right now where I am meant to be. I cannot carry the baggage of the past into the future with me. Looking back gives power to the pain. Tomorrow is a new day.

—*Failure* in one person's life can look much like *success* for another. Love can be the lens that I must use to see what I have been blind to in *myself* and *others. We are all beloved.*

—*Shame* is never helpful, and it is often something we place upon ourselves. Shame is powerful but never leads us to a healthy place. I felt ashamed because addiction had hit *our* family. It takes *courage* to stand tall and *heal* from this disease for all those involved in the situation. As more information about the medical and psychological causes of addiction is revealed, perhaps the negative stigma of addiction will decrease. We must continue to be *shameless* in our *recovery.*

—R*elapse* is a part of *recovery.* Addiction is a disease and a relapsing one that cannot be completely cured but can be managed. Addiction can go into remission, just as other medical conditions do. Science, both medical and psychological, can offer us critical research about addiction and what methods work for addicts so that they are able to understand and accept help when appropriate to do so. Suppose all I offer to my addicted loved ones is *contempt* and *conviction,* especially in the face of relapse? I would miss giving them *the understanding, compassion, and support* they need to get back to the work of recovery.

—A mother's *love* for her child *is not easily broken or destroyed.* That bond of love can become even stronger *because* of and *despite* the struggles.

—In the end, there may still be *unanswered questions.* By learning to *love the questions* and leaning into the uncertainties, I trust that God will certainly bring me to that place of understanding and peace in God's own time.

—*Laughter* can follow *tears and sadness.* Laughter can clear up the shadows and let the sunlight into you and every life that touches you. Laugh frequently. It's what leads to the next *good day.*

BROKEN SYSTEM

You were so young when you learned to play guitar,
You told mom and dad you could be a star.
You were only sixteen when you learned how to rock n' roll.
You had your first drink, and you played to impress the girls.
And then you turned eighteen,
And though you were clean-cut,
You were just burnt out and totally obscene.

Cause'
Everything you do in this world seems wrong,
You can't fight a broken system
Everything you are is in your songs,
But nobody is listening.

You're twenty-two; you should've stayed in school,
You think you're so smart, man that you're nobody's fool,
When you pick up that bottle, and you drink it down
Looking for that elusive perfect sound.
You pray every night
For success from behind the mic stand
But no one is gonna sit there
And put money in your clammy hands, no, no, no.
And everybody thinks you should just trade it in,
But you wouldn't dare,
No, I wouldn't dare.

When you put your entire world
Into a six-string
It only gives you
Pain and suffering
You want la da dee da?

I got your la da dee da.
I got your la da dee da right here.

Cause'
Everything you do in this world seems wrong,
You can't fight a broken system
Everything you are is in your songs,
But nobody is listening.

Michael M. Mehlan

Invest in Who Is Like God?

The stock is rising
The stock is rising
The cock is confused
When the sun refuses

Gone are the days lamenting
Gone are the days!
Singing sad songs like this one
but nothing has changed

The stock is rising
The stock is rising
Rub a dub, dub
Three men at the club
These perverts will be banished

"They have planted trees without fruit, in my name,
In a shameful manner."

The Hurricane
& The G O A T
The brother
The father-in-law
The Archangel
& The King

The cyst and its
Razorblade

Who is like God? Who has
The same birthday as God?

Who is the gift?
Who is full of Grace?
Who is Worthy of Love?
Who is Worthy of Love?
Find them for me

We want to make you well!
We want to make you well.
We know what well is!
And it's profitable.

The stock is rising
The stock is rising

The cock is confused
The Queen hath refused it
Off with his head
Or off with the rest
Is it a fungus or a condition?
Retribution or attrition?
Contribution or prescription?
Contrition?
Or revenge?

Who is the gift?
Who is full of Grace?
Who is Worthy of Love?
Who is Worthy of Love?

Will you find them for me?
I'll sing hymns of commitment
Will you find them for me?

I'll sing hymns
I'll sing hymns

The stock is rising
The stock is rising
The cock will now be used
To propagate the species
The seed must be sown
And then you will be sentenced
To a genderless motherhood
of unemployment

We want to make you well!
We want to make you well.
We know what well is!
And it's profitable.

"They have planted trees without fruit, in my name,
In a shameful manner."

By the power vested in me
I give you this expensive medicine
That you must purchase for eternity
On minimum wage

Rub a dub, dub
These misfits on drugs and
Who do you think they be?
A brother, a mother loved by another
None had invested in these:
ALKS, JNJ, INVVY, OPNT, AZN, MRK, PFE, etc…

Matthew D. Mehlan

THE SEPTET

I (1.)
I am good
I am at peace
I know myself
I am aware of my surroundings
I am moving even though I am still
I know my thoughts, but my path is not set by them
I know my actions, am willing to change, moving
   to right actions
I know the objects set forth before me
I know the obstacles in my path
I will not be stopped, only diverted
I am a cause
I think about good intentions
I am fully aware of my body, my brain, and my soul—
These are not illusions

II (2.)
Be able to see past the illusions
They can be blinding
Give yourself the freedom to believe (everything and nothing)
Taking what is true and piecing it together through patience
and humility
Know the reality
Acknowledge the lies
Making it a discernment
Choosing for yourself, your own path
Forgive anyone and everyone who has wronged you
No matter how serious the offense
Anger and strife are the cause for a lack of understanding
We feel it in our bodies, environment, and soul

We must be aware of these and sacrifice our emotions for
the settling of the mind
We must find the source of forgiveness
Forgiveness is the fruit of the world and our ultimate peace

III (3.)
Love one another and banish hate from your mind
Hate builds up no family for support
No one can carry the burden alone
I know what I feel
I know how to feel
I have knowledge of my range in emotions and know how
to use them
I will not use my emotions as a weapon against my friends
or enemies
I will not use my emotions as an excuse for my actions
BUT I WILL FEEL STRONGLY
Empathy, sympathy, compassion, and mercy
Grace for grace; person to person

IV (4.)
Are you afraid?
What or whom are you afraid of?
Knowing will help overcome this fear
The simplest answer is usually the correct one
But may not be the most obvious
I will make a change
To not live in fear
Even of death for which is my end
Are you hungry? Have something to eat
Are you angry? Resolve the conflict
Are you lonely? Find a friend

Are you tired? Have a rest
These will lead to fear.
We must find the end of it.

V (5.)
Are you an animal?
You are !!!
When your basic needs are not met
This drives the mind to deviant—criminal—destructive
behavior
Take care of yourself
Eat and drink, walk and move
Clean yourself--
Clean body
Clean thoughts
Clean clothes
Clean world
Now allow yourself to be more than the animal
Do not give in to the cravings that destroy you
Use your mind when your body is taken care of
YOU CAN

VI (6.)
Music and art are good
They must be learned, practiced, and part of your everyday
Part of your living
I will dance
I will sing
I will play the rhythms I feel, and I know
I will be disciplined and feel their vibration
I will show these things to be true
I will observe the colors I see

For I can only see this small portion of reality
But I must be aware and in its presence
Then it will flow out of me
Create because I can
It is in me, and I will not deny this of myself
I know I can be more

VII (7.)
Love and be loved
Solitude traps my soul in a burden of anguish
Sadness cannot be relinquished from my mind alone
For warmth and hospitality, and kindness builds up a strong family
It allows for a sense of community to rise
Receive with gladness all good things
Expect nothing from mistrust
Give all that you are able
Blood sweat, and tears for good
Expect nothing in return
And love will find you in abundance
Love is the most you can give
And once you give it
Those that have it can get nothing more from you
It is the greatest gift

I may not be a model man, but I know in my mind how;
        goals must be set and mantras must abide.
            Words have been kind to me lately.

Jolly Jackson

UNRELENTING JOY

Growing smiles,
Hugging hands
Each day stretches on forever
without seeing your learning face
"Wow, how big you've grown."
I'll say, "What a glorious day!"
I will not miss another moment
Love will find its way in,
un-avoided crushing torrents
Growing smiles,
Hugging hands
Time is but slowly passing,
the drop of single grains of sand
The journey has been hard
in these harsh and empty lands
I pray for dreams of unrelenting joy
For just one embrace from my son
The little boy—

Jolly Jackson

Michael

POSTSCRIPT—RAINBOW CONNECTION

2021

Almost home—I tell myself as I round the corner to the brick building I call my home. That word still doesn't sit right with me anymore *because home isn't a place; it's a feeling. My phone *Ding* goes off, and it's Sylvia with a text that says, "On my way." She's bringing Douggie over for his overnight at "Daddy's House." I couldn't be happier. I look forward to this day every week. My time with him is so precious to me. By the time I'm done cooking brunch on Sundays at the restaurant, I'm practically running out the door to greet his smiling face. My job is very tolling, 40-50 hours a week, hundreds of covers a day. Being a chef isn't bad; it's just exhausting. My bones almost hurt, but it's worth it. A four-year-old boy smiling and saying, "Hi, Daddy!" moves every damn atom in my body to go, "One, two, one—" just keep going, never stop.*

I pop the key in the door. I'm home. I shower, get dressed, and am back out the door to stand on the corner and wait. *Ding* "Here." Sylvia's black SUV pulls up in front of my apartment.

"DAAAADDDDDYYYY!" I hear before the rear driver-side door even slides open.

"Hey, Bug! I missed you so much!" I say as he runs over and hugs me around the neck.

"I missed you too," He says, "I'ma tell you, something Daddy."

"What's that, Kiddo?"

"I got some new cars, and, um, one's red, and they go fast, and um, um, um, they're jus' so-o-o-o cool!" in a true excited child-like fashion. The words fly around faster than my son's brain can send them to his lips. I see myself so much in this boy. I still find that sometimes I can't get the words out fast enough.

"That's awesome, Kiddo; well, let's get inside. It's cold out here. Go give your mom a hug and kiss goodbye." He runs over and hugs his mother, and she kisses him on the forehead and says,

"Have fun with your dad." She smiles, knowing that he will be happy and safe with me. This confidence in caring for my child has been a long time coming. She and I are still healing, and I wouldn't say we're friends, but we are definitely co-parenting, and that's the

best I think we could hope for. I was invited to Douggie's birthday party with her family for the first time in three years. I haven't been allowed to go before this, but now I'm invited, which means we are moving forward.

Sylvia has her life working at the hospital. She has a new boyfriend, and they are happy. We've made it to a point I like to call acceptance. We had a child together and are raising that child the best way we can. I'm clean and have a job, my own place, and a wonderful new girlfriend. I get to see my son.

We turn the corner and climb the stairs. He stomps all the way up. We get inside and warm up, and I say to him in a frog voice, "So little Douggie, what do you wanna do today?" I've perfected the best imitation of a Muppet voice to the annoyance of my coworkers and girlfriend.

"What's that voice, Daddy?' Douggie is laughing at me and thinking I'm a big goof.

"It's Kermit, the frog—you don't know who Kermit is?" I said, smiling wide.

So, I go into my record collection, find my Muppet movie soundtrack, and put it on the turntable. The opening banjo is strumming along in my head. I know this. I've known it since I was his age. It occupies a place in my mind from childhood, always a pleasant memory, a happy place for me, and I want it to be the same for my son, in my home, our home.

As the song chimes out in the background and I sing along in my best "ribbity" voice, Douggie stops and looks at me, puts his cars down, and runs over and gives me a bear hug around my legs. I'm reeling at the unexpected unsolicited hug, "What's up, Buggy?" I say, surprised.

"I love you, Daddy. You're the best, Daddy." He was obviously feeling how I was feeling, longing to have this to be the normal, for this to be what life is like for us now, father and son, happy. What do you say to a prodigal father? Douggie is glad I'm back in his life. The end is just the beginning, and so on forever. Is this the beginning? Or is it the ending? At least, this is the goal.

As the record scratching behind me comes to repose, and tears start down my cheek, I hear the words about a rainbow connection, the lovers, the dreamers, and me. These words always draw me back to my childhood.

A drug addict once told me, high as a kite, "A rainbow only ends when you're on the ground. From heaven, it just keeps going forever in a circle. The gold was at your feet the whole time." I always thought that was just some high delusional wisdom from a drug addict, but now I understand, now I see. If you believe in it, you can make it so. But it takes the faith of a child, a dreamer, to see the rainbow full of love. It takes time, hard work, and keeping your feet firmly on the ground. That's where the gold is.

"Daddy, what's wrong?"

I swallow hard and say, "Nothing is wrong, Buggy, absolutely nothing at all!" as I smile wide, joyful tears in my eyes,

"Nothing, just so happy you're here."

My whole life flashes before my eyes, every struggle, every empty space in my heart, just gone. I feel full. I have everything I believed in, everything I worked for, and I earned it.

"So, what are we doing today, Kiddo?" I ask, looking my son in the eyes, everything in the world seemingly perfect for a moment.

"It's just a good day, Daddy. Let's just play cars."

"Okay, Bug, I'm just glad you're here to see today with me." I laugh, knowing things he will never know or remember. He won't know his father as the person he was: jail, drugs, homeless, beaten, broken, and tired. He won't remember that. It was just a moment, but I will remember it. I'll remember all of it forever, and today we both found life.

"I FOUND IT! I've found myself again," I say to the lover, the dreamer, and me.

THE END #2

I cannot see the end
Not because it is far
But because it is too beautiful to look at
I cannot see the path
Not because it is hidden
But because I have no one to show me the way
So maybe, just maybe,
Can I make a path of my own?
Perhaps show myself the way?
For I know the end is bright
And it's oh, so beautiful
But it would be nice
To have some company
On this journey to find this glorious end
It's not because I need you
It's not because I want you
It's because I know you will be there
Would you like to see the end with me?

Jolly Jackson

"Joy and sorrow…light and darkness…
Simple symmetries of life that dwell in
the breath of the prayers of believers—
answers to their fervent pleas, not always
visible or understood in this mortal life."

Arlene Barker
Excerpt from *Candlemas Prayer*
(Barker, 2020)

Gail

BREATH AND LIFE

2022

"Take a breath," the instructor said on the television as I watched my early morning workout dance video. "Take a breath and move through the space around you, scooping up the energy you need and bringing it in towards you—touch your palms together and let the energy flow through you—take another breath, a deep one, and let the energy surround you—make it the energy of gratitude. What are you grateful for today?"

The stale air in the room moved in and out of my body, and I tried to calm myself. I let myself move to the music and flow with it, arms and head moving, releasing the breath moving in and out of this vulnerable body. Am I grateful today? My mind went through the list. A roof over my head. Plenty to eat. Heat. Water. A good, strong marriage. Family. Seven grandchildren. Children. Then I get stuck.

Breath continued to flow in and out of my body even as my

mind wandered. I moved through the rest of the workout, anxious to be done. What was happening? The current circumstances were bothering me. My mind wouldn't move forward today to see the gratitude beyond the immediate situation. I know that I must accept life on life's terms. I took a breath and moved on with my day, but my head and heart were stuck. Stuck in the "symmetries of life," joy and sorrow, light and darkness—

My son called us a few weeks ago. He complained that he didn't feel well, and was coughing and feverish. Because he was sick, he couldn't go to his job at a local diner. He needed the money and tips to pay his rent, and a recent breakup left him without a place to stay. He seemed desperate.

Doug and I talked it over and decided we'd ask Mike if he wanted to stay with us for a while in Indiana. Neither of us wanted him out on the streets in January.

Oh! How I wish it were possible to turn our story into a series of events that would stop at a crucial moment in the narrative, and at that moment, the story could pivot and take various turns. It would be a "choose your own adventure" story, but I would be in charge of the ending choices. With my propensity for resolutions, my options would have only positive outcomes. I want a happy ending. Period.

My mother's heart was so afraid he would find himself out on the street with no car, no phone, none of his psyche medications, and sick with what turned out to be COVID. It was a life-or-death situation, and I won't apologize for acting quickly. Mike agreed to come, and we drove up to get him and collect a few of his belongings from his apartment.

Things had been going so well for him. Having Mike here with us was a story all of its own. It has not been easy, and I instantly yearned to have my peaceful home back. I am so tired of the problematic situations that seem to follow Mike around and rear their angry head like the dragon in Mike's poetry, just as the story starts toward a happy ending. I saw a troubled young man while our son lived with us. My heart ached for him. Living in our home provided no relief from the pain of the trauma he experienced when his world fell apart.

When we picked him up, he was distraught, frustrated, lonely, and lost. One moment he'd ask for help, and then the next, he was frustrated at being here, confined to our house with no car, no money, and nothing to do but watch television. It was hard for me not to feel sorry for him, however. It would have been more difficult to send him off on his own, alone.

I watched Mike one day, taking his bow and arrows outside with a tiny handmade target, making attempts at a bull's eye. It seemed elusive. I try to be patient and loving, but I still see him as unhappy and depressed. I'd hoped he would be motivated to get some help, but the resources are hard to access, and it's challenging for those who don't have the financial means to get quality insurance. It's *his* process. He says he's trying. I'm trying, too. Patience doesn't come easy. I don't know what I expect from him. Expectations fast forward into resentments. That has never worked for us before.

Miraculously, sleep has not evaded me this time around.

We've had thought-provoking discussions about his numerous dreams and thoughts about returning to his faith. If he's not bullshitting me, it could be something *he* could hold onto during this crisis. God has held my hand through it all, and I know *I* am powerless. I still cling to hope.

The thing is—I want to wrap this story up with a bow and move on. I was doing that with my life. But the truth is, this situation has been nothing more than an inconvenience. I am trying not to let it hinder my health or sanity. I find myself face to face, looking at my son, the child of my heart, with such deep compassion. I am not in control. I *see* that he is struggling, and I know *he is powerless too.*

I still think about the waves that hit the shore repeatedly when I am near the ocean. They remind me to forgive and offer love as best I can over and over again. Those ocean waves gave me strength. I need that power, so my forgiveness doesn't become a form of *unhealthy* help. My pleas to God for my son may *not* be answered in this lifetime, "in this mortal life," or with my human understanding. I *know* that Jesus, the tender shepherd, constantly searches for the lost sheep and doesn't get too frustrated when the sheep keep getting lost. Perhaps Mike's *not* lost, just on a different path. Maybe, the tender shepherd simply has Mike over his shoulder, carrying him back to *his* own future, whatever that may be.

Mike has found a job at a local restaurant and a small apartment. He's also purchased a car and is taking steps toward his physical and mental health. I count the steps, and I watch him move ahead. *"One—Two—One—Two,"* I am grateful for each one. I add all that to my unfinished gratitude list. As much as I want to, I cannot see where the story will eventually lead.

The are many mysteries set before me to ponder. Even as I write this, my son's life is being formulated by a power I *know* exists. His life is yet to unfold. He has value and is *not* a problem to be solved but a *person worthy of love.* The uncertainty always makes me pause because, for my son, it seems to always carry a shadow over it. But I keep breathing in and out, in and out. Breath is life. Darkness seems to permeate, but it is temporary. Historically and without fail, the sun comes up each day, bringing light to the sunflowers. It will shine its light again tomorrow—I want to be here and awake to see the sunrise.

Jesus, tender Shepherd, hear me.
Bless us all tonight.
Through the darkness,
keep us safe
'Til morning light. AMEN

A bedtime prayer taught to our family by
Grandma Lee Mehlan.

ABOUT THE AUTHORS

Gail Mehlan, 70, is a retired bilingual/ESL teacher. She lives in Cicero, Indiana, with her husband, Doug of 48 years. They live close to daughter Michelle, and 4 of their 7 grandchildren. Much of this story was recorded in personal journals the author kept during the actual time of the events spoken  about. She is an avid journal writer. Gail is actively involved with her church, Roots of Life, and also enjoys sewing and getting together with her group of writing friends. Gail is still very involved with her local recovery group. Gail loves being involved with her grandchildren who bring her lots of joy and many *sunflower* moments.

Michael M. Mehlan, 36, is a musician, artist, and poet. He is a fantastic cook and a loving father to one son. He lives in Cicero, Indiana and works at a local restaurant in town.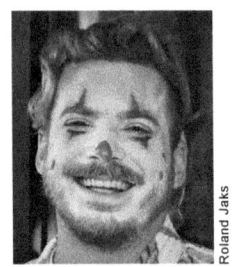

Comments, Notes, Permissions, and Resources

Introduction

Al-Anon Family Group Inc. 1992. Quote is taken from *Courage to Change*, copyright 1992 by Al-Anon Family Group Headquarters, Inc. Page 111 (April 20). Reprinted by permission of Al-Anon Family Group Headquarters, Inc. Permission to reprint does not mean that Al-Anon Family Group Headquarters, Inc. had reviewed or approved the contents of this publication or that Al-Anon Family Group Headquarters, Inc. necessarily agrees with the views expressed herein. Al-Anon is a program of recovery for families and friends of alcoholics—use of these excerpts in any non-Al-Anon context does not imply endorsement or affiliation by Al-Anon.

Part One

Are, Sarah. 2016. *The Wilderness is a Place Where We Are Brave*, Poetry by Rev. Sarah Are, Sanctified Art LLC. Reprinted with permission. www.sanctifiedart.org

Chapter 1—Darkness

Jackson, Jolly. 2020. Excerpt from *The Cracks*, Poetry by Jolly Jackson, *Jolly for Now? Rainbows, Unicorns and Devils*, Amazon Kindle. Reprinted with permission of the author.

Chapter 2—Bad Mother

Jackson, Jolly. 2020. Excerpt from *Motherhood—A War*, Poetry by Jolly Jackson, *Jolly for Now? Rainbows, Unicorns and Devils*, Amazon Kindle. Reprinted with permission of the author.

Jackson, Jolly. 2020. *Questions*, Poetry by Jolly Jackson, *Jolly for Now? Rainbows, Unicorns and Devils*, Amazon Kindle. Reprinted with permission of the author.

Chapter 3—Sometime in the Year 2001

Mehlan, Michael M. 2022. Excerpt from *None*, Poetry by M. M. Mehlan, *Jolly for Now?*, Revised Edition. GM Sunflower Creative Arts. Printed with permission of the author.

Floyd, Pink. 1975. *Wish You Were Here*. Comp. David Waters and Roger Gilmore.

Chapter 4—Why Did You Even Have Me?

Jackson, Jolly. 2020. *Under the Seas of this Revolution*, Poetry by Jolly Jackson, *Jolly for Now? Rainbows, Unicorns and Devils*, Amazon Kindle. Reprinted with permission of the author.

Chapter 5—Here I am, Lord

Jackson, Jolly. 2020. *Pills*, Poetry by Jolly Jackson, *Jolly for Now? Rainbows, Unicorns and Devils*, Amazon Kindle. Reprinted with permission of the author.

Jackson, Jolly. 2020. *Hunger*, Poetry by Jolly Jackson, *Jolly for Now? Rainbows, Unicorns and Devils*, Amazon Kindle. Reprinted with permission of the author.

Chapter 6—Help

Jackson, Jolly. 2020. *Headache#1, Headache #2*, Poetry by Jolly Jackson, *Jolly for Now? Rainbows, Unicorns and Devils*, Amazon Kindle. Reprinted with permission of the author.

Chapter 7—September 11, 2001

Jackson, Jolly. 2020. *Dry*, Poetry by Jolly Jackson, *Jolly for Now? Rainbows, Unicorns and Devils*, Amazon Kindle. Reprinted with permission of the author.

Mehlan, Gail. 2001. *Shoebox*, Unpublished poetry.

Chapter 8—Clear Lake

Mehlan, Michael. 2011. *Clear Lake*, Unpublished lyrics. Reprinted with permission of the composer.

Information on the use of DXM and "Robotripping": I did not visit a specific website the day I found the paper folded on Michael's dresser. Michael would later tell me that he stole DXM cough and cold medications to help him ease the withdrawal symptoms he experienced from other drugs he had become addicted to, such as cocaine and heroin. An internet search of "robotripping" will reveal similar information regarding the use of DXM or dextromethorphan.

Chapter 9—Phone Call

Mehlan, Matthew. 2007. Excerpt from *What They Said*, From the album, *Lucas*. Comp. Matthew D. Mehlan. Ghostly, International. Reprinted with permission of the composer.

Mehlan, Michael. 2010. *Chess with Myself*, Unpublished poetry. Reprinted with permission of the author.

Chapter 10—Oh! Oh! Oh! Another Day

Mehlan, Michael. 2010. *Chess with Myself*, Unpublished poetry. Reprinted with permission of the author.

Chapter 11—Kaleidoscope

Mehlan, Michael. 2010. *Looking at the Sun with a Kaleidoscope*, Unpublished poetry. Reprinted with permission of the author.

Jackson, Jolly. 2020. Excerpt from *I Love You*, Poetry by Jolly Jackson, *Jolly for Now? Rainbows, Unicorns and Devils*, Amazon Kindle. Reprinted with permission of the author.

Chapter 12—Escaping to Europe

Saying attributed to Confucius. Public Domain

Jackson, Jolly. 2020. *Empty Vessels*, Poetry by Jolly Jackson, *Jolly for Now? Rainbows, Unicorns and Devils*, Amazon Kindle. Reprinted with permission of the author.

Chapter 13—You've Got to have Friends

Chapter 14—God Needs More Time

Mehlan, Gail. 2004. *A Mother's Prayer*, Unpublished poetry.

Chapter 15—Arrested

Jackson, Jolly. 2020. *Prayer #1*, Poetry by Jolly Jackson, *Jolly for Now? Rainbows, Unicorns and Devils*, Amazon Kindle. Reprinted with permission of the author.

Jackson, Jolly. 2020. *Travesty*, Poetry by Jolly Jackson, *Jolly for Now? Rainbows, Unicorns and Devils*, Amazon Kindle. Reprinted with permission of the author.

Chapter 16—Being Judged

Mehlan, Matthew. 2007. Excerpt from *Sickness*, From the album, *Lucas*. Comp. Matthew D. Mehlan. Ghostly, International. Reprinted with permission of the composer.

Mehlan, Gail. 2004. *Let Go!*, Unpublished poetry.

Jackson, Jolly. 2020. *The Killer*, Poetry by Jolly Jackson, *Jolly for Now? Rainbows, Unicorns and Devils*, Amazon Kindle. Reprinted with permission of the author.

Chapter 17—Stolen Love

Mehlan, Michael. 2011. *Clear Lake*, Unpublished lyrics. Reprinted with permission of the composer.

Chapter 18—Rearview Mirror

Rearview Mirror first appeared as a short story in an anthology of local writers, poets, and musicians. 2018. *The Polk Street Review 2018: Fact or Fiction? YOU Decide.* Edited by Logan Street Sanctuary, Inc. Noblesville, IN: Logan Street Sanctuary Press. Pages 218-220.

Mehlan, Michael. 2003. *Illusion*, Unpublished poetry. Reprinted with permission of the author.

Jackson, Jolly. 2020. *Glue*, Poetry by Jolly Jackson, *Jolly for Now? Rainbows, Unicorns and Devils*, Amazon Kindle. Reprinted with permission of the author.

Chapter 19—Tough Decisions

Jackson, Jolly. 2020. Excerpt from *Glue*, Poetry by Jolly Jackson, *Jolly for Now? Rainbows, Unicorns and Devils*, Amazon Kindle. Reprinted with permission of the author.

An informational webpage from New Horizons Youth Ministries can be found on Wikipedia in a web archive file. https://web.archive.org/web/20080308055151/http://nhym.org/index.shtml

Jackson, Jolly. 2020. *Peter Pan*, Poetry by Jolly Jackson, *Jolly for Now? Rainbows, Unicorns and Devils*, Amazon Kindle. Reprinted with permission of the author.

Chapter 20—Time Out

Chapter 21—A Presence to Walk With

Smith, Michael W. 2004. *Healing Rain*, From the album, *Healing Rain*. Comp. Michael W. Smith. Reunion.

Part Two

Jackson, Jolly. 2020. *Grace*, Poetry by Jolly Jackson, *Jolly for Now? Rainbows, Unicorns and Devils*, Amazon Kindle. Reprinted with permission of the author.

Chapter 22—Among the Sunflowers

Mehlan, Michael. Date unknown. *As the Silence Fades*, Unpublished poetry. Reprinted with permission of the author.

Mehlan, Matthew. 2007. *Hey! W' Happens?* From the album, *Lucas*. Comp. Matthew D. Mehlan. Ghostly, International. Reprinted with permission of the composer.

Jackson, Jolly. 2020. Excerpt from *Walking Away*, Poetry by Jolly Jackson, *Jolly for Now? Rainbows, Unicorns and Devils*, Amazon Kindle. Reprinted with permission of the author.

Among the Sunflowers was initially written as a piece for a creative writing class that Michael took in 2007. Included here as Part 1, 2, and 3, edited to remain true to the timeline as the events occurred.

Chapter 23—The Beds Were Empty

Mehlan, Matthew. 2007. Excerpt from *Don't Worry*, From the album, *Lucas*. Comp. Matthew D. Mehlan. Ghostly, International. Reprinted with permission of the composer.

Chapter 24—New Every Morning

Families Anonymous, Inc. 2017. *Today a Better Way*. Copyright 2017 by Families Anonymous, Inc. Des Plaines, IL. Page 254 (Sept. 10) Reprinted by permission of Families Anonymous, Inc.

Chapter 25—Always Second Chances

Jackson, Jolly. 2020. Excerpt from *I Just Might be the Devil Part II*, Poetry by Jolly Jackson, *Jolly for Now? Rainbows, Unicorns and Devils*, Amazon Kindle. Reprinted with permission of the author.

Mehlan, Michael. 2004. *Among the Sunflowers*, Unpublished poetry. Reprinted with permission of the author.

Chapter 26—First Letters

The letters included in this chapter are actual transcriptions of emails and letters from Michael while he was in the Dominican Republic at Escuela Caribe. Names have been eliminated or changed to protect the individuals mentioned.

Chapter 27—The Good Servant

Jackson, Jolly. 2020. Excerpt from *With You Soon*, Poetry by Jolly Jackson, *Jolly for Now? Rainbows, Unicorns and Devils*, Amazon Kindle. Reprinted with permission of the author.

The events described in this chapter took place from 2004-2006. Michael wrote the chapter in 2021.

Jackson, Jolly. 2020. *The Girls from Santiago*, Poetry by Jolly Jackson, *Jolly for Now? Rainbows, Unicorns and Devils*, Amazon Kindle. Reprinted with permission of the author.

Chapter 28—Among the Sunflowers 2

Mehlan, Matthew. 2004. *This is My Dreams Come True*. From the album, *I'm at the Top of the World*. Comp. Matthew D. Mehlan. Shinkoyo, Inc. Reprinted with permission of the composer.

Chapter 29—Seeing the Prodigal

Jackson, Jolly. 2020. *I Loved You First*, Poetry by Jolly Jackson, *Jolly for Now? Rainbows, Unicorns and Devils*, Amazon Kindle. Reprinted with permission of the author.

Chapter 30—Thoughts

Mehlan, Matthew. 2005. Excerpt from *There are Seagulls who Live in Parking Lots,* From the album, *Git*. Comp. Matthew D. Mehlan. Ghostly, International. Reprinted with permission of the composer.

Chapter 31—Reflections

Jackson, Jolly. 2020.Excerpt from *Unrelenting Joy*, Poetry by Jolly Jackson, *Jolly for Now? Rainbows, Unicorns and Devils*, Amazon Kindle. Reprinted with permission of the author.

A Note from Gail Mehlan regarding New Horizons Youth Ministries/Escuela Caribe:

A few years after Mike's return from The Dominican Republic, I heard about a memoir published about a girl and her brother's experiences at Escuela Caribe. The book is titled *Jesus Land: A Memoir* by former Escuela Caribe student Julia Scheeres. Well-written and compelling, I could not put this memoir down and read with horror the treatment and prejudice she and her brother received at the hands of the Escuela Caribe staff. She was white, and her brother was black, adopted when he was three by her family. She and her brother had a very different experience in the program in the 1980s than what I had imagined Mike had in 2005. He said he'd heard and seen instances of abusive language and behavior from the staff but learned what he had to do to conform to their wishes.

Mike moved ahead more quickly than those students who rebelled. I recalled our conversation about how he feared his house father, who yelled a lot. The discipline for even the slightest infraction resulted in the students hitting the floor to do push-ups or run "casitas," a run up the mountain to the little house (casita), and run back. I imagine that would have been difficult physically for an out-of-shape, addicted child going through withdrawal symptoms.

Mike told me that one of the most humiliating experiences was when the house father or teacher who gave him a unit of concern, or punishment, would take the penalty for him as a sacrificial act of God's love. Mike told me he usually deserved the punishments he got, but this act of seeing someone else take the penalty to atone for his sins was horrifying. Was it abuse? I'm sure some students felt that it was. I prayed that this rigid type of discipline would ultimately help our son. Our emotionally sensitive approach to discipline had allowed Mike to wallow in a sick, addicted way of life. We had been powerless to initiate positive change with our methods at home. We felt the need to try a different approach. I even told other parents of children at Escuela Caribe that I favored the strict, sometimes harsh discipline because my son needed something different, something other than the death spiral he was on. I still believe if Mike had gone to California with his friend like he wanted to, we would no longer have a living son.

Shortly after Michael came home from the Dominican Republic in 2006, a young Christian filmmaker, Kate Logan, went to Escuela Caribe to create a film for her junior year project at an Evangelical Christian university in California. She had intended to write a "heartwarming documentary about troubled kids who were at Escuela Caribe to work through their issues." After filming on campus, she realized her film needed to tell a different story. *Kidnapped for Christ* tells the story of several students sent to Escuela Caribe by their parents. After filming there in person, the story emerged. The reporter felt that abuse was occurring, and the school held students older than 18 against their will.

The documentary showed what daily life was like at Escuela Caribe, and it was eye-opening to get an intimate look at what went on there daily. I recently watched it, and now I have a deeper understanding of what my son went through as he tried to adjust to the strict discipline, the exercise, and the strongly conservative theology that the staff hammered into the young people daily. Some students in the film believed that their time at the school changed their lives. Others felt that Escuela Caribe was abusive and punitive, especially to young LGBTQ+ students who their families rejected.

As a parent, I still feel that there were benefits to our son from his time spent in the Dominican Republic at Escuela Caribe. Perhaps I am simply justifying our decisions. After all this new information came out, we still believe we would not have done anything differently. It makes me sad that, as parents, we were put into a vulnerable, desperate situation when looking for help for our children. Finding a good treatment program is arduous. There are no easy answers, and there is no way to predict if any treatment will work for addiction.

I am disappointed that NHYM faced challenging questions that ultimately led to its demise. I wonder if they could have made some changes to their programs that would have been therapeutic but less abusive or toxic. I kept clinging to the hope that, in our situation, some benefit did come from their program. I don't want to think it was a complete waste of our resources. Michael still speaks fondly of many of his relationships and growth from that part of his journey. He was emotionally distraught when his former housefather died by suicide five years ago. I am sure there is much Mike hasn't told us. He never says it was easy.

There was a tremendously supportive group of women, mothers like me, that had troubled teens in the NHYM programs. Over the years, these mothers helped me grow and learn to cope with our difficult situations at retreats or via email. They helped me establish healthy boundaries for dealing with complex family relationships. Even today, I have very positive relationships with other mothers and staff from New Horizons Youth Ministries. I continue to pray for all of the mothers impacted by the program. I hold their children in prayer all the time.

New Horizons Youth Ministries and their affiliate camps and

schools, including Escuela Caribe, were shut down. The state of Indiana, where NHYM headquarters were located, revoked its license as a childcare facility in 2009.

https://en.wikipedia.org/wiki/New_Horizons_Youth_Ministries

Comments from Michael:

I've been thinking about my time at Escuela Caribe and the impact that experience has had on my life. I'm still processing it. There were many wonderful memories on that island and many memories that I wish I could excise from my mind.

Part of me died in the Caribbean, but a part also wanted to return to the Dominican Republic after my first year of college. I wanted to do something GOOD there. I tried to redeem my suffering and help the less fortunate. I wanted to see my experiences transformed and realized as good work.

Now I have a son with whom I want to have a blessed life. I have to LIVE harder for my son now, my parents, my family, and most of all, myself. This dad is a soldier for LIFE, for being ALIVE.

Chapter 32—Among the Sunflowers 3

Mehlan, Gail. 2005. *Solemn Peace.* Unpublished poetry.

Steve Miller Band. 1977. *Jet Airliner*, From the album, *Dreams*. Comp. Steve Miller. Capitol Records.

Jackson, Jolly. 2020. *Sunflowers and Sage*, Poetry by Jolly Jackson, *Jolly for Now? Rainbows, Unicorns and Devils*, Amazon Kindle. Reprinted with permission of the author.

Chapter 33—Possibilities

Jackson, Jolly. 2020. *Sunflowers and Sage*, Poetry by Jolly Jackson, *Jolly for Now? Rainbows, Unicorns and Devils*, Amazon Kindle. Reprinted with permission of the author.

Chapter 34—It's Not Your Life

Gibran, Kahlil. 1923. Excerpt from *On Children*. From *The Prophet*. Alfred A. Knopf.

Jackson, Jolly. 2020. *The Let's Go*, Poetry by Jolly Jackson, *Jolly for Now? Rainbows, Unicorns and Devils*, Amazon Kindle. Reprinted with permission of the author.

Chapter 35—No Sleep and a Wedding

Gibran, Kahlil. 1923. Excerpt from *On Children*. From *The Prophet*. Alfred A. Knopf.

Jackson, Jolly. 2020. *Naughty, The Price*, Poetry by Jolly Jackson, *Jolly for Now? Rainbows, Unicorns and Devils*, Amazon Kindle. Reprinted with permission of the author.

Chapter 36—Honorable Intentions

Saaveda, Miguel de Cervantes. 1612. *The Ingenious Gentleman Don Quixote of La Mancha*.

Families Anonymous, Inc. 2000. *Helping*. Copyright 2000 by Families Anonymous, Inc. Des Plaines, IL. Publication #2003. Reprinted by permission of Families Anonymous, Inc.

Chapter 37—I Don't Like Failure

Jackson, Jolly. 2020. Excerpt from *Sympathy for a Love Song*, Poetry by Jolly Jackson, *Jolly for Now? Rainbows, Unicorns and Devils*, Amazon Kindle. Reprinted with permission of the author. This excerpt was scribbled on a scrap of paper found inside the piano bench, attributed to Michael M. Mehlan. 2007.

<u>Part Three</u>

Jackson, Jolly. 2020. *The End #1*, Poetry by Jolly Jackson, *Jolly for Now? Rainbows, Unicorns and Devils*, Amazon Kindle. Reprinted with permission of the author.

Chapter 38—Astronaut

Jackson, Jolly. 2020. Excerpt from *Astronaut*, Poetry by Jolly Jackson, *Jolly for Now? Rainbows, Unicorns and Devils*, Amazon Kindle. Reprinted with permission of the author.

Note from Gail Mehlan:

For more information regarding the medal of honor story, I recommend the following book:

Pullen, John J.1966. *A Shower of Stars: The Medal of Honor and the 27ᵗʰ Maine.* Mechanicsburg, Pennsylvania. J.P. Lippincott Co.

Chapter 39—Heroin

Jackson, Jolly. 2020. Excerpt from *Astronaut*, Poetry by Jolly Jackson, *Jolly for Now? Rainbows, Unicorns and Devils*, Amazon Kindle. Reprinted with permission of the author.

Chapter 40—Darkness Continues

Jackson, Jolly. 2020. Excerpt from *My Sweet Queen Marie*, Poetry by Jolly Jackson, *Jolly for Now? Rainbows, Unicorns and Devils*, Amazon Kindle. Reprinted with permission of the author.

Chapter 41—Miracles of Life and Love

Jackson, Jolly. 2020. Excerpt from *Astronaut*, Poetry by Jolly Jackson, *Jolly for Now? Rainbows, Unicorns and Devils*, Amazon Kindle. Reprinted with permission of the author.

Mehlan, Gail. 2008. *It's Life*, Unpublished poetry.

Jackson, Jolly. 2020. *Sympathy for a Love Song*, Poetry by Jolly Jackson, *Jolly for Now? Rainbows, Unicorns and Devils*, Amazon Kindle. Reprinted with permission of the author.

Chapter 42—Holy Ghost

Holy Ghost first appeared as a short story in an anthology of local writers, poets and musicians. 2018. *The Polk Street Review 2018: Fact or Fiction? YOU Decide.* Edited by Logan Street Sanctuary, Inc. Noblesville, IN: Logan Street Sanctuary Press. Pages 187-191.

Jackson, Jolly. 2020. Excerpt from *Astronaut*, Poetry by Jolly Jackson, *Jolly for Now? Rainbows, Unicorns and Devils*, Amazon Kindle. Reprinted with permission of the author.

Mehlan, Michael and Misch, Justin. 2016. *Holy Ghost*. From the album, *Loud Noises*. Comps. Michael Mehlan and Justin Misch. Reprinted with permission of the composers.

Jackson, Jolly. 2020. *Guitar*, Poetry by Jolly Jackson, *Jolly for Now? Rainbows, Unicorns and Devils*, Amazon Kindle. Reprinted with permission of the author.

Jackson, Jolly. 2020. *Living in the Future*, Poetry by Jolly Jackson, *Jolly for Now? Rainbows, Unicorns and Devils*, Amazon Kindle. Reprinted with permission of the author.

Chapter 43—Meeting Douggie

Jackson, Jolly. 2016. Facebook. July 19

Jackson, Jolly. 2020. *LOVE and Baryons for Breakfast*, Poetry by Jolly Jackson, *Jolly for Now? Rainbows, Unicorns and Devils*, Amazon Kindle. Reprinted with permission of the author.

Chapter 44—Present Still

Jackson, Jolly. 2020. Excerpt from *Grace*, Poetry by Jolly Jackson, *Jolly for Now? Rainbows, Unicorns and Devils*, Amazon Kindle. Reprinted with permission of the author.

Chapter 45—Powerless

Powerless first appeared as a short story in an anthology of local writers, poets and musicians. 2017. *The Polk Street Review 2017: Journeys and Transitions*. Edited by Logan Street Sanctuary, Inc. Noblesville, IN: Logan Street Sanctuary Press. Pages 237-240.

Step One is reprinted with permission of Alcoholics Anonymous World Services, Inc.

Jackson, Jolly. 2020. *The Cracks*, Poetry by Jolly Jackson, *Jolly for Now? Rainbows, Unicorns and Devils*, Amazon Kindle. Reprinted with permission of the author.

Chapter 46—I Don't Want This to be Our Story Anymore

Jackson, Jolly. 2020. Excerpt from *The Cracks*, Poetry by Jolly Jackson, *Jolly for Now? Rainbows, Unicorns and Devils*, Amazon Kindle. Reprinted with permission of the author.

Mehlan, Gail. 2021. *A Loss I Have Not Grieved.* Previously unpublished.

Chapter 47—Sometimes Prayers Aren't Enough

Jackson, Jolly. 2020. *Dread*, Poetry by Jolly Jackson, *Jolly for Now? Rainbows, Unicorns and Devils*, Amazon Kindle. Reprinted with permission of the author.

Jackson, Jolly. 2020. Excerpt from *I Just Might be the Devil Part 1*, Poetry by Jolly Jackson, *Jolly for Now? Rainbows, Unicorns and Devils*, Amazon Kindle. Reprinted with permission of the author.

Chapter 48—Who is Jolly Jackson?

Jackson, Jolly. 2020. *Silence*, Poetry by Jolly Jackson, *Jolly for Now? Rainbows, Unicorns and Devils*, Amazon Kindle. Reprinted with permission of the author.

Jackson, Jolly. 2020. Excerpt from *The Ballad of Jolly and Sylvia*, Poetry by Jolly Jackson, *Jolly for Now? Rainbows, Unicorns and Devils*, Amazon Kindle. Reprinted with permission of the author.

Jackson, Jolly. 2020. *The Magicians*, Poetry by Jolly Jackson, *Jolly for Now? Rainbows, Unicorns and Devils*, Amazon Kindle. Reprinted with permission of the author.

Chapter 49—Why Did We Have Children?

Jackson, Jolly. 2020. Excerpt from *Sweet Queen Marie*, Poetry by Jolly Jackson, *Jolly for Now? Rainbows, Unicorns and Devils*, Amazon Kindle. Reprinted with permission of the author.

Miller, Donald. 2013. Facebook, March 27.

Chapter 50—Is There a Monster Under the Bed?

Jackson, Jolly. 2020. *Monsters*, Poetry by Jolly Jackson, *Jolly for Now? Rainbows, Unicorns and Devils*, Amazon Kindle. Reprinted with permission of the author.

Jackson, Jolly. 2020. *Blue Bone Disease*, Poetry by Jolly Jackson, *Jolly for Now? Rainbows, Unicorns and Devils*, Amazon Kindle. Reprinted with permission of the author.

Chapter 51—The Edge

Mehlan, Matthew. 2020. Excerpt from *The Edge*, From the album, *If the Cat Come Back*. Comp. Matthew D. Mehlan. Shinkoyo, Inc. Reprinted with permission of the composer.

Mehlan, Michael and Misch, Justin. 2016. *Little Cages.* From the album, *Loud Noises.* Comps. Michael Mehlan and Justin Misch. Reprinted with permission of the composers.

Chapter 52—Recovery is Lonely

Mehlan, Michael and Misch, Justin. 2016. Excerpt from *Little Cages.* From the album, *Loud Noises.* Comps. Michael Mehlan and Justin Misch. Reprinted with permission of the composers.

Chapter 53—The Walk Home

Mehlan, Matthew. 2008. *STEPPER, a.k.a. Work,* From the album, *Money.* Comp. Matthew D. Mehlan. Tomlab. Reprinted with permission of the composer.

Jackson, Jolly. 2020. *A Good Day,* Poetry by Jolly Jackson, *Jolly for Now? Rainbows, Unicorns and Devils,* Amazon Kindle. Reprinted with permission of the author.

Chapter 54—A Good Day

Jackson, Jolly. 2020. Excerpt from *A Good Day,* Poetry by Jolly Jackson, *Jolly for Now? Rainbows, Unicorns and Devils,* Amazon Kindle. Reprinted with permission of the author.

Chapter 55—Epilogue

Scheff, David. 2014. *Clean: Overcoming Addiction and Ending America's Greatest Tragedy.* Boston, Massachusetts: First Mariner Book: Houghton Mifflin Harcourt. Pages xv-xxi.

Lamott, Anne. 2018. *Almost Everything: Notes on Hope*. New York. Riverhead Books. Page 18.

Mehlan, Michael and Misch, Justin. 2016. *Broken System*. From the album, *Loud Noises*. Comps. Michael Mehlan and Justin Misch. Reprinted with permission of the composers.

Mehlan, Matthew. 2020. *Invest in Who Is Like God?*, From the album, *If the Cat Come Back*. Comp. Matthew D. Mehlan. Shinkoyo, Inc. Reprinted with permission of the composer.

Note from Gail Mehlan:

Matt's song entitled, *Invest in Who Is Like God?* is a song whose lyrics play on the words surrounding medical help as an investment opportunity for large pharmaceutical companies experimenting with drug treatment options potentially in the justice system. It also has name meanings such as "Chick Culling," the practice of killing all male baby chicks because they are not valuable for the poultry business, which involves gender, power, and procreation. Included in the lyric are snippets from the Gospel of Judas, Jurassic Park, the musician, Sun Ra, and the nursery rhyme, "Rub Dub a Dub, Dub," which was a type of "calling out" of otherwise respectable people for "disrespectable actions" according to Wikipedia. The letters at the end are the stock tickers for the major pharmaceutical companies. Michael's name in Hebrew, means "Who is like God?"

Jackson, Jolly. 2020. *The Septet*, Poetry by Jolly Jackson, *Jolly for Now? Rainbows, Unicorns and Devils*, Amazon Kindle. Reprinted with permission of the author.

Postscript—Rainbow Connection

Jackson, Jolly. 2020. *Unrelenting Joy*, Poetry by Jolly Jackson, *Jolly for Now? Rainbows, Unicorns and Devils*, Amazon Kindle. Reprinted with permission of the author.

Williams, Paul and Ascher, Kenneth. 1979. *Rainbow Connection*, From the album, *The Muppet Movie Soundtrack*. Atlantic-CBS Records.

Jackson, Jolly. 2020. *The End #2*, Poetry by Jolly Jackson, *Jolly for Now? Rainbows, Unicorns and Devils*, Amazon Kindle. Reprinted with permission of the author.

Breath and Life

Barker, Arlene. 2020. Excerpt from *Candlemas Prayer*. Unpublished poetry. Reprinted with permission of the author.

Bowler, Kate. 2022. Everything Happens Podcast, Episode with Ann Patchett, *Behold These Precious Days*. March 15, 2022. www.katebowler.com/podcasts/ann-patchett-behold-these-precious-days/

SPECIAL ACKNOWLEDGMENTS AND LOVE TO:

~ Doug Mehlan, my husband, for standing beside me and walking through this life and this story with me. Thank you for letting me put it out there. I hope my words convey the love I have for you.

~ Michael Mehlan, my son, for taking this journey with me to get the story out in the world, for writing so eloquently about his struggles through his poetry and his narrative. Always love. You and your son are so loved.

~ Michelle Mehlan Clarke, my daughter, for loving our family and helping us through the hard times with her deep understanding of mental health issues. Your family is precious to me. I love you.

~ Matthew Mehlan, my son, for using his gift of musical composition to express his deep comprehension and intimate involvement with this story. Your lyrics and music captured the depth of the issues surrounding us, even when we couldn't. Your family is precious to me. I love you.

~To my editor, Rachel Moulton, who worked with me and helped me transform my writing into a beautiful book. Thank you for encouraging me with the words, "You *are* a writer!"

~Tami and Keith, dear friends, who journeyed with us with faith, love, compassion and always hope.

~All parents of addicts and troubled teens, especially those mothers that I've met along the way. The path is not easy, is it?

~All of my dear friends from my mutual support groups. I love you. *It works WHEN you work it.*

~ My *Roots of Life Community* church family and my *Prince of Peace* church family, many of you have walked with us along this journey. Thank you seems inadequate.

~ All of the doctors and counselors that supported us on this journey. Your kind support and encouragement have been precious to our family.

~ To those who worked for NHYM/Escuela Caribe who were truly and honestly GOOD and loving people who helped Michael in ways he didn't understand or even realize at the time. Thank you!

~ To my special writing friends who've listened to and read multiple drafts and sections of this story over the last few years. I admire you and appreciate you cheering me on. Arlene Barker, Andrea Dunn, Cynthia Stafford, and Mariah Julio you've all become such special friends. I hope you know how much your encouragement meant to me. It saddens my heart to share that during the course of my writing and editing of this book, two of these dear souls, Mariah and Cynthia, left their physical bodies to fly with the angels. I still feel their presence as their spirits cheer me on to continue to pursue this project. I'd give anything to be able to hand them a signed copy of my book.

~ To the Indianapolis Writer's Center for your classes, workshops and support.

~ To the Oxford House in Kenosha, Wisconsin, for providing a safe place for a recovering addict to live and get back on track.

~ To Jane E. Cloud for the copy edit of this manuscript. Your comments made me feel that this project is worthy and important.

~ To David Provolo, my book cover and interior designer; you have helped me create a beautiful book, and I am very happy and proud to hold it in my hands and share it with the world. Thank you!

Recommended Reading and Other Information and Support

Al-Anon Family Groups https://al-anon.org/

Alcoholics Anonymous https://www.aa.org/

Bowler, Kate. *Everything Happens* Podcast, *Ann Patchett: Behold These Precious Days.* March 15, 2022. www.katebowler.com/podcasts/ann-patchett-behold-these-precious-days/

Doyle, Glennon. *Addiction: How do we love an addict and how does an addict love herself?*, *We Can do Hard Things* Podcast, Season 1, Episode 5. June 8, 2021. https://podcasts.apple.com/us/podcast/we-can-do-had-things-with-glennon-doyle/id1564530722

Families Anonymous https://www.familiesanonymous.org/

Logan, Kate S. *Kidnapped for Christ,* directed by Kate S. Logan, produced by Yada Zamora, Paul Levin, Kate S. Logan. Released January 17, 2014. The documentary about Escuela Caribe created is available to rent through the streaming services, Apple TV and Amazon Prime.

Wittels-Wachs, Stephanie. *Last Day*, Season 1: Addiction, Season 2: Suicide and Mental Health, Lemonada Media. September 25, 2019. https://podcasts.apple.com/us/podcast/last-day/id1468896686?i=1000449083754

Scheeres, Julia. 2005. *Jesus Land*. Berkeley, California: Counterpoint.

Scheff, David. 2014. *Clean: Overcoming Addiction and Ending America's Greatest Tragedy*. Boston, Massachusetts: First Mariner Book: Houghton Mifflin Harcourt.

BIBLIOGRAPHY

Al-Alnon Family Groups Inc. 1995. *How Al-Anon Works: For Families and Friends of Alcoholics.* Virginia Beach, VA: Al-Anon Family Group Headquaters, Inc.

Al-Anon Family Groups Inc. 1992. *Courage to Change.* Virginia Beach, VA: Al-Anon Family Groups Inc.

Alcoholics Anonymous. 1939, 1955, 1976, 2001. *Alcoholics Anonymous.* Alcoholics AnonymousWorld Services, Inc.

Are, Sarah. 2016. "Sanctified Art." *Sanctified Art LLC.* Accessed December 18, 2020. sanctifiedart.org.

Barker, Arlene. 2020. *Candlemas Prayer.* Unpublished Poetry.

Bowler, Kate. 2022. *Everything Happens Podcast.* Duke University. March 15. Accessed March 22, 2022. www.kate-bowler.com/podcasts/ann-patchett-behold-these-precious-days/.

Families Anonymous, Inc. 2000. *Helping.* DesPlaines: Families Anonymous, Inc.

—. 2017. *Today a Better Way.* DesPlaines, IL: Families Anonymous, Inc.

Floyd, Pink. 1975. *Wish You Were Here.* Comps. David Gilmore and Roger Waters.

Fur Coats for Sportsmen. 2016. "Broken System." *Loud Noises.* Comp. Michael Mehlan.

Fur Coats for Sportsmen. 2016. "Holy Ghost." *Loud Noises.* Comps. Michael M. Mehlan and Justin M. Misch.

Fur Coats for Sportsmen. 2016. "Little Cages." *Loud Noises*. Comp. Michael Mehlan.

Gibran, Kahlil. 1923. *The Prophet*. Alfred A. Knopf.

Jackson, Jolly. 2016. Facebook, July 19.

—. 2020. *Jolly for Now?* Amazon Kindle.

Lamott, Anne. 2018. *Almost Everything: Notes on Hope*. New York, New York: Riverhead Books.

2014. *Kidnapped for Christ*. Directed by Kate S. Logan. Produced by Yada Zamora, Paul Levin and Kate S. Logan.

Miller, Donald. 2013. Facebook, March 27.

Pullen, John J. 1966. *A Shower of Stars: The Medal of Honor and the 27th Maine*. Mechanicsburg, PA: Lippincott Co.

Saaveda, Miguel de Cervantes. 1612. " The Ingenious Gentleman Don Quixote of La Mancha."

Sheeres, Julia. 2005. *Jesus Land*. Berkeley: Counterpoint.

Sheff, David. 2013. *Clean: Overcoming Addiction and Ending America's Greatest Tragedy*. Boston, Massachusetts: First Mariner Books: Houghton Mifflin Harcourt.

Skeletons and the Girl-Faced Boys. 2005. "There are Seagulls who Live in Parking Lots." *Git*. Comp. Matthew D. Mehlan.

Skeletons. 2007. "Don't Worry." *Lucas*. Comp. Matthew D. Mehlan.

Skeletons. 2007. "Hey! W'Happens?!!" *Lucas*. Comp. Matthew D. Mehlan.

Skeletons. 2020. "Invest in Who Is Like God?" *If the Cat Come Back*. Comp. Matthew D. Mehlan.

Skeletons. 2008. "STEPPER a.k.a. Work." *Money.* Comp. Matthew D. Mehlan.

Skeletons. 2020. "The Edge." *If the Cat Come Back.* Comp. Matthew D. Mehlan.

Skeletons. 2004. "This is My Dreams Come True." *I'm at the Top of the World.* Comp. Mathew D. Mehlan.

Skeletons. 2007. "Sickness." *Lucas.* Comp. Matthew D. Mehlan.

Smith, Michael W. 2004. "Healing Rain." *Healing Rain.* Comp. Michael W. Smith.

Steve Miller Band. 1977. "Jet Airliner." *Dreams.* Comp. Steve Miller.

Wikipedia. 2021. *New Horizons Youth Ministries.* Accessed September 15, 2004. https://en.wikipedia.org/wiki/New_Horizons_Youth_Ministries.

Williams, Paul and Ascher, Kenneth (Kermit the Frog). 1979. "Rainbow Connection." *The Muppet Movie Soundtrack.* Comp. Paul Williams.

www.ingramcontent.com/pod-product-compliance
Lightning Source LLC
Chambersburg PA
CBHW060855120626
46553CB00001B/91